THE UNITED STATES AND DISARMAMENT

The United States
AND
Disarmament

By
BENJAMIN H. WILLIAMS

KENNIKAT PRESS
Port Washington, N. Y./London

ST. PHILIPS COLLEGE LIBRARY

327.174
W716u

THE UNITED STATES AND DISARMAMENT

First published in 1931
Reissued in 1973 by Kennikat Press
Library of Congress Catalog Card No.: 72-88946
ISBN 0-8046-1767-8

Manufactured by Taylor Publishing Company   Dallas, Texas

To
PATRICIA AND SONNY

35249

PREFACE

REFERRING to the coming world disarmament conference, President Hoover recently said: "Of all the proposals for the economic rehabilitation of the world, I know of none which compares in necessity or importance with the successful result of that conference." With regard to the same conference, Viscount Cecil has remarked that the task of disarming transcends every other political issue on earth. The present volume is written to review the problem of heavy nationalistic armaments and to consider the question of their impropriety in a period of economic internationalization. It is the purpose of the author to show how in one decade the world's greatest navies have been subjected to limitation and control through conference action—a phenomenal development which has been so aptly described by Ambassador Gibson as an amazingly rapid acceptance of a revolutionary idea. Finally, an effort is made to summarize the issues which will be laid before the world disarmament conference. These matters are considered from the standpoint of the United States which, after all, has vast human and economic reasons for seeking to promote the orderly conduct of world affairs.

The obligations of the author are manifold and only a few can be specifically acknowledged. Much valuable coöperation has been received from my colleagues in the University of Pittsburgh. Many suggestions have also come from members of my seminar on International Relations. I am indebted to the editors of *Current History* for permission to make use of an article by myself on "Sea Power and Prosperity." which appears as the

Preface

larger part of Chapter VII. I appreciate the kindness of the Foreign Policy Association in permitting me to make use of material in their Washington office which was not available elsewhere. Some of the subject matter of the book was discussed at the Norman Wait Harris Memorial Foundation Conference on American Foreign Policy at Chicago during the summer of 1930, and at that time I had the advantage of helpful criticism. The material in some places follows closely *The London Conference: Its Background and Results*, a series of radio addresses by myself which constitute a publication of the University of Pittsburgh. I have likewise drawn to some extent upon an essay written for a memorial volume in honor of Professor Giuseppe Prato and published by the Royal Higher Institute of Economic and Commercial Science of Turin, Italy.

BENJAMIN H. WILLIAMS.

UNIVERSITY OF PITTSBURGH,
June, 1931.

CONTENTS

PREFACE vii

PART I: THE SEA-POWER THEORY OF HISTORY

CHAPTER I.   Introduction: Capitalism Recoils from Suicide. 3
CHAPTER II. The Doctrine of Mahan. 9
CHAPTER III. The Age of Sea Power 21
CHAPTER IV. The Twilight of National Sea Power . . 37

PART II: AMERICAN NAVAL NEEDS

CHAPTER V.   The Defense of Territory 65
CHAPTER VI. The Protection of Trade during Belligerency. 78
CHAPTER VII. The Doctrine of Neutral Rights. 95

PART III: THE NAVAL CONFERENCES

CHAPTER VIII. Armament Limitation before the Washington Conference. 119
CHAPTER IX.   The Washington Conference 140
CHAPTER X.   The Geneva Conference 161
CHAPTER XI.   The Preliminaries of the London Conference 179
CHAPTER XII. The London Treaty. 199
CHAPTER XIII. The Ratios 226

Contents

PART IV: COÖPERATING WITH THE LEAGUE OF NATIONS

Chapter XIV. *The League Approach to Disarmament* . 237

Chapter XV. *The World Conference: General Problems, Budgets, and Supervision* 255

Chapter XVI. *Limitation of Personnel and Material.* . 281

Chapter XVII. *Conclusion* 304

APPENDICES

I. *The Washington Naval Treaty of 1922* 311

II. *The London Naval Treaty of 1930* 329

III. *Summary of the Draft Convention Drawn Up by the Preparatory Commission* 348

Index 353

PRINCIPAL SOURCES

BAKER, PHILIP J. NOEL, *Disarmament*, Hogarth Press, London, 1926.

BUELL, RAYMOND LESLIE, *The Washington Conference*, D. Appleton and Company, 1922.

BYWATER, HECTOR, *Navies and Nations*, Houghton Mifflin and Company, Boston, 1927.

Conference on the Limitation of Armament, Washington, November 12, 1921–February 6, 1922, Government Printing Office, Washington, 1922.

Congressional Record.

Documents of the London Naval Conference, 1930, His Majesty's Stationery Office, London, 1930.

Foreign Policy Association, *Information Service*.

HANNAY, DAVID, *The Navy and Sea Power*, Henry Holt and Company, New York.

ICHIHASHI, YAMATO, *The Washington Conference and After*, Stanford University Press, Stanford University, 1928.

League of Nations, *Documents of the Preparatory Commission for the Disarmament Conference, Minutes of the—Session*, Geneva (printed for the several sessions).

KENWORTHY, J. M., AND GEORGE YOUNG, *Freedom of the Seas*, Horace Liveright, New York, 1928.

MADARIAGA, SALVADOR DE, *Disarmament*, Coward-McCann, Inc., New York, 1929.

MAGRUDER, THOMAS P., *The United States Navy*, Dorrance and Company, Philadelphia, 1928.

MAHAN, ALFRED THAYER, *The Influence of Sea Power upon History, 1660–1783*, Little, Brown, and Company, Boston, 1890.

MOORE, FREDERICK, *America's Naval Challenge*, The Macmillan Company, New York, 1929.

New York Times.

Records of the Conference for the Limitation of Naval Armament Held at Geneva from June 20 to August 4, 1927, Geneva, 1927.

STEVENS, WILLIAM OLIVER AND ALLAN WESTCOTT, *A History of Sea Power*, George H. Doran Company, New York, 1920.

Sundry Legislation Affecting the Naval Establishment, 1927–1928, hearings before the House Committee on Naval Affairs, Government Printing Office, Washington, 1928.

Treaty on the Limitation of Naval Armaments, hearings before the Senate Committee on Foreign Relations, Government Printing Office, Washington, 1930.

PART I
THE SEA-POWER THEORY OF HISTORY

Chapter I

INTRODUCTION: CAPITALISM RECOILS FROM SUICIDE

IT WAS in 1916 that the United States made a dramatic change in armament policy. In that year our country was definitely launched upon the troublous waters of naval competition. For half a century the American people had almost forgotten the sea. The population had pushed westward across a vast continent. The national attention had, in the early years of our history, been turned to agriculture and internal improvements. As the Republic had entered into mature life, factories had slowly arisen in the more strategic industrial sites. Great cities came into being and the United States was moved along on the wave of industrialization. Rapid developments at the opening of the twentieth century, attaining tremendous speed in the feverish neutral years of 1914–1916, swelled the movement to the dimensions of a "second industrial revolution." An army of tireless robots, infinitely superior to human laborers in the rapidity of production and far cheaper to maintain, worked day and night to make the United States incomparably the greatest industrial producing country in the world. The prosperity of those neutral years was largely due to the fact that the increased demand and decreased production in Europe created an economic vacuum which with terrific sucking force drew powerful trade currents from the United States eastward across the Atlantic. This country was rapidly pushed, almost catapulted, into the third period of Adam Smith's three stages of economic evolution: Agriculture—Industry—Commerce.

Large groups and interests turned their attention to maritime matters. Neutrality and war dividends, rising as high in some cases as 100 or even 200 per cent, electrified the shipping and commercial interests with a new ambition. A wave of nationalistic psychology gathered force with startling suddenness. Militarism, fear, a thousand abnormal emotions, seethed in the cauldron of those war years. The President of the United States, probably the best political mind of his time, called for a powerful military force upon the sea, "incomparably the most adequate navy in the world," and later sought to justify the demand on the ground that such a weapon would become a sword of righteousness in the hands of the United States, for our country was seen as an incorruptible dispenser of international justice surrounded by evildoers. How powerful were those giant psychic whirlpools and how impotent in their grasp was man, the atom!

The combat memories of the race were stirred. New spirit animated all of the aggressively nationalistic groups in American society. Irresistible in 1917 and 1918, they continued to thrive from the momentum of war spirit and propaganda even after the restoration of peace. An urge for power swept through their ranks. A grander national destiny through arms, expressed in the softer terminology of national defense, fascinated them.

Probably the outstanding aspect of this increased nationalism was a desire for power on the ocean. The revitalized naval groups, their economic allies (the shipping interests), and their psychological supporters (the patriotic societies) joined in urging that the American people should become sea-minded. A brilliant book, *The Influence of Sea Power upon History*, 1660–1783, written by Captain Alfred T. Mahan a quarter of a century before, was the Bible of the newly enlarged cult, and the sea-power theory of national greatness came to exercise its fascination over minds which had been previously devoted to the prosaic problems of purely domestic interest.

The naval program enacted in 1916 and carried forward in the years immediately after the war placed the American problem of armaments squarely in the field of diplomacy. By the 1916 program Congress provided for the building of sixteen capital ships, each incorporating the feature of great gun power learned from the Battle of Jutland. This spectacular Act of Congress deserves to stand out as an event in American history. It set in motion programs and counter-programs. It gave rise to suspicions and alarms which were to play their part in a series of remarkable international conferences.

Before the war we Americans had been a non-militaristic nation, proud of our pacific intentions and of the sharp contrast which distinguished us from the armed nations of Europe. Our navy endangered no one and caused but little apprehension abroad. Our army was then, as it is now, too small to be considered a factor in the world's military competition. During and after the war we were swept forward by new impulses until, in the words of President Hoover, we possessed "the largest military budget of any nation in the world." Thus we took the place of pre-war Germany as the greatest spender for prospective wars. Announcements of American naval programs came to disturb the tranquillity of other continents. No longer could a realistic American keep a straight face while pointing righteously at the excessive burdens of armaments in other countries. We were one with them, a part of the world system of military rivalry.

But the economic transformations have produced another school of thought which is destined to grow stronger with the passage of time. Foreign investments have been made on a colossal scale by an army of capitalists who, for an additional 2 per cent, have given hostages to fortune by placing their money in European and other potentially hostile countries. Such investments can be destroyed by war, and the successful international financier has found his interests to be emphatically on the side of an intelligent internationalism. J. P. Morgan, whose name stands first in the catalogue of foreign lending, has had no doubt at all that the interests of his banking house are identical with pacific relations between the United States and the other great powers. American bankers have exerted powerful financial pressure upon bellicose nations of Europe, as upon France in 1923 and upon Italy in 1930–1931. A new influence for peace has gained vitality and size in proportion to the growth of syndicates and the increased flotation of foreign bond issues. The most successful industries—those of the type which spurn a protective tariff and send their machine-made products forth to compete in the markets of the world—have also discovered themselves to be advocates of peaceful procedure. It is not a coincidence that Henry Ford, whom the world looks upon as the personification of competent mass production, contrasts sharply in his international outlook with the provincial manufacturer of the old school. The distributors of oil whose fleets of tankers ride upon the narrow waters of the Suez route and skirt the coasts of Asia may be taken to represent the change in another aspect of business. Even the great octopus, formerly the embodiment of grasping and unfeeling capitalism, has reached out a friendly tentacle to make contact with a far-off communistic government whose petroleum can be purchased at a low price for distribution in the East.

The revolution in economics has brought about a strange reversal of political leadership. The progressives

CAPITALISM RECOILS FROM SUICIDE

of the American West are often highly nationalistic. In international matters they remain in the age of agricultural economy as did the Junkers of pre-war Germany. On the other hand, the improvement of relations between the United States and the other strong powers frequently finds its greatest support in the financial and commercial centers of the Northeast which, in domestic politics, have been staunchly conservative. Here again we find a parallel in Germany where Gustav Stressemann, until his untimely death, so well expressed the advanced international sentiments of the great industrialists. Unconsciously, perhaps, the world's industrial and financial leaders shrink from an unseen danger—a danger so well expressed in the words of one of the most penetrating writers of the present day: "Bolshevism waits around the corner for gentlemen who light-heartedly put the torch to modern civilization."[1] For fundamentally the efforts of big business to avert military conflict represent the struggles of a capitalist society against its own destruction.

International business has given weight and respectability to the movement for world friendship and other qualities have been supplied by other groups. The educational profession has here found an unexcelled opportunity for vigorous public work. The study of international law before the World War, for example, was notoriously dry, for in the isolation of our country such a subject seemed at no point to touch reality. The literature in this field was seldom understood, much less mastered, outside of strictly professorial circles. Knowledge combined with a world perspective gained from academic studies has given to the scholar an unusual insight into the new situation and he has come forth to take a front-rank position in the movement for friendly

[1] BEARD, CHARLES A.: "Prospects for Peace," *Harpers Magazine*, p. 328, February, 1929.

international relations and world law. Church groups, which have long been associated with the peace movement in this country, have been moved by the turn in events to give new and more vigorous support to the fight against war. They have organized and created encouragement for disarmament and the outlawry of war on a scale which will compare favorably with industrial achievements in mass production and distribution. A few farsighted philanthropists have provided a kind of immortality for their own desires for international harmony by the establishment of foundations, untiring machines which furnish their own fuel and make possible the indefinite continuance of research and peace effort upon a salary basis.

And thus as society emerges from an immature provincial economy into the broader scope of world commerce and finance we are met with a conflict between the militaristic and nationalistic schools, on the one hand, and the pacific and internationalistic, on the other. These conflicting attitudes touch our armament program at every point and must always be considered in connection with the naval problem which was placed on the American doorstep less than two decades ago.

Chapter II

THE DOCTRINE OF MAHAN

WHEN we turn to history for instruction as to the value of large fleets we are confronted with a conflicting and confusing tangle of data from which it is no easy matter to derive a simple explanation or theory. Of the vast multitude of facts concerning man's existence on earth a comparatively small number have been captured and catalogued by the historian. Meager in comparison with all transpired phenomena, these data of history are nevertheless dizzily confusing in their multiplicity. They have baffled the true historian in his attempts to explain national health and disease. Numbers of causes contribute to the growth and vitality of civilizations or to their sickness and decay. Different influences operate in each historical situation, and the world's political laboratory can never be equipped or arranged twice for identical experiments.

Communities with and without sea power have gained mastery only to lose it. If the lessons of the past mean anything, the exuberant American nation, still rising toward its zenith, will with the relentless years pass into its decline. It may take one century. It may take five. But the fixed laws of society seem to have predoomed our country to the fate of brilliancy and eclipse which has visited political units since the beginning of organized social life. "But over this surface, too," says Spengler, "the great Cultures accomplish their majestic wave-cycles. They appear suddenly, swell in splendid lines, flatten again and vanish, and the face of the waters is once more a sleeping waste."

The mind of man, unable to grapple with the complexity of history, is eternally seeking for single causes and simple explanations. Writers, prophets, teachers, and particularly propagandists have seized upon single factors which they have sought to establish as predominant causes. As we approach the consideration of the sea-power theory of history, it may be well to place it in its proper perspective by a brief survey of some of the principal single-factor explanations of political phenomena. A few of these explanations are:

The Geographic.—The contour of the land has molded the size and character of communities. River valleys, mountain barriers and passes, caravan routes, and ocean frontiers are such elements as determine the nature and measure of coöperative accomplishment. Soils and minerals have had much to do with social vitality and persistence.

The Climatic.—The climate has affected the zest for achievement, accounting for the sweeping mastery held by invigorated temperate zone dwellers over tropical peoples. Likewise, climatic changes sometimes explain the ebb and flow of entire civilizations.

The Racial.—History is a story of domination by outstanding, masterful racial stocks, such as the Nordic.

The Economic.—Political and social institutions are the products of the struggle of economic classes. The acquisitive instinct is the great motivating urge in history.

The Spiritual and Moral.—The success of a people depends upon their ideals and the soundness of their moral code. In primitive stages this is manifest as a belief in the superiority of the worshipers of a particular god.

The Great Man.—Events are shaped by the accidental appearance of intellectual giants whose genius and will dominate the political and social processes of the times.

The Doctrine of Mahan

The Military.—The success of a people depends upon their ability to use force in the defense of their so-called rights and in the imposition of their will upon their more passive and, therefore, less worthy neighbors. The reverse is also advocated, particularly in these years following the World War, *i.e.*, national or cultural survival depends upon the ability to adjust disputes peacefully and thereby to avoid suicidal wars.

None of these interpretations, unless it is the military, has space to consider sea power except as a detail in political evolution or as the manifestation of a larger principle of social force. Out of the group consciousness of the naval profession and its allied societies and industries, however, has come a theory of history which places great stress upon sea power, not only as an item in military strength but also as a prime cause of commercial and industrial prosperity. The thesis has been ably advocated. Evidence has been marshaled in attractive form to support it. While it is not of sufficient consequence to rank as one of the major theories of history, it is, nevertheless, of great importance in the consideration of the naval problem, for it underlies much of the enthusiasm for national supremacy upon the seas in all of the maritime powers.

Alfred T. Mahan, an American naval officer, has been the outstanding literary spokesman for the naval gild. In this brilliant man were combined the special knowledge of the technician, an unusual literary skill, and an evident love of research. His environment was such as to bring the subject of the justification of armaments constantly to his mind. His father had been graduated at the head of the Class of 1824 at West Point, and had served as an instructor at the Military Academy. He was thoroughly instilled with the military spirit in its best sense. Mahan spent his early years at West Point, but the sea attracted him. "As a boy," we are told by a biographer, "he reveled in stories of naval life, including the reminiscences of naval officers." Choosing a military career upon the water rather than upon the land, he entered the United States Naval Academy. During his life at Annapolis this future "naval philosopher" was described as "the smartest boy in his class." From his first tedious blockade service in the Civil War until his retirement in 1896 he performed various kinds of naval duty in many parts of the world, experiences which were to furnish the technical knowledge and background for his superb theorizing.[1] He served for a year as an instructor in the Naval Academy and for several years as President of the Naval War College at Newport. The task of teaching, however prosaic it may be, does drive one to think and tempts one to set down his thoughts in written form. Professorial lectures produced by industrious research were the means by which Mahan developed his famous system of naval values. He explained to his students the broad aspects of strategy and their relation to statecraft as he saw them, and in so doing he never forgot his loyalty to the naval profession.

In writing, Mahan found the occupation which was most suited to his particular gifts. The titles of his best known works indicate the drift of his thought: *The Influence of Sea Power upon History, 1660–1783* (1890); *The Influence of Sea Power upon the French Revolution and Empire* (1892); *The Life of Nelson, the Embodiment of the Sea Power of Great Britain* (1897); and *Sea Power in Its Relation to the War of 1812* (1905). These volumes, at least so far as their influence is concerned, have taken their place among the most noteworthy in American historical writing. Mahan's reading public was not merely national. His books were read by the admiralties

---

[1] See TAYLOR, CHARLES CARLISLE: *Life of Admiral Mahan, Naval Philosopher*, George H. Doran Company, New York, 1920.

THE DOCTRINE OF MAHAN

of the entire world. They stimulated the naval programs of England, France, Germany, Russia, and Japan, as well as of the United States, and thus added no small bit to that spirit of rivalry in armaments which at the beginning of the twentieth century set the nations building against each other. Mahan not only idealized the navy but, true to his lifelong environment, he idealized war, going so far as to assert that the right to go to war, even upon mistaken conviction, is in accordance with that "moral freedom, and the consequent moral responsibility, which are the distinguishing glory of the rational man, and of the sovereign state."[1] This seems like a strange doctrine to the present war-sickened generation and it is doubtful if a man of Mahan's genius would today concoct such a glorification of nationalistic anarchy.

Mahan was on more rational ground when he contended that historians in general have been unfamiliar with the conditions of the sea and that they have overlooked the profound influence exerted by maritime strength upon world politics. The particular object of his greatest work, *The Influence of Sea Power upon History, 1660–1783*, was to make an estimate of naval factors in the prosperity and power of nations during a period from the early part of the sailing-ship era until the end of the American Revolution.

He marshaled facts to show that in the numerous wars of the period under consideration, navies played the stellar rôles. In the Second Anglo-Dutch War, 1665–1667, the British navy, although suffering some reverses, proved superior to the Dutch fleet and the British retained New York and New Jersey which they had seized just before the formal declaration of war. In the War of the League of Augsburg, in which England and

[1] MAHAN, ALFRED T.: *Lessons of the War with Spain*, pp. 209 ff., Little, Brown, and Company, Boston, 1899.

Holland found themselves united in opposition to France, the French met with disaster because of lack of sea power. Despite their land power and great natural resources they withered away when shut off from the outside world by the British and Dutch navies. In the War of the Spanish Succession, 1702–1713, France lost valuable territory and was economically depleted. England was the great gainer by this war, acquiring Gibraltar, Port Mahon, Nova Scotia, and Newfoundland. Her commerce prospered because of her sea power, while the trade of France was destroyed. Holland was forced by pressure from land to neglect her sea power and consequently she fell behind Great Britain in the race for commercial supremacy. In the struggles of Great Britain against Spain and eventually against France, 1739–1748, England was defeated on the Continent but because of her strength on the sea she was able to make peace at Aix-la-Chapelle on even terms. The Seven Years' War, 1756–1763, was filled with the making of eventful history. During these momentous seven years, sea power wrought tremendous changes in the world map and profoundly affected the destinies of hundreds of millions of human beings in the generations to come. Because of her navy Great Britain was able to seize French possessions in Canada and India, thus adding vast territories of immense importance to her empire. France, humbled upon the water, was robbed of the fruits of the labor of her enterprising empire builders and fell behind Great Britain in the race for world power. Finally, Mahan contends that the War of the American Revolution was essentially a sea war, and that it was the navy of France that secured the freedom of the American colonies.

All of this is but a summary of an impressive array of facts, patiently sought out and beautifully assembled to prove a thesis, which may be stated in Mahan's words as follows:

THE DOCTRINE OF MAHAN

The due use and control of the sea is but one link in the chain of exchange by which wealth accumulates; but it is the central link, which lays under contribution other nations for the benefit of the one holding it, and which, history seems to assert, most surely of all gathers to itself riches.[1]

In recent years with the growth in the United States of the movement for a larger navy these views have been taken up by various writers and have been emphasized even beyond the intentions of Mahan himself. The later writers have become more confident and sweeping in their assertions that the economic prosperity of a country is dependent upon sea power. They contend that a nation must be able at all times to protect its oversea trade both when it is a neutral and when it is a belligerent. The interruption of trade spells economic disaster and such interruption can only be prevented by an adequate navy, say the men of this later school. Admiral Magruder, in his book *The United States Navy*, states the position as follows:

> The Navy is necessary to protect the vital interests of our nation. Particularly it is the guardian of the country's foreign commerce. Without foreign commerce there can be no prosperity. Life without prosperity to an American is scarcely worth living . . . A merchant marine and a protective Navy are essential to the prosperous economic life of the nation and to the welfare and happiness of every man, woman and child in the country.[2]

The idea is stated in its narrowest, most extreme, and most propagandistic form by a writer in one of the marine trade magazines as follows:

> History shows that a Navy and merchant marine are mutually dependent factors and upon both rests the success or failure of the economic expansion and development of any nation.

. . . .

[1] MAHAN, ALFRED T.: *Influence of Sea Power upon History*, 1660–1783, pp. 225–226, Little, Brown, and Company, Boston, 1890.
[2] MAGRUDER, THOMAS P.: *The United States Navy*, p. 158, Dorrance and Company, Philadelphia, 1928.

The United States and Disarmament

To anyone who has even casually read a history of the world, or studied political economy, or more specifically read Admiral Mahan's 'Effect [sic] of Sea Power on World [sic] History' or any authentic contemporary writings, it is obvious that if we expect to endure as a sovereign nation we must be prepared to defend ourselves and our commerce abroad at all times.[1]

This emphasis on the economic necessity of protecting trade by huge navies, it may be parenthetically remarked, is intended to influence the business man and is good naval strategy. It is a plan to break the line of communication and separate the forces of modern thought from the support which they have been receiving from business groups.

Returning to Mahan, the strongest feature of his works, and the same is true of the writings of others who are similarly equipped from the professional viewpoint, is the graphic portrayal of naval campaigns. By the use of charts Mahan demonstrates with great clarity the battle positions and fleet formations of decisive naval conflicts and draws some interesting deductions as to tactics. In the larger considerations of strategy he is likewise lucid and forceful. He emphasizes the part of the navy with regard to the provisioning and convoy of troops, and shows how the acquisition of oversea empires has depended upon the ability to control the sea routes.

He can, however, be properly criticised for failure at times to adhere to the methodology of scholarship, a failure which probably arises from the fundamental defect that he was writing not for abstract truth but for argumentative purposes. While the facts in his book are usually carefully correct they are marshaled predominantly on one side of the question. There is no careful balancing of factors.

It is in this regard a matter of some interest to consider the statement that the War of the American Revolution

[1] SPOFFORD, WOLCOTT: "Naval Limitation and Shipping," *Marine Engineering and Shipping Age*, Vol. 32, p. 507, September, 1927.

The Doctrine of Mahan

was essentially a sea war.[1] The evidence behind this assertion is the convoy of troops and supplies across the Atlantic by the French (an operation which the British performed on a much greater scale) and the Battle of the Virginia Capes in 1781. This battle left the French navy in temporary control of the waters off the Virginia coast and made possible the bottling of Lord Cornwallis at Yorktown. The naval victory, according to Mahan, was "the decisive blow of the war."

Now there are many historians, as for example Creasy in his *Fifteen Decisive Battles*, who feel that the decisive victory of the war was gained at Saratoga in 1777,[2] at which time the entire control of the sea was in the hands of the British. There are others who feel that, because of the strength of their land position, the American colonists would have been independent within a short time whether the Battle of Yorktown had been fought or not. The growing colonies represented an expanding force in the New World created by the impact of a pioneering people upon a virgin continent. The eight million British people across the Atlantic, burdened by the debts and responsibilities created in the Seven Years' War, could hardly have hoped to retain this buoyant and offended people more than a short time. Sea power or not, it was only a question of years.

The evidence which Mahan brings forth to prove his point is open to some critical comment. He cites the opinions of General Washington as to the importance of the French navy in the Revolutionary War. We should remember here that Washington was imploring the French to give all possible assistance. French army officers were of dubious value to the Americans because of their desires for promotions which aroused much

[1] Mahan, Alfred T.: *Influence of Sea Power upon History*, 1660–1783, p. 78.
[2] Creasy, E. S.: *The Fifteen Decisive Battles of the World from Marathon to Waterloo*, Chap. XIII, David McKay, Philadelphia, no date.

jealousy on the part of colonial officers. But the French navy created no such embarrassment. Accordingly Washington was unreserved in his solicitations of French naval assistance. In making his requests it would seem to have been unusually good psychology that he should stress the value of such assistance, and in fact, it would have been no more than human if he had greatly exaggerated the worth of the navy. Extreme statements might have been expected to be effective in persuading the French. Several letters written by Washington directly to the French or to American representatives for communication to the French are quoted by Mahan in his attempt to show that the Revolution was "essentially a sea war."[1] A knowledge of the simple rule of evidence that parties in interest are apt to exaggerate would cause us to question this testimony somewhat, even though uttered by such a respected personage as Washington.

The most elementary facts of history are proof that at least some of Washington's letters contained a radical overestimate of the services to be performed by the French navy. After Yorktown he wrote to De Grasse, the French naval commander: "It will depend upon your Excellency, therefore, to terminate the war." Later he wrote: "Whatever efforts are made by the land armies, the navy must have the casting vote in the present contest." These urgent supplications were made for the purpose of procuring further aid from the French for a southern campaign. But instead of giving such aid the French navy scudded off in the opposite direction and did not come back. In fact, it was badly defeated by the British in the Battle of the Saints in the West Indies in April of 1782. It had nothing to do with the further outcome of the American struggle in the sense which

[1] Pp. 397–400.

The Doctrine of Mahan

Washington intended. It had no "casting vote." Had the termination of the war depended upon De Grasse the cause would have been lost. But naval writers and sea-power enthusiasts at home and abroad have used the appeals of Washington without critical examination to prove the importance of navies. For example, Sir Cyprian Arthur George Bridge, in an article based largely on Mahan's work, sets forth without explanations as to time or circumstance the above-quoted words of Washington to the effect that the navy was to have the casting vote in the Revolution.[1] In all fairness the British naval author should have made clear that Washington's statement was not intended to be a scientific evaluation but rather a desperate appeal to De Grasse for aid and that this post-Yorktown estimate was completely contradicted by subsequent events.

Of course, to point out specific defects in Mahan's evidence is only sniping at a really great piece of historical writing. More fundamental is the inquiry as to whether sea power has been the effect rather than the cause of national greatness. The view of a navy as a result or symptom seems at times to be supported by cogent reasons. Thus Rome, a strong land power, within a few years constructed a fleet which vanquished Carthage, the greatest sea power of that period of history. It was the intrinsic strength of Rome which made this possible, rather than any familiarity with the sea. In the same way the United States has recently risen to the position of the world's greatest economic power, and this rise was in no sense due to a navy. But having attained a supreme position our government probably can, if it should try to do so, outstrip all other nations in naval construction. The comparatively powerful navy that we now have is the result and in no sense the cause of American prosperity.

[1] "Sea Power," *Encyclopædia Britannica*, 13th ed. Vol. 24, pp. 549, 557.

Having shown that there are certain limits and qualifications regarding the sea-power theory we are still met with the great mass of evidence assembled by Mahan, and it would be useless to deny that for the period which he considered, 1660–1783, there was a strong relationship between superiority on the seas and economic progress. That this sea strength was in some respects a result of national power no one can deny; but that it also in turn contributed substantially to the extension of that power seems equally clear. The principal reason why Mahan's theory cannot be safely applied to the present situation is that the conditions from which he built up his principles have now radically changed. The time of which he wrote was an unusual period in the emphasis which it placed upon ocean transportation and the fostering of trade by force of arms. Some historians have pointed out, however, that the changes affecting the life of man which have come about since the industrial revolution have been greater than those which had occurred previously throughout recorded history. As Shotwell has put it: "George Washington at Mount Vernon was closer to Aristotle . . . than we are to the household economy of an estate of colonial days."[1] These changes, as will be shown, have radically altered the conditions which formed the basis of Mahan's writings.

[1] SHOTWELL, JAMES: *War as an Instrument of National Policy*, p. 28, Harcourt, Brace and Company, New York, 1929.

Chapter III

THE AGE OF SEA POWER

THE period from the discovery of America until the World War was a unique epoch in the remarkable emphasis which it gave to sea power. Following the time of Columbus, the nations which possessed ships had within their hands the keys to wealth. Improvements in shipbuilding and navigation coupled with the discovery of new trade routes opened the magic doors of opportunity to those who sailed the sea and revolutionized the economic life of sea-bordering communities. Thereafter, the torpid European world, slowly rousing from its slumbers of the Middle Ages, gathered life most quickly along the coastal regions. The difference in price levels between Europe and the rich continent of Asia had created pressures for the interchange of eastern and western goods and prompted the expensive caravan trade which brought oriental merchandise to the eastern Mediterranean to meet the galleys of the Italian cities. Then suddenly it was found possible to conduct this trade far more cheaply over an all-water route in sailing ships. Simultaneously across the Atlantic a new hemisphere was discovered. The greatest mass migration of all history was to transform the Americas into productive continents and to create enormous new sources of wealth with which Europeans were to be connected by ocean highways. Riches as well as romance inspired the maritime peoples to engage in the new world trade. The commercial revolution had been ushered in.

It was largely the technological progress in navigation and shipbuilding in the fifteenth century which gave to transportation upon the sea its great stimulus of the sixteenth century. The mariner's compass and the simple astrolabe had come into use in Europe about 1300. Prince Henry of Portugal (1394–1460) brought together much of the information of his time regarding nautical affairs. Mathematicians and map makers were imported. Upon a promontory in southern Portugal, Henry established an observatory to perfect the tables of the sun's declination. The use of the compass together with the advance in methods of computing latitude inspired the seamen of the fifteenth century with much greater confidence when sailing out of sight of land.

Improvements in shipbuilding came rapidly after 1400. Small one-masted ships of 50 tons or less, half-decked sailing boats of the fourteenth century, gave way to ships of 100 or 200 tons, and in the sixteenth century vessels of 1,000 tons or more were built. The enlarged carracks and galleons were slow, pompous tubs but they could keep the sea in rough weather. The ability to carry greater quantities of supplies made possible much longer voyages. The arrangement of sails was improved. The earlier ships had one mast on which was hoisted a single square sail. During the first half of the fifteenth century vessels were built with three masts, and five or six sails were used. The triangular lateen mizzen was added to the square sail thus giving flexibility in steering.[1]

The mounting of guns aboard ship introduced a great change in fighting tactics and made necessary the abandonment of the old galley type of naval vessel. Prior to the year 1400, guns had been used by ships in a few instances. By 1500 there were large Portuguese car-

[1] The evolution of the sailing ship is described in E. KEBBLE CHATTERTON: *Ships and Ways*, J. B. Lippincott Company, Philadelphia, 1913, and *The Ship under Sail*, J. B. Lippincott Company, Philadelphia, no date, by the same author.

racks which carried as many as forty cannon. Up to this time they had been mounted on the deck; but the practice developed of carrying them between decks and firing them through portholes. Because of naval guns, fighting could take place at cannon's range and contact with the enemy could now be made by other means than the ramming and boarding tactics of galley warfare. The galley had been flexible and could navigate against the wind and therefore had been used for fighting purposes before the days of cannon. These qualities were more than counterbalanced, however, by the strength and seaworthiness of the sailing vessel and by its ability to strike at a distance. The change from the slender, unseaworthy galley, overloaded with oarsmen and scantily provisioned, to the ponderous floating fortress, bristling with artillery and moving by the power of the winds, gave to maritime people a far greater instrument for the projection of their strength upon the waters and against distant coasts.

European sea power was emphasized by the military and political weakness of other continents. In the south was Africa to be had for the taking but to be passed up for the time because of richer prizes. In the east was Asia, rich with commercial opportunities but politically disunited and unable to repel attacks from the sea made by the determined Europeans. In the west were the Americas where the products of the mines, the soil, the forests, and the sea could be taken without serious opposition by the explorers and merchant adventurers of Europe.

It is a necessary condition for the most successful sea power in the naval sense that weaker peoples exist who can be dominated by force with profit to the dominant people. The masterful and sea-conscious Europeans were in those days able to go forth in their armed ships and to batter down commercial barriers with cannon.

The defeated peoples were weak, disunited, and spiritless; and after the conquest they did not refuse to trade with their conquerors. Such commercial intercourse could not have been carried on had the exploited peoples been proud and nationalistic.

In those older freebooting days there was but little world law. Buccaneers infested the seas. Piracy had been a scourge to commerce from ancient times. Rome had been able to establish some order upon the seas but with the fall of the empire the gangsters of the deep revived their activities wherever sea-borne trade was conducted. In the age of the great commercial revolution, which we are now considering, they flourished in the coastal waters of India, on the Spanish Main, and along the southern coast of the Thirteen Colonies. More than this, in the competition between nations for the world's commerce good patriotic citizens felt moved to plunder the ships of rival nations. Thus Drake preyed upon Spanish galleons, as likewise did the Dutch "beggars of the sea," and the French Huguenot sea captains. Spain and Portugal divided the southern seas between themselves and treated as pirates those who attempted to invade their domains.

Commercial competition between the Christian nations of Europe was thus often a matter of the best arms and the fastest sail. Trade with Asia and America was too dangerous a matter to be carried on by private individuals. It became either a governmental monopoly, as in the case of Spain and Portugal, or it was entrusted to semipublic and monopolistic trading corporations, as in the case of Holland and England. These trading corporations were fighting units, mounting guns on their merchantmen and possessing the power to declare war, to make peace, to establish forts, and to maintain garrisons. Military force was to a large extent a necessary concomitant of trade.

The Age of Sea Power

The sea became the great highway of commerce during this period. Carriage by boat came to have an enormous advantage over carriage by land. The business of transportation could not be profitably conducted on a large scale off the water highways. The old Roman roads had for centuries lain in ruins and good highways had not yet been constructed in their place. Feudal dues also took the profit out of land trade. Some well-established land routes existed, such as the caravan paths from the East to the eastern Mediterranean and the overland route from Venice across the Alps into Germany. As the cheapness and ease of transportation on the water began to enlarge the volume of sea-borne commerce it diverted goods from the land routes. This process can be traced in the decline of Alexandria, whose prosperity had largely depended upon caravans from the head of the Persian Gulf or from points along the west coast of the Red Sea. The effects of this diversion are found in the drooping commerce of Augsburg and Nuremberg, interior centers of the overland trade across Europe. Venice, at the head of the European land route, waned in importance, much like a village which has been left a few miles off the course of a newly established railway.

Small sea-bordering states by exploiting the advantage of their shipping could prosper tremendously while their great land neighbors in the hinterland lay like inert giants—not dead but only sleeping. In that age of Neptune's glory the sailing vessel lorded it over the caravan and tiny maritime states like Portugal and Holland could for a brief period strut proudly in the van of the world's progress among the foremost in wealth and power.

In the sixteenth century the greatest advance was made by Portugal and Spain. The seventeenth was the glorious period of the Dutch Republic. The eighteenth and nineteenth witnessed the flowering of the supreme product of sea power, the British Empire.

The United States and Disarmament
Portugal

Portugal was the first of the maritime nations to develop and exploit the improvements in navigation and shipbuilding. Prince Henry, the Navigator, by his improvement of the nautical sciences and by his zeal in promoting the vigorous game of exploration, laid the foundations for the spectacular rise of his country. Never has one single project in education and research been repaid with such conspicuous benefits to a nation as in this case. Beginning along the northwest coast of Africa the Portuguese mariners had explored as far south as Cape Verde by the time of Prince Henry's death in 1460. Twenty-seven years later the Cape of Good Hope was rounded by Diaz, and in 1497 Vasco da Gama set out upon his historic voyage to the East. Almost eleven months after leaving Lisbon he anchored off the city of Calicut. When he returned to Portugal the following year he brought a cargo which, it is said, was equal to sixty times the investment in the expedition.[1]

Fighting was necessary to maintain this trade. The Moplahs or Mohammedan merchants, who had previously monopolized the commerce carried on with the West through the Mediterranean, did not look kindly upon the invaders. A colony established by the second Portuguese expedition under Cabral was wiped out at the instigation of these Moslem traders. When Vasco da Gama returned to India in 1502 he cannonaded Calicut and destroyed all the shipping in the harbor. The Zamorin of Calicut attacked the Portuguese and their friendly rajahs in the neighboring principalities. A few years later the great Portuguese soldier, Albuquerque, defeated five thousand troops of the Zamorin in open battle. As the expeditions of the Portuguese were largely of a military nature no private merchants were able to

[1] Day, Clive: *A History of Commerce*, rev. ed., p. 184, Longmans, Green, and Co., New York, 1922.

THE AGE OF SEA POWER

finance the necessary preparations and the trade was a governmental monopoly.[1] Fortified naval and trading stations were established along the Indian coast, but the Portuguese were not able to extend their power into the interior. It was their naval strength, the guns of their ships and the supplies brought on shipboard from Lisbon, that made their hold on the coast line possible. A Chinese writer is reported to have observed that the Portuguese were like fishes: if taken away from the water they would straightway die.

Goa became the capital of the new empire and almost rivalled Lisbon as a center of Portuguese life. The large stone houses of the rich Portuguese residents, painted red or white, were surrounded by gardens of palm trees. Merchandise from all parts of the East was brought to the Goa bazaars. Pearls and coral from the Bahrein Islands, porcelain and silk from China, drugs, tea, pepper, and cinnamon from the Spice Islands were exhibited along with the velvet and piece goods from Portugal. Slaves were sold at auction in the main streets.

For a short time Portugal was the wealthiest nation of Europe. Lisbon was the center of a prosperous shipping and shipbuilding industry. Literature and art thrived. Public buildings were erected on a magnificent scale. But the effort to maintain this great commercial establishment was too much for the small nation. Portuguese man power was drained away in the process of expansion. Depopulation was the price of empire. In 1580 the nation fell to the position of a dependency of Spain.

It is a remarkable phenomenon, however, this rise of a tiny state, possessing between one and two million subjects and weak in resources, to the position of leadership in Europe. The knowledge of maritime technology and the courage to plunge headlong into the adventurous game

[1] STEPHENS, MORSE: *The Story of Portugal*, p. 192, G. P. Putnam's Sons, New York, 1891.

of seafaring were among the principal reasons for the brief brilliancy of sixteenth-century Portugal.

Spain

Spain was primarily a land power and was influenced in much less proportion by the commerce gained through naval force than was Portugal. The union of Castile and Aragon, the expulsion of the Moors, which removed an obstacle to harmony, and the rise of industry made Spain the strongest nation in Europe during the sixteenth century. The laborers in the textile industries in Toledo increased from 10,000 to 50,000 in about twenty-five years.[1] In Seville the same industry counted 16,000 looms and 130,000 workers.[2] A large shipping and export business was likewise built up. Over 100 ships, of from 300 to 500 tons each, left Spain in the annual convoys for the colonies and the vessels which cleared for European ports were fully as numerous. Spain was powerful upon the sea due to the existence of the strong merchant marine which could be impressed for naval duty.

The colonial trade, however, was not so profitable in the long run as might have been expected. The Spanish were well schooled in the mercantilist theory that the importation of the precious metals was desirable. They were not aware, however, of the dangers which an oversupply of these metals created in the derangement of the currency. The gold and silver inflation caused by the imports of bullion sent prices soaring. The costs of production went up. The importation of manufactured goods became profitable and the reaction upon Spanish industry was disastrous. This was only one of many causes of the ruin of the Spanish economic system, but

---

[1] DAY: *op. cit.*, p. 176.
[2] WEBSTER, WILLIAM CLARENCE: *A General History of Commerce*, rev. ed., p. 127, Ginn and Company, Boston, 1918.

THE AGE OF SEA POWER

it indicates that the colonies were not an unmixed blessing. Strength on the water was more a result than a cause of strength on the land, and when the decline of Spanish sea power came it followed the weakening of the internal social and economic structure.

Holland

Holland, a name used here as synonymous with the Dutch Netherlands, was the next great sea power to emerge. When the epoch-making discoveries were taking place at the end of the fifteenth and the beginning of the sixteenth century, the lowland provinces were under the rule of the Austrian and Spanish Hapsburgs. The Dutch people, however, had a life-and-death interest in the sea. They were compelled to fight against it for their existence and they likewise made their living from it by their numerous fishing fleets. It is said that the city of Amsterdam was built on herring bones. The Dutch were also famous for their intensive agriculture and their brick and tile manufactures.

The first large participation of the Dutch in world trade came while they were still under Spanish control. Their position at the mouths of several strategic rivers, the Rhine, the Scheldt, and the Meuse, placed them in a position to handle much of the trade with German cities of the interior. The important Baltic trade also came largely into Dutch hands as the cities of the Hanseatic League lost their commercial initiative. The Dutch vessels went to Lisbon to take on cargoes of products brought from the Orient by the Portuguese. These they distributed to the northern part of Europe. Spain annexed Portugal in 1580 and in 1594 the port of Lisbon was closed against Dutch ships. The Dutch, who had for years been in revolt against Spain, now had strong commercial reasons for desiring their freedom. They intended to make their own independent connections with the East in defiance of the monopoly claimed for Portugal.

The first Dutch expedition went to India in 1595 around the Cape of Good Hope and came back two years later with valuable information regarding oriental commerce. By 1602, sixty-five ships had made the return trip and the business had shown promise of great profit. From that time on, Dutch commerce and shipping expanded rapidly.

Along with commercial developments much progress was made in manufacturing. Thousands of Flemish artisans, manufacturers, and other substantial citizens were driven by Spanish mistreatment to Amsterdam, which city soon rose to be the chief industrial and commercial center in all the Low Countries.

Meanwhile, the naval power of the Dutch had been growing with the merchant marine. In 1569, during the early part of the revolt against Spain, letters of marque were issued to Dutch vessels to prey upon Spanish commerce. These privateers, called the "beggars of the sea," took large quantities of plunder, and by capturing towns along the coast they greatly aided the cause of independence. In naval conflicts against the Spanish, success generally lay with the Dutch; and for more than half a century they intermittently dealt smashing blows at the sea power of Spain. Because of their naval superiority they were able to seize the Spanish treasure ships in the Western Hemisphere and to oust the Portuguese to a large extent from their hold in the East.

One of the greatest scholars of the seventeenth century was Hugo Grotius, the brilliant Dutch jurist, who has been called the Father of International Law. His classic work, *De Jure Belli et Pacis*, was suggested by an incident in the commercial conflict. The Dutch captain, Heemskirk, of the East India Company, captured a richly laden Portuguese galleon in the Strait of Malacca. The right of a private company to take prizes was called into question and Grotius set out to prove that the capture was lawful. The result was a manuscript, *De Jure Praedae*, which was an examination of the rules of war and of prize. Many years afterward Grotius developed this legal brief into his famous classic, *De Jure Belli et Pacis*. A special part of the argument had become a separate book. The Portuguese had contended that the eastern waters were their dominion. To sustain the capture of the Portuguese ship by the Dutch East Indiaman, Grotius argued that the ships of all nations could lawfully sail the high seas, and that therefore the Dutch had a legal right to navigate eastern waters. This section, which was Chap. XII of *De Jure Praedae*, was published separately as *Mare Liberum*.

In order to organize the commerce with the East upon a secure basis the Dutch government gave a charter to the Dutch East India Company which was formed as a merger of all the competing companies in that trade. The company was given a monopoly on the trade east of the Cape of Good Hope. The chief officer was the governor-general. The legislative body was the council. The council, in addition to its commercial functions, could declare war, make peace, erect forts, establish garrisons, and appoint administrative and judicial officers. It was a powerful quasi-political body and in its hands lay the empire of Holland in the East.

The Dutch West India Company monopolized the trade outside of Europe that lay west of the Cape of Good Hope. Day, in his *History of Commerce*,[1] describes it as a corporation of privateers which flourished for a time on the prizes taken from Spain. He points out that it opposed peace between Holland and Spain. The fact that business was conducted through such warlike agencies is a significant commentary upon the state of

[1] P. 192.

affairs in international relations and trade, and shows eloquently why sea power in the military sense was an important economic asset.

In addition to the commerce with the East Indies and America the Dutch had an even greater trade with Europe, exporting their own manufactures and importing wool and other raw materials. Their ships also carried the commerce of other countries until they had the greater part of the European shipping business. They were the "wagoners of all seas."

In due time the Dutch were to give place to a larger maritime country with greater resources. It is a strange historical process which in the centuries since the breaking up of feudalism has passed the baton of commercial and industrial supremacy from smaller to larger countries. The vital social energy which is necessary to achievement develops first in local units. Smaller masses are more quickly energized. In large areas several centers of community consciousness exist which for a time conflict with one another. It is this phenomenon which we see in Asia where Japan has achieved political unity and control long before the larger, more cumbersome, and more diversified countries of China or India. There comes a time, however, when the larger mass achieves its delayed unity. Factions become reconciled, one-time enemies begin to coöperate, and the larger nation is able to bring its greater weight of man power, natural resources, and mass effort into the competition. There are, of course, exceptions to this trend but it is well worth keeping in mind as a partial guide when we consider the successive rise of latter-day world powers.

England

The British had become formidable in their neighboring waters even before the age of discovery. Ships were to them a means of defense. The British Isles had early and repeatedly been the victim of invasion from overseas. Romans, Anglo-Saxons, and Danes had in turn landed their conquering forces on English shores. Alfred the Great has been called the Father of the British navy because he began to build ships out of the royal revenues. In 1066, however, the ships of Harold were unable to operate against the expedition of William the Conqueror, due, we are told, to the lateness of the season. Previous to the time of the Conquest and for several centuries thereafter the Cinque Ports on the southern coast were incorporated into a naval jurisdiction for the purpose of furnishing vessels in time of war to the government. These ports which, as may be implied, were originally five in number, were given numerous privileges and were required to supply the bulk of the naval forces. In addition to the Cinque Ports squadron a naval militia was drawn from the other coast towns and counties. The king's own vessels and mercenaries were a third element in the English navy.

English sea forces held a considerable control over the four seas surrounding the British Isles and foreign vessels entering these waters were required to strike their topsails and lower their flags in recognition of English mastery. In the Battle of Sluis (1340) the English fleet was victorious over the French, and Edward III called himself the lord of the sea. The British power was not continuous, however, even in the narrow seas and it was not extended to the world beyond.

During the reigns of the Tudors and the Stuarts' important developments took place in the naval forces. By the time of Elizabeth the admiralty had been converted to a belief in the sailing vessel in preference to the galley, and had also developed a liking for ships of moderate size. A 600-ton ship, it was concluded, was superior to a 1200-ton ship, because of the greater ease of management.[1] The British made revolutionary progress during this period in the use of naval artillery and their wisdom was amply demonstrated in the repulse of the Spanish Armada when the Spanish galleons, their decks crowded with soldiers ready to board the English ships, were subjected to a hot fire from the superior English guns. "Six inch guns against bows and muskets tells the tale."[2]

Despite their naval ability and seamanship the English were not as yet ready to become a great sea power. Lack of economic and political development prevented the mustering of energies for oversea operations. It is true that such adventurous spirits as Hawkins and Drake seized occasional Spanish treasure ships, but such freebooting did not result in any great national gain.

During the Tudor and Stuart reigns, however, much political and economic progress was achieved. Religious differences were settled. Sheep raising was giving way to cultivation. Domestic manufacture was increasing. Colonies were established in America and a foothold was gained in India. The devastating fight between the King and Parliament was decided in favor of the latter by the Revolution of 1688. Union with Scotland was brought about in 1707.

Competition with Holland became keen as English shipping increased but for a long time England was not able to gain equality. The Navigation Laws of 1651 were a blow aimed at Dutch shipping. Subsequent wars against Holland resulted in British victory; but it was about 1740 before the English trade equaled that of the Dutch.

By the middle of the eighteenth century the stage was set for great developments. In the Seven Years' War, Canada and India were wrested from the French because

[1] STEVENS, WILLIAM OLIVER, and ALLAN WESTCOTT: *A History of Sea Power*, p. 149, George H. Doran Company, New York, 1920.
[2] *Ibid.*, p. 162.

THE AGE OF SEA POWER

of the superiority of the English fleet. A summary of British progress through naval superiority will be found in the previous chapter in the epitome of Captain Mahan's argument. During the eighteenth century the doctrine became fixed in the British admiralty that their navy must be greater than the sea forces of the two Bourbon monarchies, France and Spain, combined.[1] In the nineteenth century the British forged ahead faster than ever. Following the Napoleonic wars they had no naval rivals. The industrial revolution came first to the British and they developed a tremendous productive power through the use of machines. In the output of manufactured goods they were supreme, and they swept forward to a conquest of their own colonial markets as well as those of many other countries. British shipping and shipbuilding preëminence became greater than ever when iron construction and steam power were applied to ships.

Just before the World War the British Empire stood out as the most illustrious example of the creation of sea power which the history of the world affords. About one-fourth of the population of the globe dwelt under the British flag. Nearly half of the world's steam tonnage was under British registry,[2] and more than half of the world's sea-borne trade found its origin or its destination within the Empire.[3] London was the world's financial center and the total pre-war exports of British capital have been estimated at about $20,000,000,000. The British navy was able to maintain a wide margin of supremacy over its nearest rivals, and, following eighteenth century precedents, a policy known as the two-power standard was adopted. This standard was es-

---

[1] MAHAN, ALFRED T.: *The Influence of America in International Conditions*, p. 112, Little, Brown, and Company. Boston, 1919.
[2] DAY: *op. cit.*, p. 381.
[3] *Ibid.*, 377.

tablished in accordance with a report on the maneuvers of 1888, rendered by three admirals, which recommended "that no time should be lost in placing the British navy beyond comparison with that of any two powers."[1]

Compared to these vast commercial and political domains of the British Empire the realms of the sea kings of antiquity, with their limited production and commerce and their puny galleys, were very small affairs indeed. The Empire was the great culmination of the sea-power period of history.

In viewing these four centuries of maritime supremacy, certain points seem to stand out clearly. Ocean transportation was exalted as the sailing vessel came to surpass by a wide margin the slow and expensive caravan. Force was necessary to economic progress because of the lawless character of the times. Large sections of the human race were politically retarded and it was found to be profitable to break down with smashing methods the obstacles which barred Europeans from trading with the backward peoples. Naturally the economic rivalries of European nations concerned themselves largely with oversea trade and possessions, and the sea became the principal battle ground on which commercial conflicts were settled.

[1] HANNAY, DAVID: "Navy and Navies," *Encyclopædia Britannica*, 13th ed., Vol. 19, p. 309.

Chapter IV

THE TWILIGHT OF NATIONAL SEA POWER

FOR more than a century prior to the World War mechanical, economic, and cultural changes had been preparing the way for a new régime in world politics in which strong navies were to lose their influence in the determination of national destiny. In the new period the dwellers on land were to be emancipated from the control of those who sailed the sea and the tremendous destructiveness of war was to rob naval effort of its profits. This revolutionary realignment is here to be dealt with under two heads: (1) the comparative growth in power of land areas and the decline in military effectiveness of navies, and (2) the economic unsuitability of military and naval force.

The Growth in Power of Land Areas and the Decline in Effectiveness of Navies

For a time after the commercial revolution, which began in the latter part of the fifteenth century, seaboard communities developed much more rapidly than inland regions. As has been shown, this was due largely to the revolutionary improvements in water transportation which quickly outstripped the slow and costly methods of moving goods by land. With the coming of the railroad and telegraph, however, the land areas were rapidly energized. Interior regions came to possess a buoyancy, vitality, and unity in sharp contrast to the stagnancy and divided localism of the pre-industrial period. This movement has continued to the present time and shows no signs of cessation. The railroad now cuts the expense of land transportation to less than a tithe of its former prohibitive cost and quickens to machine speeds the processes of domestic commerce. Telegraph and telephone systems are the nerve filaments of the sensitive social organism. The airplane has introduced a new implement of rapid transportation, the potentialities of which have been barely glimpsed in its use as a carrier of mails and passengers. It has been planned to use aërial navigation as a means of bringing together far-flung possessions of maritime powers. Because of the disasters of ocean flying, however, the plane has rather clearly demonstrated its superior utility for employment above land areas as compared with transoceanic use. Another recent invention, the radio, makes possible the instantaneous communication of the spoken word to populations spread over a vast continent, carrying unpredictable possibilities for the obtaining of mass response. This, whatever else it may mean, spells social power—a power never dreamed of in the days of the pack horse, the freight wagon, and the postrider.

Today we have the beginnings of a second age of great land empires, which differ, however, from ancient Persia and Rome in that they are to be knit together by a strong community consciousness. These are not nations on the modest scale of France, Spain, or Germany. Those countries were built of fragments which were brought together in comparatively small combinations in proportion to the strength of the unifying processes which existed at the time of their formation. In the greater sweep of industrial and social movements of today those countries are themselves but fragments, as truly as were the principalities out of which they were once constructed. They are too small for the operation of large-scale industrial and commercial enterprises on the plans of twentieth century production and distribution. A substantial part of their national energies is expended in

The Twilight of National Sea Power

the maintenance of military and economic boundaries. Nationalistic considerations stand in the way of European union. If these continue to prevail economic and political leadership will be withdrawn to other parts of the world where the new effective political unit is being shaped according to continental proportions.

In this new development occasioned by the revolution in land transportation and communication, the larger part of the twentieth century seems to belong to the United States. We may be sure that the successful nations which are to raise themselves to a plane of equal or greater productive power will also be composed of large contiguous territories whose oneness will be made possible by the unifying contrivances of machinery and electricity. Europe will come again into its own when it is able to remove its compartment boundaries and form its life upon a modern scale under a régime of economic and political rationalization. Russia, when she shall accomplish her industrial revolution, cannot be denied a leading place among the new super-nations. China, politically united and modernized with western capital, will forge ahead of maritime Japan as an express train speeding along the shore will pass a 15-knot coastwise steamer. And India! The industrial nabobs of Bombay in the twenty-first century, economic potentates and unifiers of probably more than 400,000,000 people, will enjoy many a laugh at the manner in which their ancestors trembled before the Europeans from beyond the rim of the earth who came in their frail ships and demanded homage.

Ocean transportation will have its place, an important place, now and always, but it will serve and not dominate the new order. The very life of the leading communities will not be dependent upon the sea as it was in Phœnicia, Venice, Holland, and Great Britain. Shipping and naval groups which were all-important in the economy of those countries are to have a much less proportion of influence in the great land machines.

Military science has already reacted to this change until today the shore defenses of well-developed countries have become impregnable against assault from the sea. In the past, an attacking fleet roused terror along the coasts for it appeared unannounced, struck with comparative swiftness, and the land forces were often unable to concentrate to meet the naval thrust. The effect of land transportation in diminishing the probabilities of successful invasion from the sea is well illustrated by an incident in the British defense committee in 1911 as related by Viscount Haldane, then Minister of War. The committee was making plans for military assistance to France following the Agadir incident. A difference of opinion then arose between the army and navy officials regarding the method of rendering assistance. The admiralty had plans for landing British troops on the Baltic coast of Prussia. Viscount Haldane in his autobiography asserts that these plans were derived from the analogy of the Seven Years' War of a century and a half before. The army officials took the view that this was impractical "because the railway system which the Great General Staff of Germany had evolved was such that any division which landed, even if the Admiralty could have gotten it to a point suitable for debarkation, would be promptly surrounded by five or ten times the number of enemy troops."[1]

In pre-industrial days a navy was the best defense against oversea attack, for it could engage the enemy upon the water, threaten his lines of supply, or compel him to occupy himself in protecting his own shores. The Athenian ships were "the walls of wood which alone could not be taken." Time and again has the British

[1] VISCOUNT HALDANE: *Richard Burton Haldane, an Autobiography*, p. 241, Doubleday, Doran & Company, Garden City, 1929.

The Twilight of National Sea Power

navy defended the shores of England against attacks from overseas, whether in repelling the Spanish Armada or in making impossible the Napoleonic plan of transporting an army to England by a fleet of barges. But today the installation of heavy coast artillery and fire control methods, the use of mines, both electric and contact, the development of dangerous defensive vessels, such as submarines and other torpedo craft, swift concentration systems of railways and motor roads, the ability to observe by aircraft and report by radio the movements of an enemy fleet off the coast, and, finally, the great superiority of shore-based aircraft over naval aircraft make it dangerous for the navy of today to venture within several hundred miles of a hostile shore. The power of the land, once limited to a feeble control over a scant three miles of ocean, is now projected outward radiating its vibrant energies over a broad zone of water two or three hundred miles in width.

In 1814 the British fleet was able to enter Chesapeake Bay and to destroy shipping and docks. Even the national capital was occupied, and public buildings were burned. In the World War there were only a few raids out of the dark, as at Zeebrugge and Dover, and each of these was followed by a speedy retreat. The one serious attack on land defenses, that at the Dardanelles, resulted disastrously to the British and French naval forces. The great margin of supremacy of the combined allied navies was not nearly enough to permit the landing of troops on the German coast. Since that time the development of aërial warfare has so increased the power of the forces operating from land that it has been questioned whether the British could maintain their fleet in the North Sea or the Mediterranean in case of war against nations bordering on those waters.

The fighting sciences reach their highest moral values in these improved coast-defense systems which are the bulwark of home rule. They protect against the landing of troops on foreign soil, the devastation of homes, and the atrocities practiced on men and women which are inseparable from military occupation—abuses which the best developments of military discipline seem unable to eradicate. The world has no reason to grieve over the fact that the navy has fallen in the comparative scale and that the modern industrialized nation has become immunized against invasion by foreigners from the sea.

Changes in the mechanics of maritime warfare have made it impossible that one country can control the world's wide oceans and intricate narrow seas. New instruments of warfare have given to nations bordering the sea the ability to frustrate the overlordship upon the waters of any supreme navy. These devices are swift raiders, submarines, and airplanes.

In the days of England's most complete maritime ascendancy her commerce could to a certain extent be assured of safety. The British navy scoured the seas for enemy privateers and frigates. The home bases of the foe were often bottled up with the old-time close blockade. Focal shipping points were guarded. Merchantmen were armed to repel privateers. And beyond this protection they found a degree of safety in flight, for there was not then much difference in the speeds of commercial and fighting vessels.

Today, however, the sea raider has a great advantage in speed over the merchantman. A 15-knot steamer cannot run away from a 30-knot cruiser. An overwhelming superiority in naval vessels is not sufficient to protect shipping against the activities of these commerce destroyers. If we believe the testimony of Earl Jellicoe, who during the war was the commander-in-chief of the British grand fleet, the task of dealing with the German raiders baffled the best naval science. The 114 cruisers in the British navy were not enough. At the outbreak

THE TWILIGHT OF NATIONAL SEA POWER

of the war there were twelve German war vessels outside the North Sea. These were two armoured cruisers, six light cruisers, and four armed auxiliaries. The armoured cruisers and three of the light cruisers were in the Pacific and did not operate against commerce. Two light cruisers, the *Emden* and *Karlsruhe*, and three armed auxiliaries caused most of the damage. Altogether, 250,000 tons of allied shipping was sunk before the German ships were disposed of. Later in the war three disguised German raiders destroyed 293,000 tons.[1] And all this occurred in the face of an Allied fleet that had nominal command of the sea.

One of the later raiders was the windjammer *Seeadler* commanded by the likeable and romantic Count von Luckner. Another was the *Wolf* which slipped through the British vessels in the North Sea and spent fifteen months without being intercepted. Carrying a seaplane this vessel was the first raider equipped with aërial observation. The *Wolf* sank seven steamers and seven sailing vessels and returned to port through the British cordon. An enemy with more widely dispersed home bases which could not have been closed by blockade could have set free scores of such raiders to destroy commerce.

The submarine is another obstacle to the supremacy of the surface navy. The "cut and dried" control of the seas is defied by what Kenworthy and Young call the "cut and run" system of destruction.[2] During the World War, three and finally four of the world's strongest fleets were combined against one. And yet through submarine sinkings the allies and the neutrals serving them lost

---

[1] *Records of the Conference for the Limitation of Naval Armament held at Geneva from June 20th to August 4th,* 1927, p. 29, Geneva, 1927. See also KENWORTHY, J. M. and GEORGE YOUNG: *Freedom of the Seas,* pp. 102 ff., Horace Liveright, New York, 1928.

[2] *Op. cit.,* pp. 67–68.

more than 5,000 ships aggregating more than 11,000,000 tons. Had the Germans used the submarine without restraint from the beginning they might have won the war. It also seems more than reasonable that had Germany, the world's greatest land power, been pitted in single combat against England, the world's greatest sea power, the submarine would have helped to give the victory to Germany.

The airplane is the third reason why no one nation can now control and protect ocean traffic. If trade routes lie along narrow seas, they can be dominated by the planes of an enemy whose air bases border on these waters. No matter what naval strength a nation may have it will not be able to control the sea lanes as long as such air bases can be maintained. The surface of the water may be kept clear but overhead will come the all-seeing airplanes. Enemy merchantmen and questionable vessels will be signaled to put into port for inspection. Failure to obey will mean destruction by bombing, but ordinarily this step will not be necessary and there will be no loss of life. In such waters the airplane is a much more humane weapon than the submarine and far more effective. By putting on wings the landlubber has gained a great advantage over Jack Tar in the waters adjacent to the shore, and has secured domination over those invaluable trade routes which lie along the narrow seas.

It has become impossible under modern conditions to maintain a wartime commerce against the opposition of a strong enemy. When the British at Geneva fixed their needs at seventy cruisers for the purpose of guarding their eighty thousand miles of trade routes, they were indulging in fantasies. One nation, however gallant, industrious, or competent, cannot protect an immense trade over all of the waters of the world. If a country goes to war against a strong opponent, regardless of

The Twilight of National Sea Power

how much naval effort it exerts, it will lose a large proportion of its ships and cargoes.

The Economic Unsuitability of Forceful Methods

Navies have almost entirely lost what was once their most important function, that of fostering trade. Today a people cannot get rich through naval activity. The profits which apparently accrued to nations in the colonial and commercial wars of the sixteenth, seventeenth, and eighteenth centuries have been replaced in modern warfare by destructions of capital, the loss of credit, and the ruination of markets.

Following the days of exploration, when there was comparatively little trade, when international investments were small in amount, and when rich fields of commerce lay ready to be seized, the use of the navy helped to open up greater business opportunities. Thus the bombardments which gained for Portugal a foothold on the Indian coast resulted in an increase of wealth at Lisbon. The force used by Holland to displace Portugal and by Great Britain to wrest India from France cleared the way for commerce. The occupation of the Americas by European powers meant trade expansion. In those days, it might be argued, wars were economic struggles in the true sense that a nation as a whole might gain by fighting. Of course, it may be pointed out that had the European nations composed their differences peacefully they could have advanced more rapidly. But, nevertheless, warlike activity against the weaker continents made the way for increased trade and this trade went largely to the European nations which successfully beat off the competitors of their own continent. Quarreling Europe advanced, not so rapidly as a more peaceful Europe might have done, but yet it advanced. The theory of economic gain from naval action was fully believed and it dominated governmental policies.

The growth of economic interdependence, largely a product of the years since 1850, has, however, made the old generalizations absolutely worthless. The high-powered explosives hurled from present-day long-ranged, large-calibered artillery not only mangle the bodies of men but they blow up the structure of international business organization. There now exist in each country very considerable and influential groups of citizens who depend for their prosperity upon successful and uninterrupted production abroad. Hostilities interfere with this condition. As Norman Angell has so well pointed out, war breaks down international confidence and destroys enormous wealth based on international credit.

Interdependence as measured by the volume of trade is today far greater than in previous centuries. The foreign commerce of the world in 1700 has been estimated at about $125,000,000. By 1800 this had increased to $1,400,000,000, and by 1850 to $4,000,000,000. In the latter half of the nineteenth century the curve turned sharply upward until by 1900 it had reached $20,000,-000,000 and just before the World War, $40,000,000,000.[1] In 1928 the amount was estimated at about $68,000,-000,000. The barter of the seventeenth and eighteenth centuries looks small indeed as compared with this voluminous interchange. Greater security on the sea, rapidity of communication, regularity and comparative speed of shipping, insurance, and the growth of financial machinery to serve international trade are some of the outstanding characteristics of the new organization.

Migrations of capital in recent years, irresistible and world-wide, have created a new mechanism for the international transmission of economic welfare and depression. The threads of property ownership, which in this movement have been drawn across national lines in countless numbers and directions, constitute a sensitive nervous

[1] DAY: *op. cit.*, pp. 270, 271.

THE TWILIGHT OF NATIONAL SEA POWER

system. An injury to one part of the world frequently causes a severe disturbance in another. Congress strikes at Cuban production by raising the sugar duty. The blow injures financiers in this country and depresses the securities of American corporations which own most of the sugar-producing properties in Cuba. Economic nationalism has, in this case, defeated its own purpose.

War is a more extreme illustration of the sympathetic nervous reactions caused by economic disasters. It is akin to an amputation which has devastating effects on all parts of the body. A war between the United States and a European coalition would shrivel and destroy the subsidiary nerve centers of American business in Europe where hundreds of American companies have established branch houses, and would cut asunder the connecting lines of legal titles held by Americans to billions of dollars' worth of property located on the European continent.

The confusing entanglement of international business must eventually prove to be a powerful counterinfluence to chauvinistic nationalism. Dr. Charles A. Beard in a brilliant article a few years ago enumerated the evidences of financial internationalism. He pointed out the greatly increased quotations of foreign bonds on the New York Stock Exchange. He called attention to the fact that American corporations have invested heavily in the ownership of foreign companies, which companies in turn have invested in the industries of still other countries. He reviewed the development of that comparatively recent marvel of financial cosmopolitanism, the international investment trust, which is promoted by the financiers of various countries, places its investments all over the world, and is owned by the stockholders of many nationalities. Contemplating this bewildering legal creature Dr. Beard was moved to comment:

> One might well ask how Mr. Coolidge and Mr. Wilbur, who propose to protect the American dollar wherever it is invested and

endangered, will be able to dissect the said dollar from this complex and direct the navy and marines immediately upon its locus. On the other hand, how will the company in question discover the right government to be chosen to do the protecting? Indeed the dollar, franc, mark, pound, lira, pengö, belga, krone, guilder, peseta, and zloty patriots of many countries will be perplexed in choosing their side of the next war for participation and propaganda. It is hard to imagine the alignment they can make in harmony with their interests and the form of the myth which will be necessary for the populace that is to fight and pay for the rescue.[1]

We have ample evidences of the effect of war on the modern business structure, evidences which should overwhelm and confound those who continue to preach that a nation can increase its wealth by waging so-called economic wars. Previous to 1914, the theory that gun power was a condition precedent to commerce was widespread in Great Britain. Norman Angell, writing on the eve of the World War, summarized this attitude as follows:

If she [England] has dominated the commerce of the world in the past, it is because her unconquered navy has dominated, and continues to dominate, all the avenues of commerce. Such is the currently accepted argument.[2]

Previous to 1914 there were past-minded Englishmen who believed that the rising commercial power of Germany was a menace to Britain's existence. They saw with apprehension the activities of clever German salesmen who, through superior wares and better business methods, were capturing many British markets. To these apprehensive Englishmen it seemed that if Germany could be wiped out, the result would be a great commercial gain to England.

The war which they had in mind came, and Great Britain poured forth her wealth in the conflict. Neutrals

[1] BEARD, CHARLES A.: "Prospects for Peace," *Harpers Magazine*, February, 1929, p. 327.

[2] ANGELL, NORMAN: *The Great Illusion*, p. 5, G. P. Putnam's Sons, New York, 1911.

The Twilight of National Sea Power

expanded their commerce and took over a great share of the export trade of the British. One of Britain's best markets, Germany, was partially ruined. The international chain of trade, by which German purchases from British customers had made British sales possible, was broken. The devastations wrought in the economic life of the British allies also reduced markets. Instead of entering a period of rapid trade expansion following the defeat of Germany, the British found themselves slipping downward into an era of painful depression and unemployment. Modern British thinkers have accepted the generalizations which are logically to be drawn from the hard facts of the war and have discarded the older theory that national prosperity can be promoted through force. That theory was based on older conditions, such as existed at the time of the Seven Years' War, and it is today rendered obsolete by the internationalization of business.

The case of Germany proves much the same point. Prior to the war the economic advances of the German Empire had marked out for that country what seemed to be a certain pathway to the supreme position in the world's trade. But many Germans were impatient and thought that they could smash through more quickly by military methods. As one representative of this view put it, German commerce must be carried everywhere "under the protection of German cannon."[1] The belief that the use of force was necessary to prosperity was shared by an influential school of German economists. The enlargement of the imperial navy was decided upon allegedly for reasons of trade protection. In the war which the naval program helped to precipitate, Germany lost her trade and much more. "Der Tag," in the sense of commercial and military supremacy, will

[1] SEYMOUR, CHARLES: *The Diplomatic Background of the War*, 1870–1914, p. 101, Yale University Press, New Haven, 1916.

never dawn; and the German people must resign themselves to the hope that they may share in a coöperating Europe that glory which they once hoped would be reserved for the Fatherland alone.

Wars may still be fought on the mistaken assumption that they contribute to national economic welfare. There will always be selfish minorities that will benefit from international conflict, and we may be sure that they will attempt to convince their governments that any particular war will be beneficial. At times of crisis such arguments may have some weight, for war psychology is irrational and there is no cool calculation of the tremendous costs involved.

Furthermore, pseudo-economic motives may still impel nations to war. The term pseudo-economic as used here is in need of explanation. Two rival states may find themselves competing for the annexation of a certain piece of backward territory. The dispute may become so intense that each nation will believe that it must either fight or give up its claim. A hard war will cost the winning nation far more than it can hope to gain. There will be an interruption of production. Heavy tax burdens will be imposed upon the people. And the standards of living will be lowered. In a true sense such a war will be most certainly uneconomic. On the other hand, a successful war followed by the annexation of the territory in dispute will maintain the economic power of the victorious nation at a higher level than that of its defeated rival, and this relative advantage will give great satisfaction to 100 per cent nationalists. The conquest of new territory will result in control over additional resources (in partial compensation for those that were destroyed in the war), and these resources can perhaps be used in waging a future war. Thus a certain prestige based on relative resources, power, and military success is gained.

THE TWILIGHT OF NATIONAL SEA POWER

If the nation decides to relinquish its claim to the territory without war it will lose prestige. If it fights a winning war and annexes the territory its prestige is enhanced. The flag is moving forward and not backward. This feeling of prestige appeals powerfully to ruling classes, governmental officials, patriotic societies, concessionaires, and business men resident abroad in backward countries. These groups, accordingly, sometimes exploit the sentimental side of nationalism to a point that is altogether vicious. It is false patriotism to exhort a nation to military conflict when the result is almost sure to be a weakening of the social structure, the slaughter of large numbers of citizens, and the depreciation of the standards of living in return for a certain intangible respect in imperialistically minded circles. A sacrifice of the economic welfare of millions of citizens in order to promote a sense of dignity on the part of a limited number, who cannot think in terms of realities, is poor policy, especially from the standpoint of the citizens. But, nevertheless, national prestige is still a more potent motive than it deserves to be; and wars for pseudo-economic reasons, in the sense that, while they relate to economic factors and are fought over economic spoils, they have highly uneconomic effects upon the great body of citizens, are still possible.[1]

A real cause for hope, however, lies in the fact, already discussed, that highly influential and political groups, *i.e.*, industrialists and financiers, are coming to believe that war is disastrous to their own pecuniary interests. To such men, the notion of prestige gained through war has accordingly lost much of its former weight. The motives of these men may spring from self-interest, but from the social standpoint they most decidedly represent

[1] For a penetrating analysis of so-called economic causes of war see R. G. HAWTREY: *Economic Aspects of Sovereignty*, Longmans, Green, and Co., London, 1930.

one step forward in the progress of rational thinking. The business man as such is at least more cool-headed and less willing to cut his own throat by attempting to annihilate his oversea rivals than is the sentimental "patriot."[1]

John Maynard Keynes, the British economist, has pictured the possibilities of a wonderful economic development. In progressive countries a century hence the standard of living will be four or eight times above its present level. Gradually increasing portions of the population will be endowed with wealth sufficient to remove from their lives the grim problems of economic necessity. In this paradise of our grandchildren the code of morals based on the bitter needs of grasping and holding economic goods will be changed for a more exalted and altruistic standard of conduct. All of this improvement, says Mr. Keynes, depends upon certain conditions, one of which is *that there shall be no important wars.*[2]

Another significant change which is making the use of force less profitable to the stronger nations is the growth of intercontinental equality. In the processes of international commerce, investment, and education the weak have been made strong. Mechanical methods of production, distribution, and communication, as well as the political ideas of the Western world, have been introduced into the so-called backward regions. These changes in the lives of the exploited peoples have inevitably promoted unity in thought, a capacity for coöperative action, and a more vigorous sense of national pride. As this development has progressed it has become increasingly difficult to establish and maintain trade by forceful methods.

[1] See HAMMOND, MATTHEW B.: "Economic Conflict as a Regulating Force in International Affairs," *American Economic Review*, Vol. 21, p. 1.

[2] KEYNES, JOHN MAYNARD: "Economic Possibilities for Our Grandchildren," *Saturday Evening Post*, p. 27, October 11, 1930.

THE TWILIGHT OF NATIONAL SEA POWER

In 1853, Commodore Perry went to Japan with a squadron of war vessels which overawed the seclusive Japanese. The commodore started negotiations which resulted in the opening of a market which had been closed for two hundred years. Gunboat diplomacy paid dividends in increased trade. But today such methods have no place at all in American-Japanese relations. In fact the surest way to destroy our commerce with the Sunrise Kingdom would be to dispatch a fleet of threatening warships to Japanese ports. Previous to Commodore Perry's commercial exploits Great Britain had waged war on China and by the Treaty of 1842 had been successful in opening five Chinese ports. Here again force proved to be profitable and a very substantial business was created. In 1925, however, the use of force by the British in Shanghai and Canton was met with a disastrous loss of trade due to the boycott on British goods in southern China. One author estimates that during the fifteen months of the boycott the British city of Hongkong lost $300,000,000 in trade. Property values and shares in Hongkong industrials dropped $500,000,-000. "Certainly in October, 1926," says this author, "even after the boycott had ended, Hongkong had all the appearances of a deserted village. Business was dead. Buildings were empty, offices were closed, and there was very little activity of any kind."[1]

The powers still maintain war vessels in Chinese waters but they must use them with considerable care. And the time cannot be far distant when they will be eliminated from that trade altogether. Already observers from Shanghai report that British and American commercial leaders of the most conservative type—often referred to as "die-hards"—have radically revised their notions

[1] ORCHARD, DOROTHY J.: "China's Use of the Boycott as a Political Weapon," *Annals of the American Academy of Political and Social Science*, p. 260, November, 1930.

regarding the use of force. They now appear to have accepted the theory that friendliness to their customers is more profitable than the threat of military intervention. When Chinese unity shall be attained, foreign gunboats will be withdrawn from the rivers of China and armed force will play no greater part in our trade with that country than it now does in our trade with Japan.

In the Americas the power of the fleet in the development of trade was once likewise great but it has now diminished to a vestigial condition. From the discovery of America to the proclamation of the Monroe Doctrine, sea power and commerce went hand in hand in the New World. The business prospects of Portugal, Spain, Holland, France, and England rose and fell with the successful activities of their armed ships. The increase in the strength of the countries in the Western Hemisphere brought an end to this situation. European war vessels are no longer on station along the Spanish Main. Warships still have a function related to economics in American countries, as is shown by the use of the Caribbean squadron of the United States in stabilizing conditions in the waters of Central America. Even in this small field of action the display of force is not always financially profitable. One of the greatest blunders of all American diplomacy occurred when President Roosevelt rejected patient negotiation for the use of a naval threat in the Panama affair. When the Colombian Senate refused our offer of $10,000,000 for the canal zone, the United States turned from the procedure of peaceful purchase and a gunboat was dispatched. A revolution was begun by French interests in Panama. When Colombian troops approached to quell the disturbance, an American naval officer refused them the right to land. The revolution succeeded and the new Republic of Panama leased us the zone for $10,000,000. Later we paid Colombia $25,000,000. Thus, instead of buying the zone for possibly $15,000,000 plus some minor concessions to Colombian pride, the United States chose the way of the gunboat, paid eventually $35,000,000, and incurred a much greater liability in the ill will of Latin America. In resorting to sea power we selected a method which may once have been effective but which proved in 1903 to be a blundering and costly means of attaining a very simple end. Had President Roosevelt possessed the requisite tact and patience, with all the diplomatic cards in his possession, and particularly with the alternative of the Nicaraguan route, he could have acquired a canal right of way for less money and could have increased the regard for the United States in Latin America, which taken all together would have been a much more profitable bargain.

A great deal has been written about the rôle of the American naval officer in diplomacy, and it is a very picturesque subject. But if we examine the cases in which the naval officer has performed this service we find that they fall under two heads: (1) Cases of dealings with countries where naval diplomacy was once possible but no longer exists as in negotiation with weaker peoples which have now either increased in strength or which have been brought under the protection of stronger powers. Under this head fall the dealings with the Barbary pirates, with Hawaii, and our early relations with Japan. (2) Cases in which the possibility of naval diplomacy still exists, as in the Caribbean or Central American republics. Admiral Caperton's manipulation of the Haitian government in 1915 is an example. Here the percentage of American commerce affected is not large. Furthermore, such naval activity does not in any sense call for an increased fleet. The operations are minor in character and are generally conducted with ships that are too old for the first line.

Altogether, as a greater intercontinental equilibrium appears and as backward peoples develop a consciousness of equality, the power of navies to increase commerce and trade is gradually lost.

The growth of law and order throughout the world has likewise eliminated much of the necessity of naval power. Private self-help has now gone from the seas while national self-help to promote maritime interests has shrunk greatly in importance. Private redress was at one time permitted by usage and it was fully approved by governments. The early letters of marque gave to shipowners who had been injured by foreigners the right to take compensation by seizure of foreign shipping even in times of nominal peace. Thus in 1295 a subject of the King of England, whose cargo of figs had been seized by Portuguese sailors, was given license by the King to take Portuguese goods until he had been repaid.[1] Less formal was the system of raids without open official permission which were conducted against the commerce of rival countries. Such quasi-piratical practices were frequently given secret governmental sanction for they injured the trade of competitors. In days when there were no public fleets of consequence these activities kept the shipowners in trim to bear the burden of the fighting when war should be declared. Sir Francis Drake despoiled the galleons of Spain and his freebooting was regarded with approval by his countrymen. Private redress received a severe blow in England when Sir Walter Raleigh was thrown into prison on complaint of the Spanish ambassador and executed for an attack upon a Spanish port in South America. In due course unlicensed activity of this kind was outlawed. Likewise, letters of marque and reprisal given in times of peace

---

[1] STARK, FRANCIS R.: "The Abolition of Privateering and the Declaration of Paris," Vol. VIII, p. 50, *Studies in History, Economics, and Public Law*, Columbia University, New York, 1897.

The Twilight of National Sea Power

were discontinued. Privateering survived for some time and letters of marque, granted to harass enemy commerce in times of war, continued to be issued until the middle of the nineteenth century. The practice received its deathblow when it was renounced in the Declaration of Paris in 1856. Thus the private shipowner lost his legal right to seize merchandise upon the seas.

The decline of piracy has likewise taken away an important function of the public navy. This scourge to commerce, which formerly furnished a striking argument for the maintenance of public armed ships, has now practically passed away. Pirates defied the law with surprising persistence until in comparatively recent times the great growth of commerce, the need for security, and the increase in the strength of the groups interested in legitimate sea trade brought about their downfall. Where once there had been willing buyers for stolen goods and a certain amount of public sympathy the pirates found themselves confronted by the lack of markets and the cold hostility of the law. The British navy played a conspicuous part in the clearing of the seas. As commerce grew in importance, the merchants became more determined that they should not be robbed, and they stirred their governments to greater activity. Navies became more vigorous and law triumphed over lawlessness as the growing volume of trade created the necessity for secure conditions. Accordingly, a commercial vessel can now navigate the oceans unarmed. This is a very significant change from the days when merchant ships were forced to sail under the protection of war vessels, or to carry their own armament.

The naval function of sea police, although very much diminished, still exists. Should the nations disarm entirely their action would be followed by a revival of piracy backed by modern methods of organization and finance. But the levels at which navies are maintained today are much more than ample to deal with the problem. In fact, national sea power is not absolutely necessary for this task for it could be well performed by a system of international police.

As a final evidence of the trend of the times away from that fiery nationalism which is so destructive of a harmonious economic order let us consider the movement toward world organization which has gathered such surprising momentum in the last decade. A recent list of principal international conferences, exclusive of meetings of public international unions, shows one hundred such meetings for the ninety-six years from 1818 to 1913 inclusive. In the nine years from 1920 to 1928, inclusive, the convention method of settling world problems made remarkable progress and seventy-five such conferences are recorded.[1] The great increase in frequency is characteristic of the coöperative movement of the new age. To this we must add the large amount of international business transacted by the Supreme Council, the Council of Ambassadors, and the regular organs of the League of Nations, which activities are not included in the above-mentioned post-war list.

The rise of the League of Nations most truly represents in an institutional way the progress of internationalization. When the victorious allied and associated powers became the nucleus of the League, there was a decided attitude of hostility toward it, not only from the defeated nations and from old-fashioned nationalists but from idealistic pacifists as well. Fears that it was to be merely a special militaristic compact to enforce an unjustifiable peace have, however, been definitely allayed. In the years since the war the League, representing fifty-four members, has gradually

[1] HILL, NORMAN L.: *The Public International Conference*, pp. 229–233, Stanford University Press, Stanford University, 1929.

THE TWILIGHT OF NATIONAL SEA POWER

taken a central place in directing the processes of international life. Each year the Assembly of all the members convenes in Geneva to consider questions affecting the welfare of the world. A series of annual meetings, comparable in scope to the Hague Conferences but filled with a better spirit of coöperation have thus become a regular part of the world's routine. At least four times each year the League Council meets to take action upon an agenda which is crowded with pressing international issues. While all the time in Geneva a permanent and busy secretariat, with a total staff, including the clerical services, of about 670 persons drawn from 51 countries, grinds out the day-to-day grist of investigations and conference preparations.

The League has already performed invaluable services for a sick world. It has considered some 30 political disputes and has brought about a settlement of many of them, including some which in all probability would have led to war. It has organized nine reconstruction loans which have amounted to $400,000,000, and has helped to repatriate some 400,000 war prisoners. It has supervised mandates and special districts and has been the best friend of oppressed minorities. More than 2,000 treaties have been registered with the Secretariat which has published about 100 volumes of treaty texts, thus providing an incomparable source of current treaty information. It has brought about conferences on the most vital issues in international affairs, including such subjects as the traffic in arms, disarmament, health, labor conditions, and world economics. It has sponsored the fight against the drug traffic and has waged war against epidemic diseases.[1] It has without any doubt proved to be the greatest intelligent agency for inter-

[1] For a survey of League activities see *Ten Years of World Cooperation*, Secretariat of the League of Nations, Geneva, 1930; and SWEETSER, ARTHUR: "The First Ten Years of the League of Nations," *International Conciliation*, No. 256, January, 1930.

national coöperation which the world has seen. In the words of General Smuts:

> Mankind has, as it were, at one bound and in the short space of ten years, jumped from the old order to the new, across a gulf which may yet prove to be the greatest divide in human history . . . What has been done can never be undone. One epoch closes in the history of the world and another opens.[1]

The American student who turns to consider the coöperation of the United States with the League since our government began to deal with the Secretariat in 1923 is invariably surprised at the extent of our participation in activities sponsored from Geneva. This, however, should occasion no particular amazement for it is inconceivable that a nation like the United States, which is bound up with international affairs in a thousand ways, could ignore the political organs of internationalization.

The World Court which is adhered to by forty-five members has provided a modern mechanism for the solution of judicial disputes. The new tribunal is decidedly more effective and promising than are the arbitration systems which date from pre-war days. Thus far it has rendered sixteen judicial decisions and has handed down eighteen advisory opinions many of which have resulted in the elimination of international quarrels.

The Kellogg Pact renouncing war as an instrument of national policy has been ratified by fifty-six governments. Six others have signed or have signified their intention of signing the treaty which leaves only two nations outside the scope of the agreement. The pact is a drastic amendment of international law with regard to the right to wage war, and has at least provided a legal basis upon which a workable system of outlawing war may be erected.

The bold self-help of past centuries has lost its efficacy and its respectability. The use of war to obtain

[1] Quoted in SWEETSER, *loc. cit.*, p. 60.

The Twilight of National Sea Power

a desired end, once a well-recognized remedial measure, is coming to be looked upon as an aggression against the international community whose system and interests are thereby threatened. The nations best equipped for life in this integrating world must eventually prove to be those with the coöperating attitude. Powerful, solitary states, whose navies are a threat to peace upon the seas and whose armies cause alarm on land, are as unfit for success in the dawning age of internationalism as the self-reliant outlaw in a period of encroaching civilization.

PART II
AMERICAN NAVAL NEEDS

Chapter V

THE DEFENSE OF TERRITORY

THE value of war and armaments must be recomputed in the light of the modern international economic system which has been created by specialization in production, rapid transportation, and instantaneous communication. There are good reasons why this country, from the standpoint of its own interests, should be a chief sponsor of the reduction of armaments. The United States rose to first place in the economic scale without the aid of military power. During the period of rise, which was most rapid in the neutral years from 1914 to 1917, our navy was commonly described as third-rate. This country owes no gratitude to sea power as a means of attaining wealth. Americans now have a greater stake than any other people in the successful and pacific working of economic internationalism. Nor are the usual fears regarding national defense and the memories of invasion so strong as to interfere with an intelligent control and limitation of the war machine. Under existing armaments this country has a wider margin of security than any other power, due to defensible coast lines, large population, wealth, and the enormous war potential of American industry. The United States is therefore relieved to a great extent from the alarms which inhibit the modernization of thought in certain other countries. Furthermore, a mutual reduction of armaments will tend in some respects to increase that security by decreasing the forces which might threaten the American position.

The United States and Disarmament

A reasonable national security must, of course, be an absolute essential to any successful attempt to reduce military power. There are certain interests which, in the public mind, are too vital to be jeopardized. The policy toward which the American government seems to be veering makes ample provisions for these. The present chapter and the two which follow discuss the question under the heads of the defense of territory, the defense of trade in war time, and the defense of neutral trade.

Incomparably the most important function in the American scheme of national defense is the safeguarding of continental United States against attack. Although there is no quantitative method of measuring national interests it seems conservative to say that at least 95 per cent of the human and property values of the nation are located in the continental homeland. Here 122,000,000 American people live. Here is located the great mass-production machinery of the American economic structure. Alongside of the enormous wealth, resources, and social interests of this vast region the possessions of the American people located abroad are of comparatively little consequence. Of course, the whole world economic system contributes materials and markets to the American economy, and any major dislocation of the international scheme will throw some parts of the American machine out of adjustment. We cannot shut ourselves up at home and thus escape the economic effects of a war of any consequence whether we are parties to it or not. There is no human way to prevent loss in such a case. Navies and diplomacy are alike inadequate. The question of protection against such disaster is primarily not that of national defense but that of maintaining world peace. Certain steps to reduce the commercial loss arising from extra-continental interferences in case war should come will be dealt with later. At this place,

The Defense of Territory

however, the question of territorial defense only is to be considered.

Fortunately the problem of the protection of the United States against invasion is not a difficult one. No other nation in the world can face this task with the same confident assurance. Our principal frontiers are our coast lines, fronting the Atlantic and Pacific oceans. Under modern conditions of defense, an invasion and landing along the shore of an industrial country by an expeditionary force from across such great stretches of water is almost unthinkable. Plans for invasions of this sort existed in the archives of war councils prior to the World War, but modernists in the military game have discarded such schemes as relics of another period of history. There is no reasonable likelihood that an alien power would be able to carry the coast of the United States against the defense of battle fleet, coast artillery, torpedo craft, mine fields, and shore-based aircraft.

It would, however, involve certain risks in this day of the airplane, to permit the existence of a hostile navy in the adjacent seas. There is the danger that aircraft carriers, under fleet protection or operating independently, might reach a position within two or three hundred miles of the coast from which a devastating air attack could be launched. The United States need not fear such an invasion from the sea as that made up the Chesapeake by the British in the War of 1812; but there exists, nevertheless, the possibility of an aërial raid over a commercial and industrial center, such as New York City, which could easily inflict damage greater in amount than the entire cost of the War of 1812. The navy has, from the standpoint of the defense of territory, an important function to perform in prohibiting the entrance of enemy naval forces into the proximity of American shores and in repelling them if they so intrude.

The United States and Disarmament

The function of territorial defense is classified by naval administrators under two heads, local defense and general defense, or, in other words, defense by naval districts and by the battle fleet. Local defense is a minor naval activity under present conditions. Naval districts, into which the coast line is divided, maintain shore establishments which include: radio stations; observation equipment; landing fields; fuel, ammunition, and mine depots; and submarine bases. The vessels assigned to such districts are small submarines, submarine chasers, old destroyers, mine vessels, aircraft tenders, scouting craft, and local vessels which may be taken into the government service in time of war. The naval district extends out to sea sufficiently to include the coastwise sea lanes. It is the function of these local forces to fight enemy craft in the district waters and to coöperate with the army in repelling attacks upon the coast. In time of war scouting patrols are used to detect the approach of an enemy and under-water listening posts are employed. Contact mines, nets, and booms are installed and mine sweepers are provided Such local forces would, in conjunction with air and land defense, make it exceedingly difficult for enemy vessels to remain in proximity to the coast line. Torpedo craft, particularly submarines, would subject the enemy vessels to danger of attack day and night.[1]

In addition to the local defense system, and far greater in importance, is the battle fleet, which would seek to defend the coast by conducting operations against the enemy fleet. The battle fleet may venture thousands of miles from the shore for the purpose of defeating or containing the hostile naval forces, or it may assume a position in the vicinity of its own coast for the purpose of intercepting the enemy ships should they attempt to

[1] *Joint Action of the Army and Navy*, Chapter V, prepared by the Joint Board, Government Printing Office, Washington, 1927.

The Defense of Territory

approach. In the past, there have been disadvantages in the policy of passive waiting. With the meager facilities for reconnaissance and communication, the immobile defensive fleet was largely in the dark as to the movements of its foe while all the advantages of singleness of purpose and definiteness of action lay with the attackers. Today, however, the fast scouting vessel and the patrolling airplane, assisted by radio communication, have greatly increased the facilities for watching the movements of a hostile navy and for reporting the findings immediately to the naval command. The fleet which ventures out of its own waters to attack an enemy has lost much of its former advantage of secrecy. Accordingly, any naval policy of aggressive oversea action based on the experiences and successes of naval operations in the past is apt to be erroneous.

The present American policy of maintaining a navy equal to the strongest single rival, the one-power standard, should, for purposes of the defense of territory, provide a wide margin of security. Other things being equal, the fleet which fights near its own coasts has a decided advantage over one which is distant from its base. The advantages of nearness to base lie in the proximity to fuel, supplies, repair facilities, and, in some situations, aircraft support from shore. Two equal fleets fight on even terms only when equidistant from their respective bases. As they move away from this central point, the fleet which is drawing near its own shores gains strength while the other is correspondingly weakened. Accordingly, in a policy of defensive waiting, the American fleet would possess a considerable combat superiority over an invading enemy. This superiority would be lost and the advantage would pass to the hostile forces if our battle fleet should cross the line of equal strength and make contact with the enemy in the vicinity of his own shores.

The present disposition of warships shows that the defense of continental United States is not considered a difficult matter by the strategists of the Navy Department. The fact that the battle fleet is maintained in the Pacific, leaving only the scouting fleet in the Atlantic, is ample evidence of this attitude. There is almost no possibility that the Pacific coast can be carried by naval assault. The location of the larger part of American naval forces in the Pacific is an indication that the uppermost purpose in the minds of those who direct our policy is not defense of territory but naval action in Far Eastern waters or perhaps the effect which the presence of the battle fleet in the Pacific may have in our diplomacy with Japan. Thus the disposition of the fleet shows that this country is in the exceedingly fortunate situation of comparative indifference to naval attack upon our home territory.

Next to the safeguarding of continental United States, the protection of the Panama Canal is of supreme defense importance. The canal has great strategic value. It permits the transfer of war vessels from one ocean to the other. The obstruction of the canal would prevent this transfer, and might, under some circumstances, be equivalent to the sinking of several hundred thousand tons of naval vessels. The canal has also great commercial value. Through it pass the water routes connecting the two coasts of the United States, those from Atlantic and Gulf ports to the Far East or to the western coast of South America, and those from the Pacific coast to Atlantic and Mediterranean ports. Thus for strategic and commercial reasons the United States cannot permit the capture of the canal.

There is no likelihood that an enemy could wrest the canal from the United States. Such a movement could not be accomplished without first seizing American bases in the Caribbean. This would be a tremendous disaster

THE DEFENSE OF TERRITORY

to the United States, for it would cut off our trade with South America. Considering the effort which the United States would certainly exert because of the vital importance of this region and allowing for the enormous advantages which our forces would possess over those of an attacking enemy, it may be set down that the seizure of the Caribbean and Panama area by hostile forces is practically out of the question under present naval ratios.

The blocking of the canal by well-directed bombs is not, however, beyond the bounds of practical possibility. The obstruction of the canal by air bombardment might be accomplished should the enemy possess an ally among the northern countries of South America, or it might result from an enemy naval raid from overseas. During the maneuvers around the canal early in 1929, the aircraft carrier *Saratoga* of the forces attacking from the Pacific approached the canal at high speed under cover of night and in the darkness of the early morning let loose some forty-five planes at a distance of ninety miles from the entrance to the canal. Theoretically these planes bombed the locks.[1] In actual war, moreover, the planes could have taken off at a distance of three or four hundred miles from the canal. The carrier could have retired immediately with all speed leaving the planes to deliver their attack and then to fly into neutral territory for internment. It is not inconceivable that a fast enemy ship disguised as a merchantman with its decks camouflaged to conceal airplanes would be able to come within attacking distance of the canal. This hazard could be reduced to the minimum by maintaining, in case of war, extensive air and water patrols in the Caribbean and the most improved types of air defenses at the canal.

The Panama Canal maneuvers of February, 1931, demonstrated the increasing part which aviation has

[1] *New York Times*, January 27, 1929.

come to play in plans for the protection of the canal. The maneuvers were staged to solve the highly artificial problem of an attack by the battle fleet of a Pacific power seeking to conduct a large convoy to the coast of one of the Central American republics. Having gained a foothold within striking distance of Panama, the attacking forces would have been able to menace the canal with planes which they were theoretically prepared to unload and set up at the newly acquired base. The defending forces were those of the United States Scouting Fleet, which was composed of one battleship and a force of cruisers, destroyers, and submarines. To these were added the aircraft carriers, *Lexington* and *Saratoga*, and the dirigible, *Los Angeles*. The burden of the assault upon the invading fleet and its convoy fell to the lot of over two hundred planes which were carried upon the decks of the carriers and cruisers. Under war conditions additional aërial support would have been available from the army air forces at the canal.

In the Pacific the problem arises as to how far the United States should attempt to extend or maintain its naval power in the face of increasing Asiatic nationalism and race consciousness. There are strong reasons to doubt the wisdom of building a stronghold in the Philippine Islands to await the shock of a coming conflict seven thousand miles away from territory inhabited by the American people. The trusteeship of the United States in the Philippines should be regarded as a temporary matter from which a retreat may be made in an orderly fashion that will bring credit upon this country, and it should not therefore be bolstered up by a strong permanent military establishment. It is exceedingly difficult for a powerful country to relinquish its control over a weaker people in a graceful and creditable manner as is well proved by the embarrassments of the British in India. The example of Great Britain in the West

The Defense of Territory

Indies, however, is worthy of note. At one time England had undoubtedly aggressive aims in that region. At the time of the War of American Independence the Caribbean was a naval zone of some importance. One of the most striking British victories was that of the Battle of the Saints in 1782. As time went on, Great Britain acquired British Honduras, the Bay Islands, and a protectorate on the Mosquito Coast in Nicaragua, looking forward to the time when a British canal would pierce the isthmus. Such a development would have given Great Britain control over one more of the great world trade routes. The growing power of the United States finally made the plan impractical. The Clayton-Bulwer Treaty and the Hay-Pauncefote Treaty were the diplomatic steps of England's dignified retreat. The British naval bases in the Caribbean have been allowed to fall into a state of practical obsolescence. The naval establishment at Bermuda, although built up after the Civil War, was greatly reduced after the Spanish-American War. The defenses at Bermuda and Jamaica are not sufficient to offer any real resistance to a naval attack. The fact is that the British have practically capitulated in this region.

For the same reason the United States would do well to retrench gradually in the Far East until a graceful withdrawal can be accomplished without shock to American pride. Such a withdrawal would be to the eternal credit of the United States, and would be evidence of a higher grade of intelligence than governments have ordinarily been able to show in the handling of imperial affairs. The Philippines have not been a paying proposition. Commercial developments which were forecast in 1898 have not materialized. Manila has not come to rival Hongkong as a distributing center in the Far East. Such Philippine trade as the United States has been able to divert to itself by means of tariff preference has not been of sufficient consequence to balance the liabilities which this country has found it necessary to assume. It is estimated that the annual profit to American citizens from commerce, investments, and personal service amounts to less than $10,000,000 per year, whereas the United States contributes at least $4,000,000 per year for the maintenance of government in the islands.[1] If we should add to this the interest on the cost of acquisition and pacification which would amount to more than $20,000,000 per year, and also a fair rate of interest on the capitalized liability in national defense, it is apparent that the Philippine account of the United States would show a decided loss.

The liability in national defense of these possessions is enormous. With present equipment in the Philippines and with present ratios in naval vessels, the islands cannot be defended against Japan. The 10:6 ratio in capital ships and aircraft carriers and the Washington Treaty agreement not to increase fortifications represent an abandonment of the Philippines so far as their immediate defense against a strong Far Eastern power is concerned. From Formosa, which lies about three hundred miles from the Philippines, the Japanese could conduct an assault by sea and air against which the United States has no adequate protection. While the harbor defenses at Cavite are strong, the Japanese could effect a landing elsewhere on the island and capture Manila from the land side. With the rapid development of the mechanics of warfare the American defenses, already a decade behind the times, are slowly but surely becoming obsolete. Under the Washington Treaty it is impossible to add air defense facilities. As a naval officer recently testified: "Aviation has been developed considerably since 1922, yet we can not even add a ramp, or

[1] BUELL, RAYMOND LESLIE: "Philippine Independence," Foreign Policy Association *Information Service*, Vol. VI, Nos. 3 and 4, p. 75, 1930.

The Defense of Territory

a hauling out ways, in the Philippines now for our six planes that we have out there; we can not put up another radio station to communicate with them."[1]

Should this country engage in war with a Far Eastern power the Philippines would be immediately taken and would later be regained after an expenditure which might easily run as high as twenty or thirty billions of dollars. The acquisition of the islands thus appears to be the most severe blow ever dealt to the American defense system. Prior to 1898 the oceans had been a protection to the United States. In that year, the American government in a moment of imperialism deliberately abandoned this protection and extended its territories seven thousand miles overseas. Unless a prudent policy is followed we shall ultimately be forced to pay for this lack of foresight.

The major error in the calculations of the United States in 1898 was the failure to estimate the possibilities of Asiatic nationalism. This was an easy mistake to make. Subsequent developments, because of the inadequacies of political science, were at that time practically unpredictable. Accordingly, the McKinley administration based its action on the apparently sound premise of western supremacy and Asiatic political incompetence.

This premise is now being revealed as false. The possibilities of political power in Asia have risen beyond anything which could have been foreseen in 1898, and the end is not yet. Ordinarily when the defense of the Phillippines is discussed, Japan is the enemy in mind. Eventually much more powerful nations than Japan will develop in the Far East. A united China, confident of her future and with a nationalistic spirit which has been forecast by the firm attitude toward western nations assumed by the Kuomintang, will ally herself in time with the aspirations of other Asiatic peoples. A strong

[1] *Treaty on the Limitation of Naval Armaments*, p. 302, hearings before the Senate Committee on Foreign Relations, Government Printing Office, 1930.

China will be a natural leader for the suppressed nationalities of Asia against American, British, French, and Dutch rule. Before a Chinese Monroe Doctrine in Asia, Western imperialism will eventually be helpless. It will be well when that time comes if the United States will present no shining target at which a fervent Asiaticism can aim.

The natural base in the Pacific which the United States should defend as its farthest outpost is found in the Hawaiian Islands. Pearl Harbor, located 2,100 miles from San Francisco, affords opportunity to develop a splendid outer fortification against sea attack. The harbor is ample in size and is approached by a dredged channel through which the *Saratoga* or *Lexington*, the largest vessels in the American fleet, can enter. For a century American naval officers have regarded Pearl Harbor as a strategic point of the first importance. In recent years it has been built up as the strongest and most adequate naval station outside of continental United States. The base is defended with heavy guns and is equipped with barracks, good roads, electric lights, sewers, and a water system with a distilling plant. It possesses a radio station, a submarine base, an air station, and an oil depot. A large drydock and machine shop exist for repairing battleships, although it is said the present drydock is not adequate for the largest ships.[1] With this base standing out in the Pacific 2,100 miles from the United States it appears that the difficulties of an attack upon our Pacific coast from Japan would be insuperable.

Hector Bywater, an English authority on the naval problem, has devoted a great deal of attention to the question of war and strategy in the Pacific. According to his view the hazards of a hostile expedition from Japan

[1] For a discussion of naval bases see WILLIAM T. STONE: "Outlying Naval Bases," Foreign Policy Association *Information Service*, Vol. V, No. 15, 1929.

The Defense of Territory

conducted against the islands would be so great as to make such a movement next to impossible. The Japanese would be forced to risk the destruction of their fleet, and thus imperil their national defense, in an attack across 3,400 miles of water. During the slow journey over this distance the fleet with its auxiliary ships and troop transports would be subjected to attack by submarines and aircraft from the bases in Hawaii. Upon reaching the islands they would have to reduce the batteries of heavy guns and howitzers at Oahu, and in the encounter the advantage would unquestionably lie with the shore defenses. If the forts could be silenced, the landing of troops would have to take place at a point where they would not be subjected to fire from such fixed batteries as would remain in action. This would necessitate the use of small boats in the debarkation process. The troops would then be forced to face a devastating machine gun barrage on the beach. If they could survive all of this they would have to defeat the division of American troops which is maintained on the island.[1]

It seems farfetched to suppose that the Japanese, whose very existence depends upon naval defense, would imperil their precious vessels so far from home and under such unfavorable conditions. If they should be successful their victory would be of little ultimate consequence. Considering all of these factors it is safe to conclude that the Pacific coast of the United States, with its powerful outpost at Pearl Harbor, is the most securely defended stretch of commercially important coast line anywhere in the world.

[1] BYWATER, HECTOR: *Navies and Nations*, p. 199, Houghton Mifflin Company, Boston, 1927.

Chapter VI

THE PROTECTION OF TRADE DURING BELLIGERENCY

NATIONAL defense in its primary sense means the protection of the homeland against invasion, but in the first stages of economic internationalism the term takes on new meanings. A modern specialized state draws upon the world for its food and materials. If it be a maritime and industrialized state, such as Great Britain or Japan, the imports from the territories of other people or from oversea possessions come to be indispensable. In such cases, under the system of nationalistic wars, the maintenance of the open sea lanes is as necessary as the guarding of the coasts against invading enemies.

With the growth of power on land and in the air, however, naval defense of world trade routes which pass near to hostile shores becomes difficult, if not impossible. The position of the strictly maritime nations is, therefore, precarious. Changing world conditions have robbed them of their protection; and, unless a system of world security is established, the survival of these oceanic types as great world powers is highly problematic.

Food

Countries whose rising industrialism causes them to rely upon foreign food supplies during a period when the mentality of the world has not advanced beyond the psychology of private wars frequently pay a heavy price for their prosperity. The industrial revolution of the last century was not the first to produce situations of this sort. When ancient Athens became a commercial and indus-

Protection of Trade during Belligerency

trial center, the population of Attica migrated to the city in such numbers that the local food production was no longer sufficient for the needs of the people. The docks of the Piraeus were crowded with grain ships from the Black Sea and from all over the Mediterranean world. So long as the Athenian galleys were able to protect the sea routes, all went well. But when the galleys failed, starvation loomed ahead. In 404 b.c. the Peloponnesian fleet under Lysander captured the Athenian galleys and blockaded the Piraeus. This maneuver cut off the incoming supply ships. A Spartan army intercepted provisions from the land. After a few months of starvation the Athenians were forced to submit and their empire fell. The fierce localistic mentality of the Greek city states had not been modified in accordance with the economic internationalism which had made the Athenians so dependent upon their neighbors.

The rapid, cheap, and dependable transportation of the modern era has brought about an exchange of foods and raw materials on an incomparable scale. Trains and motor trucks cross boundary lines with shuttle-like rapidity and mammoth ocean liners bring exotic products into the life of every advanced people. Political thought is still strongly influenced by the nationalistic and separationist tendencies which began with the breaking up of the Middle Ages. But international dependence has made private war as unprofitable and as painful to the advanced nation as it was to dependent Athens.

The weakness of nations which seek the enormous advantages of internationalized economics under a political system of nationalistic cutthroat competition was amply demonstrated during the World War. That conflict in one important aspect was a struggle for food and materials. Each side tried to isolate the other from the world. Germany had come to rely upon outside sources for important raw products. When these were shut off by blockades and trade agreements the result was food rationing, semi-starvation, and greatly reduced industrial efficiency. The rations permitted to the masses of civilians in the German cities during 1917 and 1918 were in total calories about 60 per cent of normal and this reduction was followed by a drastic shrinkage of human work power to less than two-thirds the capacity of the pre-war German laboring population. High death rates traceable to subnutrition produced losses which may have been equal to from one-fourth to one-eighth of the war casualties.[1] The civilians drowned by German submarines were few in comparison with the hosts thus prematurely swept away.

In return, the Germans struck a heavy blow at their enemies by raiding the incoming British supply ships. Like ancient Athens, England, because of rural depopulation and city growth, had become dependent upon the outside world for food. Three-fifths of her supplies including grain, meat, and dairy products from the furthest seas were annually imported. The Germans risked all to bring England to her knees. During the month of April, 1917, "the blackest month of the war," the total losses of allied and neutral shipping from submarines amounted to 395 ships of 840,000 tons. The daily list of vessels sunk en route to England gave the British people ample cause for the gravest anxiety. The success of antisubmarine devices saved the situation. But it must be remembered that Great Britain, with the most powerful naval force ever assembled, was for a time faced with the prospect of defeat through starvation.

The United States representing the new continental type of nation, has a vast agricultural hinterland which gives it a relatively secure position in the matter of food supplies. Corn and wheat fields are connected with the

[1] TAYLOR, ALONZO E.: "Results of the Blockade upon Germany," *World's Work*, Vol. 38, pp. 595–596, October, 1919.

Protection of Trade during Belligerency

centers of population by fast lines of transportation. The principal food products of the temperate zone are grown in amounts which permit of an excess for export. Following are the figures for the chief food exports in 1929:

Wheat, including flour	$192,300,000
Fruits and nuts	137,500,000
Meat products	78,800,000
Fish	23,500,000
Dairy products	17,900,000

On the other hand, the country has come to rely upon imports of food of a tropical and subtropical nature which either cannot be produced in this country at all or which cannot be grown here profitably in sufficient quantities to supply the American demand. Our principal food imports for 1929 were:

Coffee	$302,400,000
Sugar, cane	209,300,000
Fruits and nuts	86,600,000
Cacao or cacao beans	49,500,000
Vegetables and preparations	47,800,000

A glance at these lists indicates that the food problem should not be an urgent one for the United States in time of war. Coffee is the most vulnerable spot in the food list, by far the larger part of the American supply being shipped from Santos in Brazil which is the greatest coffee-exporting port in the world. Should the United States be engaged in a war with Great Britain, this trade would be subject to interruption by raiders operating from the British bases in the Falklands and South Africa. Whether in time of war it would be profitable and desirable to reroute the coffee trade by rail to the head of navigation of the Rio São Francisco whence it would reach the ocean more than a thousand miles to the northeast of Santos is a question which transportation and naval men would be faced with in the contingency of an Anglo-American war. Under any plan of commerce in such a war the cost of coffee to the American consumer would soar to the levels of luxury prices. This would be checked somewhat by the growth of coffee production in Mexico and countries adjacent to the Caribbean. The effect on the public in the United States would not in itself be disastrous. The withholding of a beverage would upset well-formed habits and would be irritating, but it might result in strengthening the morale for the time being. In the long run, if the war did not progress satisfactorily, we may predict from German experience that such a deprivation would add to the psychology of unrest.

Sugar, another imported food of great importance, comes mostly from Cuba, although there is considerable production in continental United States and the insular possessions. In the year 1928–1929 the production of cane and beet sugar was for Cuba, 5,775,000 tons, while 1,279,000 tons were produced in continental United States and 1,975,000 tons in the insular possessions. The United States is fortunate to have in Cuba such a conveniently located source, and from the standpoint of national defense the raising of the tariff on sugar is unwise. Increased tariffs will cause the United States to obtain a smaller percentage of sugar from Cuba and a larger percentage along the less defensible trade routes from the Philippines and Hawaii and thus weaken our best located supply.

Other food imports of a tropical nature such as fruits and cacao can be procured from relatively secure sources in the Caribbean, Central America, and the northern countries of South America. Thus the food problem would not be a serious one to the United States, even in time of war. This is all the more true because of the fact that the large food-producing countries of Mexico and Canada lie on the American borders.

Protection of Trade during Belligerency

Raw Materials

War has become largely a contest between scientists. Chemists, engineers, industrialists, and metallurgists have thrown their skill into the competition of military technology. Man power is overshadowed by machine power and the military technique of the past is as nothing in comparison with the science of industrialized warfare. A pigmy behind a machine gun, at the controls of a bombing plane, or among the retorts of a laboratory is now endowed with the destructive power of a regiment of giants.

The modern war machine has been built up to a large extent by the international movement of materials. No nation has been able to construct its military equipment entirely out of its own resources. The less advanced countries import rifles, explosives, airplanes, and practically all the implements of war. Such nations, when shut off from the world by blockades, find their military power immensely reduced. The United States has adequate industrial facilities for making war appliances, but this country is dependent upon outside sources for a number of the essential materials which enter into the processes of manufacture.

Minerals present a greater problem than vegetable materials. Many agricultural products which are not originally found in this country may be introduced here and grown with success. Those products which, because of climatic considerations, cannot be grown in the United States, can with few exceptions be propagated in the American tropics. Minerals, on the other hand, are not located uniformly in climatic zones, but are often found in comparatively limited spots. This lack of uniformity in distribution, taken together with the fact that minerals cannot be reproduced, has made necessary vast shipments of ores and metals, amounting to nearly a third of the world's mineral tonnage, across political boundaries.[1]

The continued industrial efficiency of the United States depends to a large extent upon international trade in minerals. About 40 per cent of the world's mineral production and consumption takes place in the United States.[2] But the minerals consumed do not coincide altogether with the minerals produced and consequently this country is both an exporter and importer of these commodities.

The Committee on Foreign and Domestic Mining Policy of the Mining and Metallurgical Society of America classifies the minerals for which this country is dependent upon foreign sources as follows:

1. Those which exist in the United States but in amounts which are inadequate to our needs: antimony, asbestos, ball clay, kaolin, chalk, chromite, corundum, garnet, certain grades of graphite, grinding pebbles, manganese, mercury, mica, monazite, Naxos emery, nitrates, potash, precious stones, pumice, tungsten, vanadium, and zirconium.

2. Those minerals which are entirely or almost entirely lacking in the United States: nickel, cobalt, platinum, tin, gem diamonds, black diamonds, or "carbonado," and diamond dust and bort.[3]

As an illustration of the importance of some of these minerals of which so little is popularly known let us consider the case of manganese. The steel industry is dependent upon manganese which is used in the manufacturing process as a deoxidizer and a desulphurizer. In some cases it is also used as an alloy to impart greater resistance to the finished steel. No other element has been discovered which can perform these various services at

---

[1] LEITH, C. K.: *World Minerals and World Politics*, p. 13, Whittlesey House, McGraw-Hill Book Company, Inc., New York, 1931.

[2] *Ibid.*, p. 48.

[3] *International Control of Minerals*, published jointly by the American Institute of Mining and Metallurgical Engineers and the Mining and Metallurgical Society of America, New York, 1925, p. 13. LEITH: *op. cit.*, p. 185.

PROTECTION OF TRADE DURING BELLIGERENCY

permissible costs. "In short, manganese, in the present state of the art, is indispensable for the production of good steel in large quantities."[1] The scanty manganese resources of the United States make importation absolutely essential. The ore can be mined in this country under the pressure of high prices, but such production would tend to exhaust local supplies and could not long be adequate to the needs of steel manufacturing which is one of the most important basic industries in the waging of war. According to the testimony of Colonel William P. Wooten, the initial ordinance and transport equipment of a modern soldier requires about one ton of steel. World War experience showed that from two to two and a half tons were expended annually by the Western European belligerents for each soldier in the field.[2] Thus, manganese, as an essential to the steel industry, becomes an important war material. In case of a war with Great Britain, both the Russian and Indian supplies would probably be denied to the United States. In such a case, rising prices would bring about an increase in domestic production and the Brazilian ores would be drawn upon as far as possible.

Aside from minerals, the United States is entirely dependent upon outside sources for such necessary industrial materials as rubber, manila, sisal, and shellac. Rubber is obtained from British and Dutch possessions in the Middle East, but sources in Liberia and Brazil will doubtless some day be available. The Brazilian producing section lies in the valley of the Amazon and the rubber exports will be shipped to the United States over a trade route which, it seems, may be made com-

[1] *International Control of Minerals*, p. 53.
[2] WOOTEN, COLONEL WILLIAM P.: "Raw Materials and Foodstuffs in the War Plans and Operations of the Army," pp. 269–270 in WILLIAM S. CULBERTSON: *Raw Materials and Foodstuffs in the Commercial Policies of Nations*, The Academy of Political and Social Science, Philadelphia, 1924.

paratively secure. Manila is procured from the Philippines, sisal from Mexico, and shellac from India.

It would be impossible to point out all of the raw materials which the United States would desire to import in a future war or to appraise with any accuracy the success which the government would probably experience in its efforts. Changing technology will create new industries and require the importation of materials which are now unimportant. All of the increased skill of the scientist of tomorrow will be used to create synthetic materials as substitutes for those which cannot be imported. Thus, if war should come, it would bring about demands which cannot be predicted and would necessitate the concentration of energies to supply the requirements in ways which cannot be foreseen. From the experience of past wars, from the ever increasing specialization and internationalization of economic life, and from the unmistakable decline of surface sea power, however, it can be easily deduced that in a future conflict a belligerent nation will not be able to maintain its vital industries intact, and that it must look forward to no end of embarrassment, waste, and industrial dislocation because of the impossibility of guarding adequately the essential sea routes.

In order to import the required materials in war time it becomes necessary to keep certain of the trade routes free from surface raiders and submarines. This is a task which is admittedly difficult under modern conditions of warfare. During the World War, German surface raiders destroyed half a million tons of shipping in spite of the overwhelming control of the seas by the Allies. At one time the British had twenty-nine ships upon the track of the raider *Emden*, and altogether seventy vessels were at different times in search of this elusive but destructive ghost of the waves. The British made splendid efforts to protect their trade routes. The 114 cruisers which they

Protection of Trade during Belligerency

possessed at the beginning of the war were not sufficient to give entire security. The Battle of Coronel, fought off the coast of Chile on November 1, 1914, was lost because Rear Admiral Cradock, in his anxiety to protect the route along the Chilean coast over which the nitrate trade was moving, hurried into action against superior forces. The defeat in this engagement alarmed the British admiralty. Two battle cruisers were almost immediately dispatched to reinforce the naval detachment at the Falklands and on December 8, 1914, they participated in the battle which destroyed the German squadron. The *Dresden* escaped, however, and continued its activities for several months. Later in the war, three German raiders put out to sea in disguise and destroyed fifty-eight allied ships. The *Wolf* sank or captured twenty ships in fifteen months, the *Seeadler*, twenty-three in seven months, and the *Möwe*, fifteen in two months.[1]

Submarines were far more effective in the destruction of commerce than were surface raiders and, as before stated, they accounted for more than 11,000,000 tons of British, Allied, and neutral shipping. Troop transports and commerce vessels under the protection of destroyers moved with comparative safety, but lone steamers by the score fell prey to the torpedo. In the critical months of 1917, 40 per cent of the imports to Great Britain were cut off. One-fourth of the ships leaving English ports at this time did not return. The weapons employed by the Allies which finally reduced the effectiveness of the submarine were convoys, mines, counter-submarine attack, airplanes, guns carried on merchantmen, and listening devices. The Germans fought at a disadvantage for the reason that the movements of their vessels were greatly reduced by the blockade of their home bases. A submarine campaign carried on by a strong nation

[1] STEVENS and WESTCOTT: *op. cit.*, p. 369.

whose bases cannot thus be closed would prove much more difficult to check.

Hereafter the airplane will doubtless be used to interfere with commerce. It has been predicted that in a future war merchant ships will not be able to sail within several hundred miles of a hostile shore or of seas under control of the enemy. Should they attempt to pass through such waters the patrolling airplanes of the enemy will signal them to proceed under threat of bombing to a spot where they can be safely searched.

The greatest single step in the protection of commerce, should this country become involved in a maritime conflict, would be the defeat or bottling-up of the opposing fleet. If such a course were to be determined upon at all costs the United States naval forces would proceed to seek out and engage the enemy, probably in its own waters. There would be a certain hazard in thus jeopardizing the American fleet in an area where the advantage would be with the enemy. If successful, this strategy would not entirely solve the problem of commerce protection for it would not dispose of surface raiders and submarines.

Against the surface raider the best available weapon is the cruiser. In 1927, when the Navy Department was advocating a program of forty-three cruisers, it was planned to dispose of the number as follows: Twenty-eight were to be used with the fleet, six were to guard the convoys moving to and from the fleet, and nine were to be assigned to the task of commerce protection. The latter were to guard the focal points of American commerce, such as the principal harbors of the United States, the Panama Canal, and the Hawaiian zone.[1] At present the plans of the United States call for a somewhat smaller

[1] *Sundry Legislation Affecting the Naval Establishment*, 1927–1928, pp. 515, 696, 789, hearings before the House Committee on Naval Affairs, Government Printing Office, 1928.

Protection of Trade during Belligerency

force of cruisers, and the number to be assigned for commerce protection in time of war in line with the former ratio would probably be about seven or eight. This force would be greatly augmented by converted merchantmen, but even thus increased it would not be adequate to give complete defense against the raiders of a strong naval power. No number of cruisers which this country is likely to build would provide safe conditions over all the major trade routes under modern conditions of warfare.

As a guard against submarines the destroyer force of the American navy would find ample opportunity for its utmost activity. Merchantmen would be armed for defense. Aircraft patrols would be used far more than formerly to protect coastwise commerce and to guard such sea routes as could be reasonably left open.

An enumeration of the principal trade routes over which the sea-borne commerce of the United States passes will indicate that the task of their protection against a strong naval power is beyond the ability of any nation today. These sea lanes are: (1) the coastwise route extending all the way from New England ports to Puget Sound through the Panama Canal; (2) the North Atlantic route to British, French, North Sea, and Baltic ports; (3) the Mediterranean route, leading to Mediterranean ports and through the Suez Canal to the East; (4) the Northern Pacific route to China and Japan; (5) the Southern Pacific route to Australia, New Zealand, and the smaller islands in the South Pacific; (6) the route to the eastern ports in South America; and (7) the route to the western ports of South America.

In considering the prospects of maintaining commerce over these routes it would seem that in a war with a great European power the United States would be thrown back to a large extent upon the economy of the Western Hemisphere. Such a war would find the North Atlantic and Mediterranean routes forbidden to our commerce. In a war with a strong Far Eastern power the North Pacific route would be blocked and the South Pacific route would be exposed to the activities of raiders. On the other hand, reasonable protection could probably be given to coastwise trade, to trade with Caribbean countries and along the western coast of South America, as well as to trade with the east coast of South America as far south as the mouth of the Amazon. A commercial advantage would doubtless be gained if this protection could be extended by means of convoys as far as the mouth of the Rio São Francisco. Farther south, along the important southeastern coast of South America, which includes the ports of Rio de Janeiro, Santos, and those of the Rio de la Plata, our commerce would be subjected to destruction by raiders from any naval power possessing African bases. The British have a defended base with a drydock and fueling facilities at Simonstown in South Africa. They also possess a naval station with fueling facilities at Port Stanley in the Falklands. To a layman it seems probable that in a war with Great Britain the United States would contemplate sending a squadron down the west coast of South America to round the Cape and capture the Falklands. If such a maneuver could be conducted with success it would mean much for the protection of American trade and the destruction of that of the enemy along the coast of Argentina and Brazil.

It is evident that the United States cannot maintain a naval force which will be able to defend all important trade routes under all possible eventualities. A large part of our trade will be destroyed in a war with a strong naval power, no matter how great our armaments may be. The principal reason why no nation now can control the seas is the growth of land power. Naval officers, with their eyes focused on the sea have not kept up with this development. The plan of the British navy which existed as late as 1913 to land troops on the Baltic coast of Germany in case of war with that country was hopelessly out of date. The plans of American naval men, frequently expressed, to make the waters of the earth secure to American commerce are equally obsolete. Wherever trade routes that feed the United States run near to enemy territory such routes cannot be defended for our trade. Enemy raiders on the water, under water, and in the air will operate with such vigor in the proximity of their land supports as to place at a great disadvantage our naval forces cruising at a distance from American bases. This is a comparatively recent development in naval warfare, for the time is not remote when Great Britain, the mistress of the seas, could defend her trade routes even in sight of enemy land. Thus the British kept open the Mediterranean to a large extent during the Napoleonic Wars, a feat which could not be repeated in a modern war between England and France.

If war should come, the United States must expect a failure of certain imports, an upset of the productive system, and a striking rise in prices. In return the United States would attempt to destroy the trade of its enemy. Commerce raiding would become the most popular enterprise of the time. And in company with the other belligerents this country would participate in an orgy of destruction which would have for its ultimate effects the weakening of countries whose industries and markets contribute to our prosperity.

Markets and Investments

The loss of markets and investments during war time is a separate problem which, in general, cannot be solved by naval defense. The destruction of markets includes loss of trade with the enemy countries, loss of trade with those countries to which the trade routes cannot be protected, and the loss of exports to other neutrals due to the fact that the energies of the nation would be diverted from peaceful occupations to those of war.

The experience of Great Britain during the World War shows that even a dominant naval power cannot maintain its export trade. Prior to the war Great Britain exported each year about 5,000,000 tons of iron and steel. During the war these shipments dropped to 2,000,000 tons. The diversion of industries to war purposes, the scarcity of shipping, and rising costs made it impossible to maintain normal commerce. Neutrals were willing and anxious to take over the business. Before the end of the war other countries were building up the machinery to compete for the world's markets. Following the war it became impossible for the British to recover the entire volume of their 1913 export trade. As the economic dominance of Great Britain was based to a large extent upon the export of manufactured goods, this loss of sales meant a decline in relative world position.

The experience of the United States after entering the World War was abnormal. The declaration of war made it possible for this country to continue its enormous export trade partly through the medium of governmental loans to the allies. Of course, so far as the interallied debts are written off the payment for these goods will fall upon the people of the United States. In another war, in which we would be a principal belligerent, this situation of continued trade can hardly recur. The United States will, in all probabilities, have the painful experience of watching neutral countries thrive on our losses just as we prospered from the inability of the belligerents to continue their normal exports during the early years of the World War. A war between the United States and a strong European combination would doubtless be accompanied by tremendous industrial development in

Protection of Trade during Belligerency

South America and Asia. The destructions of war would diminish the purchasing power of the world and the post-war struggle for trade would be a desperate economic conflict. The sequel for the United States would be unemployment and political unrest. Communism in the United States is today only a puny threat, but it would probably thrive at the close of a serious war. One need but glance superficially over the pages of history to observe the correlation which has existed between wars and political instability.

The relation of the countries of South America to the commercial needs of the United States must be regarded as of utmost importance. Coffee, rubber, and manganese are to be obtained from Brazil; tin from Bolivia; oil from Colombia, Venezuela, and Mexico; vanadium from Peru; platinum from Colombia; sisal and graphite from Mexico; hides from Argentina; nitrates from Chile; and in the Caribbean and Central America can be procured tropical fruits, nuts, cacao, and sugar. The maintenance of cordial relations with these countries is a matter of prime importance. Furthermore, the outlay of American capital in developing the resources of Latin America helps the defensive position of this country. Let us take the case of rubber, for example. Imports of crude rubber from British Malaya or the Dutch East Indies could be cut off in case of war with a strong European naval power. Shipments from Liberia or the Philippines would likewise be subject to interference. Rubber grown in the valley of the Amazon, however, would constitute a comparatively safe supply. Furthermore, the access to materials in Latin America will become easier with the development of rail, highway, and aërial transportation in that area.

In laying plans for commerce protection, one course suggests itself above all—the maintenance of peaceful and cordial relations with the world. No other policy is so profitable. In addition certain subordinate methods must be kept in mind. Plans for substitute materials should be developed to replace those which may be cut off in the contingency of war. The defense of trade routes should be kept in mind in the disposition and construction of warships. Naval ratios, ample for American defense, are necessary principles in our diplomacy. But when the emphasis on naval expansion becomes so great as to interfere with the maintenance of friendship with other nations, it threatens to do infinitely more harm than good to American commerce.

Chapter VII

THE DOCTRINE OF NEUTRAL RIGHTS

A THIRD danger which causes some apprehension, particularly among past-minded Americans, is the possibility of the destruction of our neutral commerce when other nations are at war. American thinking upon problems of maritime law has generally been in terms of neutrality. If the people of this country come to fear war in the future with a great rival, say in South America, then undoubtedly plans will be laid to cut off the trade of that rival, and the rights of the belligerent will be emphasized. In the past, however, isolated America has generally thought of the possibility of sea war only as holding forth a threat to the interests of the neutral. It is a popular belief that the War of 1812 was fought to avenge interferences with our neutral trade. Delegates sent by the American government to conferences dealing with the law of the sea have carried instructions to safeguard the rights of neutral merchants. The second demand in President Wilson's Fourteen Points called for the establishment of the principle of the freedom of the seas. Congressional opinion has at times been expressed that the problem of naval limitation should wait until a conference of sea powers can be held to enact into law the doctrine of the immunity of private property at sea. This article of belief is of major importance in the American diplomatic creed and has ranked with such outstanding dogmas as the Monroe Doctrine and the Open Door.

Advocates of greater sea power have found the freedom of the seas a most useful argument in recent years. In the hope of attracting the support of powerful business groups they have contended that the prosperity of this country depends upon keeping the seas open at all times for American commerce. The influence of this policy upon plans for naval construction is of the highest importance. A capable exponent of the naval view, Rear Admiral W. L. Rodgers, declared a few years ago:

> The principal diplomatic service of the American Navy will always be found in its support of neutrality and the neutral rights of commerce. This support is a fundamental policy which directs the shipbuilding program of the Navy Department. For the Navy must be adequate to guard its commerce when other nations are at war.[1]

In Congress also the defense of commerce rather than the defense of territory has been strikingly emphasized. In the cruiser debates of January, 1929, Senator Borah expressed the importance of this phase of the subject in the following words:

> So, Mr. President, while we are considering this bill we really have in our minds the sole question of how we are going to protect our commerce. I do not think many think of the use of the Navy in any other light . . . the moving, controlling question is how to protect our commerce against the inroads of those who may be engaged in war.[2]

Those who favor the doctrine in its old form point out that during the period of American neutrality in the World War our commerce with countries in northern Europe was strictly regulated by the British government. Congressman Britten of the House Committee on Naval Affairs has considered that this experience justifies the building of a strong navy. A few years ago, during a committee hearing on naval legislation, he said:

[1] RODGERS, W. L.: "The Navy as an Aid in Carrying Out Diplomatic Policies," *United States Naval Institute Proceedings*, Vol. 55, pp. 102–103, February, 1929.

[2] *Congressional Record*, Vol. 70, p. 2183, January 24, 1929.

The Doctrine of Neutral Rights

In order to ship furniture, shoe polish, etc., from my own district to Norway in American bottoms from our own ports, I had to go to the British embassy here for a permit to ship them. The application had to indicate the character of the material, how it was to be packed, the size of it, and the cost. That information was turned over to the commercial office of Great Britain in London. The permit itself was issued in London. Do you think that a powerful nation upon the seas would countenance such an insult? No; it never would have asked that permission.[1]

There are, on the other hand, many students of modern international developments who sincerely question the value of the neutral rights doctrine and the wisdom of a naval race to prepare for its defense. These doubts arise from the conviction that the doctrine has done considerable more harm than good to American commerce in the past and they also spring from the belief that a world organization will some day be prepared to take action against an aggressor nation. If, in that emergency, an isolated country like the United States should strenuously assert its so-called neutral rights, such a position would amount to making common cause with an outlaw against the organized world. Leaving aside the extent to which the giving of aid to an aggressor would be a blow at the international community, we can readily estimate that it would provoke friction and would most likely become quite disadvantageous to this country.

At the outset let us cast aside the notion that the doctrine of neutral rights or the freedom of the seas is an abstract principle arising from some great moral urge. The question is rather one of self-interest. In war the productivity of the belligerents is suspended while their wants increase. Accordingly, the prices paid for neutral goods soar far above peace-time figures. Like the Christian trader whose vessel to the South Seas

---

[1] *Sundry Legislation Affecting the Naval Establishment*, 1927–1928, pp. 1345–1346.

carried both Bibles and wooden idols, the neutral merchant, responding to the lure of war profits, sends forth explosives and firearms, on the one hand, and medicines and foodstuffs, on the other, with equal alacrity. Each belligerent, however, feels that its existence is at stake and can be expected to attempt the commercial strangulation of its enemy. This involves drastic interference with neutral trade. And thus it is that neutrals, attempting to gain an honest dollar, will have plenty of reasons for controversy with belligerents. These disagreements are inevitable and run entirely true to fixed principles of human nature. The mechanistic character of all the factors involved is amply proved when in another and later war the former neutral becomes a belligerent and the former belligerent becomes a neutral. In such case their previous lofty indignations are completely reversed. For the purpose of this chapter the matter will be presented as an attempt to answer the question: Has the doctrine of neutral rights been an aid to the economic interests of the United States and is it apt to promote such interests in the future?

An examination of the history of the neutrality of the United States which looks beneath the surface of official statements will reveal unexpected information regarding the operation of the doctrine. The economics of neutrality is a doubly deceptive study. A first glance at American experience would incline one to believe that in a great war the trade of the neutral nation is all but driven from the seas by the belligerents and that to avoid commercial ruin the neutral government must definitely assert its rights, either by force or by vigorous diplomacy. On second glance we find that except for losses to individuals in a few particular lines of trade this destruction of neutral commerce is a myth. In fact, the United States as a neutral has prospered and its wealth has increased. On still further examination we find that in

THE DOCTRINE OF NEUTRAL RIGHTS

the two major instances of American neutrality this prosperity has been only temporary. The neutral has been finally and inevitably drawn into the whirlpool of war, thus destroying its gains and much wealth in addition. The very force which the neutral has used in entering the quarrels of others in order to safeguard its swollen profits or to avenge interference with them has brought about the destruction of those profits.

On two major occasions this country has been a neutral during a general European war, and in each instance American merchants have sought to maintain their normal trade and in addition to supply the disputing nations with increased amounts of merchandise at a considerable profit. Such commercial activities have received governmental support. Thomas Jefferson, as President of the United States, expounded the position of his administration in the following words, which may be roughly taken as a formulation of the general American contention:

... when two nations go to war, those who choose to live in peace retain their natural right to pursue their agriculture, manufactures, and other ordinary vocations; to carry the produce of their industry, for exchange, to all nations, belligerent or neutral, as usual; to go and come freely, without injury or molestation; and, in short, that the war among others shall be, for them, as if it did not exist.[1]

When war broke out between France and Great Britain in 1793, the young American nation was still suffering from the desperate financial and commercial conditions into which it had been brought by the Revolution. The country was heavily in debt. Merchants and shipowners complained that their business was depressed by foreign restrictions against American trade. The Constitution had gone into operation, it is true, and Hamilton's noteworthy financial reforms had been

[1] MOORE, JOHN BASSETT: *A Digest of International Law*, Vol. VII, p. 677, Government Printing Office, Washington, 1906.

adopted, but only by placing enormous burdens upon the treasury. The war lasted with slight intermission from 1793 until 1815, and American neutrality appeared to the financial leaders in the harassed American republic as a mirage of material blessings. The statistics of those years indicate emphatically a boom era.

Lucrative opportunities were opened to American shippers, and the insistent demand for ocean carriers was reflected in the expansion of the merchant marine. The American tonnage, which had been 478,377 in 1790, was increased to 1,424,783 by 1810.[1] The national shipping was then, as it is not now, an index of American prosperity. A computation in 1807 of the earning power of the merchant marine showed that the annual return amounted to much more than the value of the ships. It was even estimated at one time by George Cabot that if a single vessel out of three escaped capture at the hands of the sea-scouring belligerents, the result would be a handsome profit.[2] Fascinating stories of almost fabulous returns come out of this period. For instance, the *Catherine* of Boston, 281 tons, and worth possibly $7,000, in 1808 made a net profit of $115,000 in a single voyage.[3] Despite the efforts of each belligerent to intercept the trade with its enemy the American shipping centers hummed with activity, and countinghouse clerks worked long hours to compute the profits. "America became almost the exclusive carrier for the world."[4]

Imports and exports likewise showed a remarkable increase. In 1792, the year previous to the outbreak of the war, the American imports were valued at $31,500,000

---

[1] U. S. Bureau of Navigation, *Merchant Marine Statistics*, p. 24, Government Printing Office, Washington, 1930.

[2] MORISON, SAMUEL ELIOT: *The Maritime History of Massachusetts*, 1783–1866, p. 191, Houghton Mifflin Company, Boston, 1921.

[3] *Ibid.*, p. 194.

[4] ADAMS, JAMES TRUSLOW: *New England in the Republic*, 1776–1850, p. 240, Little, Brown, and Company, Boston, 1926.

THE DOCTRINE OF NEUTRAL RIGHTS

and the exports at $20,753,098. From these figures they gradually increased until in the peak year of 1807 they amounted to $138,500,000 and $108,343,150 respectively.[1] The increase was due mainly to four factors: the rise in prices, the large *entrepôt* trade resulting from the shortage in foreign shipping, the growth in the quantity of goods produced for foreign consumption, and the larger demand for imports which followed the increase in the purchasing power of a prosperous people.

The national finances also benefited remarkably. The customs duties, which constituted by far the largest source of national income, increased from $3,443,000 in 1792 to $16,363,000 in 1808.[2] The national debt, which was $80,000,000 in 1793, fell to $45,000,000 by 1812, in spite of greatly increased expenditures which included such an item as the $15,000,000 paid to France for Louisiana.

Albert Gallatin, the great financier of this period, regarded the condition of neutrality as an exceedingly remunerative one. "Whilst it lasts," he said, "we are enabled to pay for a larger quantity of foreign luxuries, we import more, we consume more, and the revenue receives a temporary increase. The return of peace, as it will diminish our profits, the value of our exports, and our ability of paying, will also diminish our consumption, our importation, and our revenue."[3] The financial historian, Albert S. Bolles, summarized the effects of neutrality as follows:

. . . the wars which raged in Europe produced a favorable effect. American commerce rode the waves of an unexpected and brilliant prosperity. As the United States was a neutral nation, she fattened on

[1] Import and export statistics in this chapter are taken from the volumes of *Commerce and Navigation of the United States*.

[2] DEWEY, DAVIS RICH: *Financial History of the United States*, 4th ed., pp. 110, 123, Longmans, Green, and Co., New York, 1912.

[3] *Writings of Albert Gallatin*, Vol. III, p. 84, J. B. Lippincott & Co., Philadelphia, 1876.

The United States and Disarmament

the miseries of the European nations, and her commerce increased with astonishing rapidity.[1]

The attempts by Great Britain and France to shut off the American trade with each other were strenuous and to a certain extent effective. Questionable blockades, the extension of contraband lists, impressments, and, finally, seizures, which could be justified under no doctrine of international law save that of reprisals, were resorted to. During all this time the United States was protesting against the rather arrogant actions of both belligerents in the obstruction of neutral trade. The legalist, who is interested merely in the questions of law involved and whose descriptions of the controversy are largely based on the remonstrances sent out from the Department of State, sometimes writes under the apparent illusion that the trade of the United States was practically wiped out by the belligerents. This is a mistake, of course, for American commerce had never been so prosperous. Vigorous diplomatic representations were made, which was quite proper. These protests were only partially effective and other means were resorted to. An unofficial naval war, an embargo, nonintercourse, and finally a declaration of war were in turn employed.

The War of 1812 was begun allegedly to defend American trade against the illegal commercial restrictions of the British and as a protest against the impressment of American seamen. There was much in the conduct of both the French and the British to provoke the United States. But as an economic venture, based upon the interests of the merchant marine, the war was a total failure. Neutrality, the goose that laid the golden egg of inflated commerce, was killed. The total imports and exports, which were maintained at $115,557,236 during the fiscal year of 1812, had dwindled to the miserable sum

[1] BOLLES, ALBERT S.: *The Financial History of the United States from 1789 to 1860*, 4th ed., p. 85, D. Appleton and Company, 1894.

The Doctrine of Neutral Rights

of $19,892,441 by 1814. The national debt rose from $45,000,000 to $123,000,000.

That the war was not waged wisely or sympathetically in behalf of commerce is likewise indicated by the fact that the merchants who were engaged in foreign trade and whose private interests were at stake were opposed to hostilities. The shipowners felt that the war was disastrous to their interests, and the sentiment in the New England states inclined toward secession. Those were the bitter days of the Hartford Convention. The supporters of the war were mostly of the agricultural party, and were doubtless moved by the feelings of political humiliation growing out of insults to the government which they controlled. There is also a very strong suspicion that some of the war group were animated by "land hunger." The prospect of annexing Canada and Florida appealed to the party of the South and West.[1] The war leaders have been described on the one hand as defenders of their country's honor and on the other as "war hawks." They were, however, not generally from the business classes and the War of 1812 was in no accurate sense a war for the promotion of commerce. If American prosperity depended upon such naval action as this it would, indeed, be in perilous straits.

A century later the World War began with the United States in a neutral position and there was no direct reason for participation in the conflict. American fortunes during the period from July, 1914, until April, 1917, reproduced with some important variations the experiences of this country during the Napoleonic wars. After a slight depression, due to the initial dislocation following the outbreak of hostilities, the demand for American prod-

---

[1] See HAMLIN, C. H.: *The War Myth in United States History*, pp. 33 ff., Vanguard Press, New York, 1927; and BEARD, CHARLES A. and MARY R.: *The Rise of American Civilization*, Vol. I, pp. 410 ff., The Macmillan Company, New York, 1928.

ucts began to make itself powerfully felt. Munitions and foodstuffs, in particular, were desperately needed by the belligerent nations. Nothing in history is comparable to the colossal requirements of this emergency. American production was stimulated as by a powerful hypodermic injection. For the last fiscal peace-time year, that which ended June 30, 1914, exports from the United States were valued at $2,364,579,148. For the year ending June 30, 1917 (which with an allowance for nearly three war months may serve to show the conditions of the last year of American neutrality), they rose to $6,290,048,394. Correcting for the advance in prices, the exports of the last neutral year almost doubled those for the year before the war. The so-called favorable trade balance during this period increased fivefold. The exports of breadstuffs, chemicals, iron and steel and their manufactures were tremendously expanded. The explosives industry was the most rapidly growing war baby with an increase in exports from $6,272,197 to $802,789,437, the latter figure bearing in relation to the former the ratio of 128 to 1. The exports of firearms were multiplied more than twenty-seven times, increasing from $3,442,297 to $95,470,009.

American firms who had specialized in trade with Germany and Austria were dismayed to find their business completely strangled. Exports to Germany, which were $344,794,276 in the year ending June 30, 1914, dwindled to $28,863,354 in 1915, to $288,899 in 1916, and were $2,199,449 in the fiscal year ending June 30, 1917. The exports to Austria for the first three of these years were $22,718,258, $1,238,669, and $146,302. For the next year the exports to Austria did not register at all in the tables of the Department of Commerce. Peace-time exports of $367,512,544 to the two Central Allies were thus wiped out due to the methods of Great Britain which were in violation of traditional international law.

The Doctrine of Neutral Rights

There were losses and business disruptions in individual cases in the United States and there were some embittered minorities which complained loudly against these restrictions.

On the other hand, the enormous growth of commerce with the Entente which controlled the seas was such as to compensate many times over for the lost trade with the Central Powers. The following table shows the export trade with the principal allied nations:

Year ending June 30	United Kingdom	France	Italy	Russia
1914	$ 594,271,863	$ 159,818,924	$ 74,235,012	$ 30,088,643
1915	911,794,954	369,397,170	184,819,688	37 474,380
1916	1,526,685,102	628,851,988	269,246,105	178,694,800
1917	2,046,812,678	1,011,667,206	360,608,356	428,688,107

In contrast to this undreamed-of development of American business the complaints of the State Department regarding the restrictions placed on commerce by both belligerents convey the impression that illegitimate blockade methods and contraband lists were so oppressive that they well-nigh extinguished neutral traffic. It is not contended that it was the intention to convey this impression or that the complaints were not thoroughly justified. But such is the psychology of argumentation that continued emphasis on one's wrongs is apt by a process of auto-conviction to delude the complainant himself, into the belief that his contentions are the whole truth. Apart from all questions of morals or legalism and regarding the matter strictly from the commercial viewpoint, the outstanding fact remains that American trade and industry were tremendously aided during the period of neutrality. At no time in American history had commerce been conducted with such abandon and profit.

The United States and Disarmament

Under the stimulus of expanded exports the stocks in many American industrial corporations rose to unprecedented heights. E. I. du Pont de Nemours and Company declared a 100 per cent dividend on common stock in 1916, and this was possible, as the president of the corporation said, in spite of the regrettable fact "that the United States government has made our stockholders victims of excessive taxation."[1] So prosperous were the munition makers that a 12½ per cent tax which reduced the dividends to a mere 100 per cent was considered no mean blow at private industry. There were evidences that dealers in securities considered neutrality to be the condition most favorable to American prosperity. After the sinking of the *Lusitania* on May 7, 1915, when much sentiment was manifested for a declaration of war upon Germany, there was a severe break in prices on Wall Street. Rumors of peace negotiations in March, October, and December, 1916, in turn caused breaks in stock prices, the last one being described by a prominent financial writer, Alexander D. Noyes, as "something like a small panic."[2] The United States had built up a huge system of war industries and many industrial leaders had begun to dread the slump which would come with peace.

Under cover of legal neutrality the American nation was working night and day for the Allied cause and was being paid for its efforts in a most handsome manner. The following letter by Thomas Lamont, printed in the *Manchester Guardian* of January 27, 1920, and quoted by Harry Elmer Barnes in his book, *The Genesis of the World War*, shows rather clearly the pro-ally character of American finance at this time:

---

[1] *New York Times*, Feb. 14, 1917. He was referring to the munitions tax of 12½ per cent on net profits which went into effect in 1916.

[2] Noyes, Alexander D.: *The War Period of American Finance, 1908–1925*, p. 153, G. P. Putnam's Sons, New York, 1926.

THE DOCTRINE OF NEUTRAL RIGHTS

At the request of certain of the foreign Governments the firm of Messrs. J. P. Morgan and Co. undertook to coördinate the requirements of the Allies, and then to bring about regularity and promptness in fulfilling those requirements. Those were the days when American citizens were being urged to remain neutral in action, in word, and even in thought. But our firm had never for one moment been neutral: we didn't know how to be. From the very start we did everything we could to contribute to the cause of the Allies. And this particular work had two effects: one in assisting the Allies in the production of goods and munitions in America necessary to the Allies' vigorous prosecution of the war; the other in helping to develop this great and profitable export trade that our country has had.[1]

As time went on, however, neutral prosperity threatened to play out. The problem of finance became greater than could be borne by the allied exchequers. The huge surplus of American exports over imports had been balanced by a combination of methods. In round figures, one billion dollars in gold had been shipped into the United States and almost two billion dollars in American securities had been returned from allied countries. This, in addition to the earnings of European shipping and various other invisible debits, had not been sufficient to balance the account. Borrowing had been resorted to. In 1915, a $500,000,000 loan to Great Britain and France jointly had been floated by New York bankers. In 1916, France had borrowed $100,000,000 more and Great Britain $500,000,000. By these loans of more than a billion dollars the international account had been substantially balanced and at the end of 1916 the pound sterling was as high as $4.75. But there came a time early in 1917 when the allies had very nearly exhausted the means of payment. The stock of gold in Europe had been depleted until further shipments from those countries had become dangerous to their currencies. Furthermore the transportation of gold was imperilled by

[1] Barnes, Harry Elmer: *The Genesis of the World War*, pp. 611-612, Knopf, New York, 1927.

submarines. Additional financing by the sale of American securities had become difficult. Credit was low. Large overdrafts had been made by Great Britain upon J. P. Morgan & Company, finally reaching $400,000,000 before the United States entered the war. By March, 1917, it appeared that the Allies could only with great difficulty pay for their immense imports and that their purchases must be drastically cut unless new and unusual means of financing should be found.

In a significant cablegram on March 5, 1917, Walter Hines Page, ambassador to Great Britain, warned President Wilson that there was very serious danger of a credit collapse. Page stated that he had learned from his inquiries that the situation was "most alarming to the financial and industrial outlook of the United States," that it appeared as if the ability to pay for purchases was being exhausted, and that transatlantic trade would "practically come to an end." "The result of such a stoppage," he said, "will be a panic in the United States." In the last paragraph of this cablegram occurs the extraordinary sentence: "*It is not improbable that the only way of maintaining our present preëminent trade position and averting a panic is by declaring war on Germany.*" The cablegram is of such significance that the complete text is here set forth:

> The inquiries which I have made here about financial conditions disclose an international situation which is most alarming to the financial and industrial outlook of the United States. England has not only to pay her own war bills, but is obliged to finance her Allies as well. Up to the present time she has done these tasks out of her own capital. But she cannot continue her present extensive purchases in the United States without shipping gold as payment for them, and there are two reasons why she cannot make large shipments of gold. In the first place, both England and France must keep the larger part of the gold they have to maintain issues of their paper at par; and, in the second place, the German U-boat has made the shipping of gold a dangerous procedure even if they had it to ship. There is,

The Doctrine of Neutral Rights

therefore, a pressing danger that the Franco-American and Anglo-American exchange will be greatly disturbed; the inevitable consequence will be that orders by all the Allied Governments will be reduced to the lowest possible amount and that trans-Atlantic trade will practically come to an end. The result of such a stoppage will be a panic in the United States. The world will therefore be divided into two hemispheres, one of them, our own, will have the gold and the commodities: the other, Great Britain and Europe, will need these commodities, but it will have no money with which to pay for them. Moreover, it will have practically no commodities of its own to exchange for them. The financial and commercial result will be almost as bad for the United States as for Europe. We shall soon reach this condition unless we take quick action to prevent it. Great Britain and France must have a credit in the United States which will be large enough to prevent the collapse of world trade and the whole financial structure of Europe.

If the United States declare war against Germany, the greatest help we could give Great Britain and its Allies would be such a credit. If we should adopt this policy, an excellent plan would be for our Government to make a large investment in a Franco-British loan. Another plan would be to guarantee such a loan. A great advantage would be that all the money would be kept in the United States. We could keep on with our trade and increase it, till the war ends, and after the war Europe would purchase food and an enormous supply of materials with which to reëquip her peace industries. We should thus reap the profit of an uninterrupted and perhaps an enlarging trade over a number of years and we should hold their securities in payment.

On the other hand, if we keep nearly all of the gold and Europe cannot pay for reëstablishing its economic life, there may be a world-wide panic for an indefinite period.

Of course we cannot extend such a credit unless we go to war with Germany. But is there no way in which our Government might immediately and indirectly help the establishment in the United States of a large Franco-British credit without violating armed neutrality? I do not know enough about our own reserve bank law to form an opinion. But these banks would avert such a danger if they were able to establish such a credit. Danger for us is more real and imminent, I think, than the public on either side the Atlantic understands. If it be not averted before its manifestations become apparent, it will then be too late to save the day.

The pressure of this approaching crisis, I am certain, has gone beyond the ability of the Morgan financial agency for the British and

The United States and Disarmament

French governments. The financial necessities of the Allies are too great and urgent for any private agency to handle, for every such agency has to encounter business rivalries and sectional antagonisms.

It is not improbable that the only way of maintaining our present preëminent trade position and averting a panic is by declaring war on Germany. The submarine has added the last item to the danger of a financial world crash. There is now an uncertainty concerning our being drawn into the war; no more considerable credits can be privately placed in the United States. In the meantime a collapse may come.[1]

After the United States entered the war the now famous inter-allied loans were granted. This support from the strongest financial government in the world eased the credit situation and made it possible for the export of goods to continue. There was no panic, and to that extent the reasoning of Ambassador Page was clear enough.

It is impossible to resist a few comments at this point as to the part which economic motives played in the entrance of the United States into the war against Germany. Some skeptics have said that the American government declared war in order to save certain rich bankers whose funds were tied up in the allied cause. Sentimental nationalists recoil in horror from such a suggestion and staunchly maintain that this country was guided entirely by moral and legal reasons. Although it is yet too early to speak confidently upon the matter it may be provisionally concluded that both of these groups are wrong. It can hardly be supposed that the administration of President Wilson would be willing to throw away many billions of dollars belonging to the American people in order to safeguard private investments of a billion dollars or so.

On the other hand, it seems a reasonable conclusion that the channels of American action were to a very

[1] Hendrick, Burton J.: *The Life and Letters of Walter H. Page*, Vol. II, pp. 269–271, Doubleday, Page & Company, Garden City, 1925.

The Doctrine of Neutral Rights

definite extent fixed by economic facts. For commercial and financial reasons the United States could hardly have gone into the war in 1917 on the side of Germany and against the power controlling the seas. It is true that in 1812 this country declared war upon the mistress of the seas. Such action was highly detrimental to American trade, however, and was bitterly resented by the commercial classes. In 1917 the financial, industrial, and commercial groups were enormously increased in strength and they had greatly outdistanced the agricultural faction in political influence. No government could have sacrificed their interests. Even a rumor of war against Great Britain would have meant a panic, and actual entry into war against that country would have spelled almost complete destruction of American foreign trade and the loss of outstanding loans. And all of this would have been true had the United States navy been doubled in size.

The United States had then either to stay neutral or to join with Great Britain. But when the world is aflame it is difficult for a nation which is intimately connected with the struggle by commercial ties to remain out of the conflict. A thousand points of friction exist. Propagandists on both sides try to destroy the sentiment of neutrality. There were, in 1917, strong commercial and financial interests which were anxious to see the allied cause prosper. Perhaps Mr. Page was not the only one to feel that war against Germany was the best way to avoid a financial panic. Then there was also the moral indignation which was aroused by the excesses on both sides, the most dramatic depredations being the German submarine attacks which resulted in the destruction of commerce and in the killing of American citizens. These excesses were matched by the less sensational but more methodical and deadly illegal blockade methods of Great Britain. All of this aroused the fighting instincts of the American people and inclined them to leave the status of neutrality behind. But for economic reasons the pressure to bring the United States into the war could move this country in but one direction, that is, against Germany.

The war came and it proved to be far more costly in the long run than had been anticipated. Profits of the neutral period were surrendered in the expense of preparing an army and navy. Regardless of the entire accuracy of his estimates there is much substantial truth in the remarks of President Coolidge on Armistice Day, 1928:

> It is sometimes represented that this country made a profit out of the war. Nothing could be further from the truth. Up to the present time our own net war costs, after allowing for our foreign debt expectations, are about $36,500,000,000. To retire the balance of our public debt will require about $7,000,000,000 in interest.
>
> Our Veterans' Bureau and allied expenses are already running at over $500,000,000 a year in meeting the solemn duty to the disabled and dependent. With what has been paid out and what is already apparent it is probable that our final cost will run well toward $100,000,000,000.[1]

Summarizing American experience during two great periods of neutrality it may be said that, despite the attempts of each belligerent faction in Europe to shut off trade with its enemy, the commerce of the United States during such times has increased tremendously. With the world blazing in war, however, the temptation to be drawn into the quarrels of other nations has proved irresistible and the gains of neutrality have been destroyed. The argument that American neutral prosperity can be maintained and promoted only by the building of a large navy to engage in war, if necessary, against a strong maritime power seems to be open to grave doubts.

[1] *New York Times,* Nov. 12, 1928.

The Doctrine of Neutral Rights

Whatever else such a plan may be, it is distinctly not a business proposition. In addition to these lessons gleaned from the past there is now the prospect of difficulty if this country should insist on trading freely with a nation which has been adjudged an outlaw by the organized international society.

It would be folly, of course, to suggest that the United States should make no attempt to protect neutral commerce and that this country should submit meekly to every indignity which an inflamed belligerent would care to heap upon us. Considering the national pride of the United States, such a course is beyond serious consideration. So long as the system of private wars exists, human nature being what it is, there seems to be no practical alternative but to follow our former policies, protect neutral commerce so far as we can, and then drift blindly into war. But a way out of this dilemma has been clearly shown in recent years in the movement for world organization which would abolish private wars and all of the law of neutrality incident thereto. The United States has entered partially into this movement by sponsoring the Multilateral Treaty for the Renunciation of War. It still remains for practical methods to be adopted which will give effect to this splendid expression of the will for peace. If the treaty can be made effective it will go far to insure the freedom of the seas, for it is only through peace that commerce can be really protected and made profitable.

One of the most practical methods thus far suggested to support the Multilateral Treaty is the Capper Resolution which would make it unlawful to export articles for use in war to any country which, in the opinion of the President, has violated the treaty. It likewise would withdraw the protection of the United States from American citizens who give aid and comfort to the offending nation.

The United States and Disarmament

The Capper Resolution would mark a wise change in our policy toward the unprofitable doctrine of neutral rights. The resolution in its present form, however, would not be entirely adequate for the serious task of war prevention. It is possible that under the resolution the President might disagree with other nations as to which of two warring nations is the violator of the treaty. It is also possible that, acting for the United States separately, the President would be unwilling to designate the offender because of the seriousness of such action. A nation which would individually seek to apportion the blame in a crisis of this kind would run the risk of being roundly censured as an uninvited meddler. A matter of such gravity as accusing a sovereign nation of being an international outlaw should be considered only in consultation with other powers. The Capper Resolution suggests the negotiation of agreements with other governments which will pledge them not to protect their nationals in giving aid and comfort to a breaker of the Multilateral Treaty. This would leave the matter to the individual judgment of the many signatories of the pact. It does not seem possible that so vital a decision would in practice be arrived at in that way. The need for coöperation at such a critical point is overwhelming.

American consultation with other powers in passing on the violation of the pact would appear to be a wise precaution for the protection of our own interests. A decision by an international conference for the application of the pact would carry more weight than the separate and perhaps conflicting actions of the various governments alone. The conference would be less likely to shrink from determining the malefactor than would individual nations, for each conferring power would feel a much greater sense of security in taking this sort of action in coöperation with others. And, above all, any prospective aggressor, fearing that its conduct would be examined before such a formidable array of nations, would be more apt to refrain from taking the rash step of violating the treaty.

The United States, in the present state of feeling in this country, would be compelled by force of circumstances to ignore the nomenclature of the League of Nations. Of course, the League Council will be called together when a rupture between two nations occurs and will bend its best efforts to avert war. If war comes the Council will have to determine whether the action of an aggressor is in violation of the Covenant. The proposed conference which the United States would attend under such circumstances would be separate from the Council. But actually the governments which are members of the League would proceed in the conference with full knowledge and in complete harmony with the action being simultaneously taken in the Council. The machinery of the conference to apply the Multilateral Treaty would of necessity gear with the machinery of the League. When a decision is reached by the conference, sanctions can be applied by League members according to League methods and by the United States under some such measure as the Capper Resolution. The United States would not have to agree with the other governments represented in the conference and certainly it would not be bound by decisions of the Council. It would have an absolute veto to protect its own independence of action. But if this country should be honestly inspired by a desire to prevent war, it would, under the above outlined arrangement, be able to coöperate in a sympathetic manner with the existing machinery for peace.

National individualism and freedom of action offer no solution for the problem of war. For this reason the United States' doctrine of neutral rights points backward toward disorganization and chaos. Fear of conflict with the American policy has already done much to block international progress and in 1925 contributed to the failure of the Geneva Protocol for Arbitration, Security, and Disarmament. It is only through the coöperation of the members of the international society that peace and freedom of the seas can be maintained. Why then should not the United States, seeking primarily its own commercial welfare, coöperate to end the era of international anarchy and private war in which the Devil takes the foremost as well as the hindmost and in which disaster falls upon the neutral as well as upon the belligerent?

PART III
THE NAVAL CONFERENCES

Chapter VIII

ARMAMENT LIMITATION BEFORE THE WASHINGTON CONFERENCE

PRIOR to the World War the movement for the mutual limitation of armaments among the great powers had produced no tangible results. The decade before the war was a period of rising industrialization, and the building of machines for armed conflict on land and sea kept pace with the growth of factories and the development of transportation. Mechanical invention had made war so highly destructive that it could no longer be used profitably as an instrument of national policy. The multiplication of international commercial and financial transactions had created a world economic structure. But mentally the human race had not emerged from the period of militarism and nationalism. The industrial revolution still awaited its complement in an intellectual revolution. It was commonly felt that the new capitalism led even more certainly toward war than the older agricultural economy. The struggles for markets and raw materials, according to this well-accepted view, made armed conflict inevitable. This theory, of course, had much historical evidence to support it. The practical political world believed that war was an effective implement for promoting the business interests of a people. The pre-war period was, therefore, just the wrong time for armament limitation because the new industrialization of war, which tended to upset the world's equilibrium, was guided by the old nationalistic philosophy of armed competition.

The United States and Disarmament

During the pre-war period there were, of course, many protests against the military and naval preparations that were being conducted so feverishly. The pious and the altruistic were on the side of peace. Religious societies denounced war as wicked. Radical people, such as the Socialists, considered war to be only the instrument of the capitalist class. They advocated an international boycott of war by the workers. Small intellectual minorities, thinking ahead of their time, clearly perceived the folly of war as an agency for advancing the national interest. Norman Angell in his book, *The Great Illusion*, published in 1911, analyzed the factors behind the armament competition and with remarkable insight refuted the contention that military methods can be used today to achieve economic advantages. There were also certain nations with a respectable military standing which found it a difficult business to maintain the rapid pace set by such an ambitious and industrially equipped country as Germany. These nations whose position was threatened by the growth of armaments had naturally strong reasons for maintaining the *status quo* by agreements not to increase military budgets. But even in such countries the existence of military classes and the effect of powerful nationalistic sentiments were such as to make a clear and effective policy for peace and armament limitation impossible.

Despite all of the various groups and interests which condemned armament competition, only a small fraction of which have been mentioned here, the evils of the modern system of national competition in militarism with all its brutality and economic devastation were not graphically or realistically understood, and there was no overwhelming demand for reform. Least of all did business leaders understand their great interest in peace. Their conversion was a condition precedent to the success of the movement. And so, although the brink of the precipice seemed to lie dimly ahead yet the stark reality of the disaster which awaited at the base of the cliff was not sufficiently appreciated to cause genuine alarm and to compel the governments to change their course. The Hague Conferences were excellent illustrations of the feeble condition of the movement against armaments in those pre-war days. The First Hague Conference was called by the Czar because of the pressure of armament costs. Regarding the new light which the opening of archives has thrown on the calling of the conference, Dr. Charles A. Beard has said:

> The proposal for the conference originated in the Russian war department, apparently with General Kuropatkin, after a survey of the beautiful new artillery equipment which Germany had completed with a view to overcoming by weight of metal the superiority of Russia and France in man power. Staggered by Germany's achievement and aware that Austria-Hungary would soon follow the example, the Russian general faced a dilemma: a common reduction in armaments or an enormous expenditure to bring his country up to the new level of machine efficiency. With the peasants already bowed to earth under oppressive taxation which took away almost half of their income, the additional drain on the treasury might make trouble—even though France would help with generous loans.[1]

In his invitation to the nations of the world the Czar deplored the expensive drain of military and naval competition and set forth the necessity of action in these words: "To put an end to these incessant armaments and to seek the means of warding off the calamities which threaten the whole world—such is the supreme duty which is imposed upon all states." The first topic mentioned in the circular issued by the Russian government on January 11, 1899 was: "An understanding stipulating the non-augmentation, for a term to be agreed upon, of the present effective armed land and sea forces, as well as the war budgets pertaining to them; preliminary study

[1] BEARD, CHARLES A.: "Bigger and Better Armaments," *Harpers Magazine*, Vol. 158, p. 135, January, 1929.

of the ways in which even a reduction of the aforesaid effectives and budgets could be realized in the future."[1]

When the conference was organized, the question of disarmament, which was considered to be the most important problem for consideration, was, with other matters, referred to the First Commission. Because of its difficulty, however, it was placed last upon the agenda. After a month's time the subject was reached, and an impassioned speech supporting the Russian proposals was made by General den Beer Poortugael, representing the Netherlands, who realistically sensed the dangers of the armament race. He declared:

> If I said that the States are hastening inevitably to their ruin it is because the more their armed forces increase, military budgets swallow billions, peoples are crushed under the weight of taxes, the States are dragged more and more over the steep of the abyss into which they will finally perish; they are exhausting and ruining themselves.[2]

Colonel Gilinsky of the Russian delegation then submitted specific measures for carrying out the Czar's plan with regard to land forces, and suggested a five-year agreement not to increase the number of troops or the size of the military budget. Captain Scheine of the Russian navy proposed that the size of the naval budget of each power should be determined for three years, and that during this period no increases above the fixed limit should be made. He likewise urged the principle of publicity of naval statistics.

The Russian proposals, moderate as they were, had an unpleasant sound to the ears of the German delegates. Colonel von Schwarzhoff, representing the German government, delivered a strong speech in opposition. Replying particularly to the remarks of General Poor-

[1] *The Reports to the Two Hague Conferences of 1899 and 1907*, p. 3, Oxford at the Clarendon Press, London, 1917. Also HULL, WILLIAM I.: *The Two Hague Conferences*, p. 45, Ginn and Company, Boston, 1908.

[2] *Proceedings of the Hague Peace Conferences. Conference of 1899*, p. 302, Oxford University Press, New York, 1920.

tugael, he denied that armaments had become too burdensome. "The German people," he informed the commission, "are not crushed beneath the weight of expenditures and taxes; they are not hanging on the edge of a precipice; they are not hastening towards exhaustion and ruin." Following this burst of unrealistic optimism the Colonel outlined certain difficulties which stood in the way of reaching an agreement on army limitation. There were a large number of elements, he said, which should be considered in arriving at the total of military power, such as the length of service of troops, the duration of enrollments of reserves, the number and situation of fortified places, and railway systems. The weight of these would be difficult to estimate, but they could not well be separated from the question of troops. The enumeration of these technical difficulties constituted the perfect defense tactics of the expert who did not wish to come out openly against the principle of armament limitation. The same sort of maneuvers has been repeated many times in the experience of post-war days.

The Russian proposals were submitted to two technical committees, one to examine the military proposal and the other to consider the naval suggestion. The military committee consisted of three generals, three colonels, one lieutenant colonel, and two captains. Of course, the Russian plan did not have a gambler's chance. It is not fair, however, to cast the burden of the blame upon the military officers when neither the civilian representatives at the conference nor the populations back of them were awake to the situation. In due time the military committee reported that because of the difficulty of estimating the numerous elements entering into land strength the Russian proposal could not be accepted.

The second committee likewise rejected the plan for the limitation of naval budgets and for publicity of naval statistics. Only the vote of the delegate from the Netherlands was favorable. The committee felt that if the various parliaments should attempt to fix the size of the budget for three years they might, in ignorance of each other's intentions, be unduly suspicious and accordingly set the figures at a high level for reasons of safety. Hence, instead of stopping competition the plan might greatly stimulate it.

After hearing the reports of the two committees the first commission adopted a high-sounding and meaningless motion: "The commission is of opinion that the restriction of military charges, which are at present a heavy burden on the world, is extremely desirable for the increase of the material and moral welfare of mankind."[1] Another motion referred the questions of military and naval armaments to the governments for thorough study. The plenary conference merely approved these motions. So far as armament limitation was concerned the First Hague Conference was a complete failure.

In the short space of eight years between the first and second conferences the armament budgets of the principal countries were raised 27.5 per cent. Two important wars were fought. The world was moving onward toward the brink of the precipice.

In the program for the Second Hague Conference the Russian government expressly excluded the question of the limitation of military and naval armaments. There were two reasons why the Czar and his advisers had capitulated to the forces of militarism. In the first place, the subject threatened to arouse discord among the delegates. Germany was opposed to the consideration of the question and threatened to stay away from the conference if it should be placed upon the agenda. In the second place, the Russian government desired to build up its own armaments after their depletion in the Russo-

[1] *Ibid.*, p. 319. For the action of the plenary session see pp. 90, 233. See also HULL: *op. cit.*, p. 65.

Armament Limitation

Japanese War. Great Britain, however, supported by the United States, urged the consideration of the question. In the fourth plenary session, Sir Edward Fry introduced the subject in a speech in which he pointed out that naval and military burdens had increased since the first conference. In 1898 the expenditures for armaments in the European countries, the United States, and Japan had been 251 million pounds sterling, whereas by 1906 the same countries were spending 320 millions. "Such," he said, "is this excessive expenditure, which might be employed for better ends; such, Mr. President, is the burden under which our populations are groaning; such is the Christian peace of the civilized world in the twentieth century."[1] The result of this excellent speech was a weak but pious resolution "that it is highly desirable to see the governments take up the serious study of this question." The resolution represents the meager record of the second conference on the subject. Instead of dealing with the realities of armament competition the conference busied itself with such matters as the preparation of a code of land warfare.

It is only fair to say that the conferences accomplished something of value in the creation of the Permanent Court of Arbitration, thereby making a distinct advance in the movement for the judicial settlement of international disputes. The Court of Arbitral Justice, also provided for by the Second Hague Conference but which did not go into effect due to the lack of a method of electing judges, was certainly a contribution to the movement for pacific settlement and furnished the basis for the present World Court. But the conference completely failed to stem the tide of growing armaments. It is no wonder that when the time set for the calling

---

[1] *The Proceedings of the Hague Conferences. Conference of* 1907, Vol. I, p. 89, Oxford University Press, New York, 1920. See also HULL: *op. cit.*, 72.

of a third conference arrived it found the nations engaged in the most desperate war of history.

We turn now more specifically to the naval competition between Great Britain and Germany and to the ineffectual attempt to stop it. The principal facts in the naval situation preceding the World War were the long-established British mastery of the seas and the German challenge to that mastery. The doctrine of the necessity of naval supremacy was deeply rooted in the psychology of the British people. It had been more or less associated with English national ambition since the time of Alfred the Great. A hundred dramatic naval battles from Sluis to Trafalgar, cherished in British memory, had created a mental attitude on the subject which no amount of internationalistic arguments could greatly affect. But as the industrial revolution spread from the British Isles to other lands, conditions were created which placed the doctrine of British supremacy in jeopardy. At about the end of the nineteenth century the naval situation was again in flux. The revival of the French fleet, the growth of the Russian fleet, and the entrance into naval competition of Germany, the United States, and Japan began to threaten the British position.

In 1898 the first German Naval Act was passed. Two years later and immediately after the failure of disarmament in the First Hague Conference, the Act of 1900 definitely launched the German Empire upon an ambitious naval program for the alleged purpose of safeguarding German trade. The memorandum which was appended to the 1900 navy act stated:

An unsuccessful naval war of the duration of even only a year would destroy Germany's sea trade, and would thereby bring about the most disastrous conditions, first in her economic, and then, as an immediate consequence of that, in her social life.[1]

[1] HURD, ARCHIBALD and HENRY CASTLE: *German Sea Power, Its Rise, Progress and Economic Basis*, p. 346, Charles Scribner's Sons, New York, 1913.

Armament Limitation

The policy behind the 1900 program was the creation of a fleet which, while not equaling that of Great Britain, would nevertheless be able to endanger the British position. The memorandum summarized this aim in the following words:

> To protect Germany's sea trade and colonies in the existing circumstances there is only one means—Germany must have a battle fleet so strong that even for the adversary with the greatest sea power a war against it would involve such dangers as to imperil his position in the world.[1]

Thus in the year following Colonel von Schwarzhoff's proud boast that Germany was not overburdened with armaments, we find a great expansion occurring in the Imperial navy for the protection of German business. Like German missionaries in China, the German merchant was being "used" for purposes of military and naval expansion. An illustration of the way in which the Junker philosophy of force was clothed in the raiment of commercial terminology may be found in a well-known text-book written for American use by a German scholar. The author comments as follows:

> German industry and commerce represent an enormous investment. Every sensible merchant insures his business in proportion to its value. The expenses for the Imperial navy are like the premium of an insurance policy. The government and the people of Germany act like cautious merchants spending a large amount of money for their insurance, *i.e.*, the battle fleet.[2]

The appeal to the business man on the grounds of the commercial value of sea power is sometimes based on dangerously misleading comparisons, as is well illustrated by the application of the insurance simile to German naval expansion. The schedules of reparation payments are a harsh reminder of the fallacy of such

[1] *Ibid.*, p. 348.
[2] Krüger, Fritz-Konrad: *Government and Politics of the German Empire*, pp. 164–5, World Book Company, Yonkers-on-Hudson, 1915.

reasoning. Instead of collecting the value of the insurance policy the "cautious merchants" of Germany will for many years be paying for the losses of their neighbors caused partially at least by the growth of German militarism. Thus the alleged premium became a cause of loss instead of a guarantee against disaster.

An incident of the Anglo-German competition was the laying down of the *Dreadnought*, or all-big-gun ship, by Great Britain in 1905. This type rendered obsolete the pre-*Dreadnought* battleships. According to certain naval authorities the development was a blunder on the part of Great Britain as it cleared the slate of previous capital ships, and gave Germany a fresh start on an equal basis. "Great Britain had to write off seventy-five ships, Germany only twenty-eight," says Bywater. "More than this, Germany was in a position to resume the naval race on equal terms."[1]

As German competition grew stronger the British admiralty adopted a new policy of a 60 per cent superiority over Germany for vessels of the dreadnought type with "other and higher standards" for smaller vessels. The British also began increasing the caliber of guns from 12 inches to 13.5 inches and then to 14 and 15 inches, while the Germans evidently continued to be satisfied with the 11 and 12 inch guns. This difference in gun power was later held to be an important factor when the two fleets met at Jutland. In 1914 the British navy possessed 41 ships of the dreadnought class built or building while the Germans had 27 of such ships.[2]

The British had a very marked superiority over the German fleet, but they were too shrewd to be satisfied with that. In addition to a costly building program the government began to make political agreements which removed threats to British interests in other parts of the

[1] BYWATER: *Navies and Nations*, p. 28.
[2] *Ibid.*, p. 178.

world. Powerful armies and navies were brought into alliance with England, and the concentration of almost the entire British naval force in the North Sea was made possible. The writer remembers seeing, in the summer of 1913, a part of the British fleet operating in its maneuvers from the mouth of the Humber. For miles the lines of these powerful ships stretched out into the waters of the North Sea in anticipation of a conflict on this historic and strategic battle ground. Only one opponent could have been the object of these maneuvers. The "blue" or defending forces stood in the place of the British navy and the "red" or attacking fleet represented the sea power of Germany.

In 1902 the first alliance was made with Japan. The enemies then in prospect were Russia and Germany. But when the alliance was renewed in 1905, Russia had passed from the scene as a naval rival and the single opponent in mind was Germany. As a result of the alliance all of the British battleships maintained in Far Eastern waters were withdrawn. In 1904 the famous political agreement was made with France which paved the way for a redistribution of naval forces in 1912. The French Brest fleet was transferred to the Mediterranean while the British withdrew most of their Mediterranean squadron to the North Sea. Because of the important part which the Mediterranean plays in British policy, some of the latest and most powerful vessels in the navy had been stationed at Malta. After 1912, however, the reduced British Mediterranean forces contained no battleships, although they included three battle cruisers in addition to some smaller craft. This reapportionment of naval vessels was felt by the French to have placed a moral obligation upon Great Britain to defend the North Sea and Atlantic coasts of France in return for the protection of British Mediterranean interests by the French fleet.

The United States and Disarmament

The five greatest navies in 1914 were in order of strength, the British, German, American, French, and Japanese. By shrewd and careful diplomacy Great Britain had brought into alliance three of these navies and before they could be successful they were yet to combine four of the five.

As the race became more pronounced the public mind of Great Britain was being prepared for a conflict. Traditions of supremacy, centuries old, were being shaken by an enemy which was strategically situated to strike a crushing blow at the British Isles. A frequent topic of conversation in London was the coming war between Great Britain and Germany. Admiral Mahan wrote a few years before the war:

> The rivalry between Germany and Great Britain today is the danger point, not only of European politics, but of world politics as well . . .
> No such emphasized industrial and maritime competition between two communities has arisen since the time of Cromwell and the later Stewart kings, when England wrested from Holland her long possessed commercial supremacy, supported by a navy until then unconquered.[1]

In 1912 there came an attempt to end the dangerous competition by direct diplomatic conversations. The Agadir incident of 1911 had aroused many people in both countries to the seriousness of the situation. Early in 1912, Sir Ernest Cassel went to Germany with a verbal note proposing a settlement of the problem on the basis of (1) restriction of the German naval program and a recognition that naval superiority was essential to Great Britain, (2) a sympathetic discussion of Germany's colonial ambitions, and (3) reciprocal assurances debarring either power from joining in aggressive designs or combinations against the other. In the note of reply from

---
[1] *The Interest of America in International Conditions*, pp. 163–4.

ARMAMENT LIMITATION

the German government further direct negotiations were suggested. As a result Viscount Haldane, British Minister of War, was selected to go to Berlin.[1] Haldane represented to the German government the seriousness of the naval situation and expressed the hope that the Germans would modify their building program. He evidently held out to Germany the hope of an economic outlet in an African empire. He further stated that if Germany were to fight France she could not count on the neutrality of Great Britain unless Germany were the victim of attack. Viscount Haldane could make this statement with considerable confidence for the year before he had been engaged in the formulation of plans in collaboration with French army officers for sending troops to France in case of an attack by Germany. He warned that if Germany should continue to build, the British would have to lay down two keels for every new German keel. The Germans on their part were willing to modify their building program if Great Britain would agree to be neutral in any war between Germany and a third power and to promise not to be a party to a combination against Germany. To this Haldane could hold out no hope of agreement. He returned to London without having settled the question. The subsequent negotiations came to nothing and another failure in armament limitation was recorded.

[1] Accounts of these conversations written by some of the principal actors are: WILLIAM HOHENZOLLERN: *The Kaiser's Memoirs*, Harper & Brothers, New York, 1922; VISCOUNT HALDANE: *Before the War*, Cassel & Co., Ltd., London, 1920; GRAND ADMIRAL VON TIRPITZ: *My Memoirs*, Dodd, Mead and Company, 1919. FAY, SIDNEY BRADSHAW: *Origins of the World War*, The Macmillan Company, New York, 1930, contains an account of the negotiations based largely on *Die Grosse Politik der Europäischen Kabinette, 1871–1914*, Sammlung der Akten des deutschen Auswärtigen Amts, Berlin, 1922–27. See also *British Documents on the Origins of the War, 1898–1914*, Vol. VI, Chapters XLVIII and XLIX, edited by G. P. GOOCH and HAROLD TEMPERLEY, His Majesty's Stationery Office, London, 1930.

The United States and Disarmament

The Kaiser had given Viscount Haldane the plan for the new German Fleet Law, the contents of which caused some stir among British naval men. The plan of the new law was to raise the number of active squadrons in the German navy from two to three so that the greater part of the fleet could be maintained in commission and ready for war at all times. This plan was in due time placed before the Diet although it has been stated from German sources that four battleships were eliminated as a result of Lord Haldane's persuasions.[1] The introduction of this law brought about increased building in England. Winston Churchill, the energetic First Lord of the Admiralty, succeeded in having the British naval budget raised until it amounted to more than 50 million pounds sterling. Had the two countries expended one-tenth the money and energy in the attempt to avoid war that they were willing to spend in the movement to prepare for war the result might have been different.

Two years later the war came and British supremacy on the seas was a considerable factor in the result. Not only did it enable Great Britain to repel attacks against the British Isles, but it guarded the sea lanes to a certain extent and made possible the importation of some of the supplies which were so urgently needed. An enormous trade was conducted with the United States which constituted a strong bond to tie the American Republic to the allied cause, and a virtual blockade of Germany was set up.

The importance of the British navy in the allied victory can be easily overemphasized. It was assisted by three other strong navies and by the armies of Great Britain, France, Russia, Italy, and the United States. As has been suggested, if Germany, the world's greatest land power, had been pitted singly against Great Britain,

---

[1] Dawson, William Harbut: *The German Empire*, 1867–1914, Vol. II, p. 490, The Macmillan Company, 1919.

Armament Limitation

the world's greatest sea power, the result most probably would not have been a victory for Great Britain.

No sooner was the war over than the British attention was directed to the possible growth of a much more formidable naval power than Germany. Up to the time of the World War the American navy had developed slowly. The United States could boast of no modern battleship in 1889. Gradually the growing wealth and commerce and increased American participation in world affairs were reflected in an enlarged naval tonnage. The controversy with Great Britain over the Venezuelan boundary in 1896 emphasized the naval weakness of the United States for the contemporary forecasts of the narrowly averted struggle necessarily conceded an easy British triumph on the seas. The incident, accordingly, gave a stimulus to the sentiment for a larger navy and by 1898 this country had five modern battleships and two large armored cruisers. The war with Spain brought the exploits of naval men graphically before the American people. The names of Dewey, Sampson, Schley, and Hobson were on every tongue. The enthusiasm for greater power upon the sea ran high. The United States navy ranked second until the development of the German fleet. It then took its position in third place although the margin over the navy of France was slight.

During the World War the amazing changes in the commerce and finances of the United States were accompanied by an equally sweeping transformation in naval plans. The 1916 program enacted by Congress provided for ten battleships, armed each with twelve 16-inch guns, and six battle cruisers, armed with eight 16-inch guns and capable of a 34-knot speed. These ships were planned to embody the lessons of the Battle of Jutland which was fought just prior to the enactment of the program. Up to that time the belief had gained ground that the submarine had greatly reduced the importance of the big ship. At Jutland in May, 1916, the success of the heavily armored vessel with large-calibered guns had inclined naval men to return to their faith in the powerful capital ship. In addition to the ten battle ships and six battle cruisers the program provided for ten scout cruisers, 110 smaller combat craft, and several other auxiliary vessels.

The Act of 1916 would have given the United States a great preponderance in heavy ships. A forecast of the anticipated naval situation of 1923, made prior to the Washington Conference by Congressman Britten of the House Committee on Naval Affairs, showed that altogether the American fleet would have possessed thirty-three capital ships as compared with thirty-five in the British navy. The American ships, however, would have been larger and would have had greater gun power. The American displacement on the average would have been 6,638 tons per ship greater. The number of big guns per ship would have averaged 10.3 for each American ship and 8.97 for each British vessel. The American guns would have averaged 14½ inches in caliber as contrasted with 13⅔ for the British.[1] This comparison led Hector Bywater, the able British naval writer, to observe in 1921:

> On the basis of modern armored vessels completed, building, and authorized, the British Navy has already declined to second rank. And in this connection it is important to note that the modern armored vessel—the capital ship—remains, in the deliberate opinion of the British Admiralty, the unit on which sea-power is built up.[2]

The 1916 program was never completed because of the Washington Conference, but it was, nevertheless, a significant fact in international relations. For the first time since the Napoleonic Wars the British navy was threatened with a position of inferiority.

[1] BYWATER, HECTOR: *Sea Power in the Pacific*, pp. 10 ff., Houghton Mifflin Company, Boston, 1921.
[2] *Ibid.*, p. 12.

Armament Limitation

The motives behind the American naval expansion program were two-fold. In the first place there was much bitterness against both of the belligerent parties for their actions in restricting American trade. Even after this country had joined the allies many Americans continued to hold resentment against the British for the way in which they had summarily ordered American vessels and other neutral ships with American cargoes into British ports. Furthermore, when the world was aflame rumors of all sorts spread like wildfire and it was feared that at the end of the war the victorious countries might turn their attention to the western hemisphere.

If we read the Congressional debates regarding this revolutionary naval bill we are struck with the fact that the sea-power theory was enthusiastically accepted by many of the Congressmen. The world was in flux. The influence of naval strength on national greatness was a subject of current discussion. Senator Swanson, ranking majority member and spokesman for the Naval Affairs committee and whose coastal constituents at Norfolk look upon the navy as their greatest industry, said to the Senate:

> I deeply feel that the fate of this Republic, the preservation of our institutions and the maintenance of our well defined foreign policies are dependent upon the strength and success of our Navy. America and her Navy, for weal or for woe, are united in indissoluble wedlock.
>
> The history of the world teaches one sure lesson—that naval supremacy ultimately means national preeminence and triumph. More than ever before sea power is the best and strongest military power. The rise and fall of nations and empires teach the same lesson—that national safety and national success are inseparable from naval strength and power.
>
> . . . .
>
> With a foreign commerce exceeding that of any other nation, we, above all other nations, need an adequate navy to give this proper protection. There is not a citizen in this Republic whose material prosperity is not more or less dependent upon our Navy.
>
> . . . .

The United States and Disarmament

This great war vastly increased our foreign trade and reviving our home industries, has given us wealth almost unspeakable. When this war is concluded this Nation will be rich beyond the wildest dreams of avarice. If we have naval and military strength we will be able to hold our wealth, power, and prestige. If we are weak in this respect the day of our despoilment will inevitably come.[1]

Fourteen years later Senator Swanson came to question this unreserved opinion of the value of naval supremacy, and to his eternal credit he was able to alter his judgment in the face of new conditions and new evidence as to the futility of force in national economic policy.

Senator Borah became a flaming apostle of military power, assuring the Senators that the fall of Athens was due to the lack of interest in military affairs on the part of Athenian citizens and the decline of Venice must be traced to the indifference of Venetians to preparedness. Weakness, he said, was a cause of war and a strong navy was an assurance of peace.[2] The passage of time has likewise led to a radical revision of Senator Borah's views on the value of armaments and in late years this most eloquent of American legislators has frequently cast his influence on the side of reductions in the naval establishment.

The American 1916 program had its effects in England and Japan. When the plan was first enacted Great Britain was immersed in war. But when the keels of the sixteen capital ships were laid down between 1919 and 1921 the British government was just recovering from the shock of the conflict and was beginning to look to the future. The British would, no doubt, have been well pleased to have preserved the *status quo* at the end of the war. They were then more powerful upon the seas than were all of the other nations put together.[3]

[1] *Congressional Record*, Vol. 53, p. 10,923, July 13, 1916.
[2] *Ibid.*, (July 17, 1916), p. 11,173.
[3] Great Britain possessed forty-five capital ships as against not more than forty ships of equivalent power in other navies, BYWATER: *Navies and Nations*, p. 118.

ARMAMENT LIMITATION

But their warships were fast becoming obsolete and other nations had developed competitive programs. Across the Atlantic there was now looming up a more powerful rival than Germany had ever been, for the United States had not only projected the greatest navy in the world but also possessed the economic strength to carry out the plan with comparative ease. The British were not ready to accept this new situation. The deep feeling with which the doctrine of naval supremacy was regarded was given expression by the able cabinet official, Winston Churchill, who, speaking shortly after the armistice, said:

> Nothing in the world, nothing that you may think of, or dream of, or anyone may tell you; no arguments, however specious; no appeals, however seductive, must lead you to abandon that naval supremacy on which the life of our country depends.[1]

The British admiralty considered plans for vessels which would have greatly surpassed the powerful American ships. At the Geneva Conference reference was later made to designs which had been drafted in England for battleships of 45,000 tons with 18- or 20-inch guns.[2] Bywater mentions an estimate by a British constructor that the capital ship of the future would have 57,000 tons displacement and would be armed with eight 18-inch guns.[3] Ichihashi states that at the time of the Washington Conference the British government had designed and collected material for two super-Hoods of about 50,000 tons each.[4]

In Japan, the American naval program produced sensational effects which exceeded the apprehension

---

[1] BYWATER: *Navies and Nations*, p. 21.

[2] *Records of the Conference for the Limitation of Naval Armament, Held at Geneva from June 20th to August 4th, 1927*, p. 21, Geneva, 1927.

[3] *Navies and Nations*, p. 29.

[4] ICHIHASHI, YAMATO: *The Washington Conference and After*, p. 56, Stanford University Press, Stanford University, 1928.

created in England. For years there had been serious tension in American-Japanese relations. The immigration question, the alien land laws, and the clash of policies in China had been sufficient to arouse suspicions on both sides. Japanese opinion had regarded the American occupation of the Philippine Islands as in the nature of a threat, much as some Americans had regarded a Japanese commercial and industrial project in Magdalena Bay. Following the war the most important part of the American navy, the battle fleet, had been transferred to the Pacific Ocean. The prospect of an enormous increase in the size of the fleet combined with the possibility of powerful bases in Guam and the Philippines, therefore, created panicky fears among the Japanese.

In 1920, the Japanese government approved a project along the lines of the then existing 8-8 plan. By building two capital ships each year the Japanese expected in time to have forty-eight ships not over the age of obsolescence, which was fixed at twenty-four years. The forty-eight ships were to be divided into three squadrons, each consisting of eight battleships and eight battle cruisers. By 1927 this program would have required an expenditure of $400,000,000 per year, which, considering the meager resources of Japan, would have been a crushing sum.[1]

The large naval expenditures of this country, the bitter resentment which undoubtedly existed in the British admiralty, and the inflamed state of mind in Japanese naval circles, all combined to make it appear that the continuance of the American program was highly undesirable. Under these circumstances it was the height of statesmanship for the United States to invite her chief naval rivals to attend a conference to discuss the limitation of armaments. In June, 1921, Congress passed

[1] BUELL, RAYMOND LESLIE. "*The Washington Conference,*" p. 139, D. Appleton and Company, New York, 1922.

Armament Limitation

the naval bill which carried an amendment, introduced by Senator Borah, recommending a conference for the reduction of naval expenditures and building programs. In accordance with this suggestion, President Harding asked the leading naval powers, Great Britain, Japan, France, and Italy, to send delegates to Washington to consider the problem of naval limitation. In addition, the scope of the conference was broadened to include Pacific and Far Eastern questions, and China, Holland, Belgium, and Portugal were invited to participate in the deliberations of the conference on these problems. On November 12, 1921, the delegates met in the first plenary session of the conference.

Chapter IX

THE WASHINGTON CONFERENCE

THE conference method of dealing with international questions has almost unlimited possibilities. In the solution of problems of mutual interest among nations it represents the substitution of intelligent direction for disorganization and chance. The use of this method in attempting to bring rational order into world affairs has been given great stimulus in the years following the war, and in no field has it been used more strikingly than in that of naval limitation. Before 1914, as has been shown, the efforts to stop the growth of armaments were sporadic and ineffectual. Since the war there has been hardly a year in which there has not been a notable meeting of an international conference or commission to give serious and prolonged consideration to the matter. And a continuation of the series of important gatherings to grapple with the question is definitely upon the program for the future. Some of these meetings have accomplished real gains and others have been unable to achieve any concrete or immediate results. Practically every discussion has, however, helped to clarify the subject, and has made a later solution easier. The whole movement bears unmistakable marks of progress. Only by comparison with the past can we judge the trend of the movement. The present situation is certainly far more encouraging than was that at the time of the Second Hague Conference in 1907 when the subject could not be placed on the agenda for fear of breaking up the conference.

The efforts of the League of Nations will be dealt with separately in Chaps. XIV, XV, and XVI. Aside from the

THE WASHINGTON CONFERENCE

work of the League there have been three important conferences which have met at Washington (1921-1922), at Geneva (1927), and at London (1930).

The Washington Conference was an epochal event in international politics, for it reached the first important agreement among the great powers for the limitation and reduction of armaments. It established the method and set the standard for practically all the immediately effective work on this subject for a decade, and its precedent will probably influence the movement for many years to come.

From the beginning the Washington Conference was dominated by the personality of Secretary of State Charles Evans Hughes. Mr. Hughes was fairly well in tune with the sentiments of the large business groups centered in New York City. As has been said, one of the guiding principles of the international bankers is friendship between the United States and the greater powers. If they have not always shown the same desire to placate the sentiments of the smaller and weaker nationalities of the Caribbean it is because the economic loss from bad feeling in that quarter is not so certain; and economic gains, for the immediate present, at least, have been promoted by strong action. Mr. Hughes can easily be adjudged the most persuasive and convincing of American statesmen who have tried their arts in the field of conference diplomacy. His mastery of the new method was amply proved at Washington in 1921-1922 and at Havana in 1928. At the latter conference his performance was little short of miraculous when he wellnigh convinced the assembled delegates from Latin America that, in spite of marines in Haiti and Nicaragua, the United States was not imperialistically inclined.

At Washington, Mr. Hughes was desirous of removing certain particular causes of friction which were pregnant with danger, and he wished, in general, to build up the intangible asset of good will. To do this he was willing to sacrifice the large capital ships which were in the process of construction, for he felt that because of the bitterness which they were certain to promote they were a liability to the expanding American economy. Realistic thinking was necessary to grasp this proposition which runs decidedly counter to the older systems of thought.

Doubtless the great climax of Mr. Hughes' successful career came at the opening of the Washington Conference. In a speech delivered on November 12, 1921, he outlined in detail practically all that was to be accomplished in the way of naval tonnage limitation. He offered to abandon the American program of capital ship construction in return for concessions from Great Britain and Japan on a somewhat smaller scale. His speech was in part as follows:

> The first [consideration] is that the core of the difficulty is to be found in the competition in naval programs, and that, in order appropriately to limit naval armament, competition in its production must be abandoned. Competition will not be remedied by resolves with respect to the method of its continuance. One program inevitably leads to another, and if competition continues, its regulation is impractical. There is only one adequate way out and that is to end it now.
>
> It is apparent that this cannot be accomplished without serious sacrifices. Enormous sums have been expended upon ships under construction and building programs which are now under way cannot be given up without heavy loss. Yet if the present construction of capital ships goes forward, other ships will inevitably be built to rival them and this will lead to still others. Thus the race will continue so long as ability to continue lasts. The effort to escape sacrifices is futile. We must face them or yield our purpose.[1]

Secretary Hughes then presented a specific and practical program for reduction, the main points of which were as follows:

---

[1] *Conference on the Limitation of Armament, Washington, November 12, 1921–February 6, 1922,* p. 58, Government Printing Office, 1922.

The Washington Conference

1. That all capital ship building programs, either actual or projected should be abandoned;
2. That further reduction should be made through the scrapping of certain of the older ships;
3. That, in general, regard should be had to the existing naval strength of the powers concerned;
4. That the capital ship tonnage should be used as the measurement of strength for navies and a proportionate allowance of auxiliary combatant craft prescribed.[1]

Becoming more concrete, he detailed a program for the scrapping of American, British, and Japanese capital ships and further specified which ships each of the three powers should retain. The limitations on the French and Italian navies were reserved for later consideration. Here, indeed, was a departure from the grandiose generalities and meaningless professions of goodwill which had been the bane of previous disarmament discussions. Nor was there the resort to bickerings over minor technicalities in guns and characteristics of ships which is often the defense of the unwilling technician. The method of disarmament was free-handed and sweeping. The British writers, Kenworthy and Young, said about it: "He was sinking in a few sentences more tonnage in battleships than all the battles of the world had sunk in a century."[2] Ichihashi, who was present and attached to the Japanese delegation, wrote: "It electrified the calm session; some were shocked, some were even alarmed, but others were pleased. It made the day a memorable one in history."[3] Seasoned journalists, whose lives have been devoted to dramatizing political events for their newspaper readers, have sought to depict the effect of the speech. Mark Sullivan in his book, *The Great Adventure at Washington*, has devoted many pages to describing the reaction to "that inspired moment" of various personalities in the

[1] *Ibid*, p. 60.
[2] *Op. cit.*, p. 155.
[3] *Op. cit.*, p. 35.

plenary session. According to his description, Admiral Beatty of the British Navy "came forward in his chair with the manner of a bulldog, sleeping on a sunny porch, who has been kicked in the stomach by the foot of an itinerant soap-canvasser." Lord Lee reached around excitedly for pencil and paper.[1] Miss Tarbell testifies that the Japanese "took it without a flicker of an eyelash,"[2] while Louis Seibold wrote: "There was no discounting the surprise of Prince Tokugawa, Baron Kato, and Ambassador Shidehara. The Italian, Portuguese, and Belgian envoys appeared to be greatly pleased if a trifle startled."[3] Well might these veteran writers wax enthusiastic, if slightly at variance, for they had lived through a climax in the drama of history.

The Hughes plan for reducing the capital ships of the three powers to the ratios of 5:5:3 was adopted. The tonnage figures which were first suggested by the Secretary of State were scaled slightly upwards to make it possible for the Japanese to retain the newly completed *Mutsu*, a ship which, it was stated, had been constructed partially from contributions of Japanese school children. Japanese naval officers had taken great pride in this modern 16-inch gun battleship. Accordingly, the *Mutsu* was retained and the feelings of the Japanese school children were spared, but the other powers were given compensation in additional tonnage.

The ratios for France and Italy, after some heavy pressure upon the French delegates, were finally set at 1.67 each as compared with 5:5:3 for the United States, Great Britain, and Japan. Hereafter, for convenience, the ratios of the five powers will be referred to as 10:10:6:-3.33:3.33. The numbers and tonnage of capital ships to

---

[1] SULLIVAN, MARK: *The Great Adventure at Washington*, pp. 27, 28, Doubleday, Page & Company, Garden City, 1922.

[2] TARBELL, IDA M.: *Peacemakers—Blessed and Otherwise*, p. 45, The Macmillan Company, New York, 1922.

[3] SULLIVAN: *op, cit.*, p. 29.

The Washington Conference

be retained by each of the powers were eventually fixed as follows:

Country	No.	Tonnage
United States	18	525,850
Great Britain	20	558,950
Japan	10	301,320
France	10	221,170
Italy	10	182,800

It will be noted that the tonnage left to the powers did not correspond entirely to the ratios agreed upon. Thus the American tonnage was 33,100 tons below that of Great Britain. The reason for this discrepancy was that the British vessels retained were slightly older than those left to the United States. With the larger tonnage given to Great Britain it was estimated that the two fleets of capital ships were of about the same strength.

The tons in which the fleets were measured were not the same but varied somewhat according to systems in use in the different navies. The treaty included a definition of standard displacement as that of the ship complete, fully manned, engined and equipped ready for sea, including all armament and ammunition, equipment, outfit, provisions and fresh water for crew, miscellaneous stores and implements of every description that are intended to be carried in war, but without fuel or reserve feed water on board. The ton agreed upon was the long ton of 2,240 pounds.[1] When this standard ton was later applied to measure the existing fleet it was found that the older British method of measurement had included fewer items than the treaty definition of displacement while the American method had included more. The British ships, when translated into standard tonnage, accordingly ran somewhat higher than the treaty figures

[1] Chapter II, Part IV of the treaty. See Appendix I.

and the American ships ran somewhat lower. The revised figures as of December 31, 1929, which were accepted as correct by the American delegates to the London Conference, showed 532,400 tons of capital ships for the United States. This included some 30,000 tons that had been added through the modernization of ten American ships since the Washington Conference. The British capital ship strength was set down as 608,650 tons.[1] Thus, even with the increase from modernization, the American ships were 76,250 tons behind the British.

The discrepancy, however, was of only temporary importance. After the year 1931, when replacements of capital ships were to be permitted,[2] the tonnage of the various powers was expected to fall in line with their respective ratios until in 1942 they would be exactly in accord with their allotments. Measured in treaty tons the 1942 strength would be as follows:

Country	No.	Tonnage
United States	15	525,000
Great Britain	15	525,000
Japan	9	315,000
France	5	175,000
Italy	5	175,000

All of this reduction required the destruction of many capital ships. American critics of the Washington Conference have pointed out that the United States gave up much more than did the other powers. This is true. A comparison of the tonnage destroyed is difficult to reduce to exact mathematical terms because of the variation in the definition of displacement which then existed in the different navies, and because of other

[1] For an estimate of the comparative tonnage just prior to the London Conference see below, p. 188.

[2] France and Italy were, however, given the right to lay down one capital ship each in 1927 and 1929.

THE WASHINGTON CONFERENCE

variable factors such as the age and gun power of the existing vessels which were destroyed and the percentage of completion of the doomed ships which were in process of construction. The following figures set forth the number of the scrapped ships and their tonnage, but, because of the difference in definition of tons involved, the statistics are only approximately accurate:[1]

Country	No. of capital ships destroyed	Tonnage
United States	28	845,740
Great Britain	24	583,000
Japan	16	435,328
Total	68	1,864,068

Of the sixteen powerful capital ships of the 1916 program, eleven were scrapped, or, if you include the *Lexington* and *Saratoga*, battle cruisers which were not destroyed but were converted into aircraft carriers, the number is thirteen. Senator Hale, chairman of the Senate Committee on Naval Affairs, estimated that of these ships, which were all in process of construction, the battleships were 43 per cent and the battle cruisers were 16 per cent complete.[2] This is what is referred to when critics of the Washington Conference speak of the sinking by the United States of the most powerful fleet afloat.

In addition to limitations upon capital ships, the tonnage for air-craft carriers was restricted as follows:

United States	135,000
Great Britain	135,000
Japan	81,000
France	60,000
Italy	60,000

[1] ICHIHASHI: *op. cit.*, p. 106. These figures do not include the tonnage of six ships, two American and four British, which were later scrapped upon the completion of other ships.

[2] *Congressional Record*, Vol. 70, p. 1051, Jan. 3, 1929.

The United States and Disarmament

Auxiliary combat craft, including cruisers, destroyers, submarines, and other smaller types of ships, were not limited at the Washington Conference. In his opening speech, Secretary Hughes had suggested figures of limitation for auxiliary vessels as well as for capital ships, but this part of the program met with little enthusiasm from the other powers. The most apparent reason for the failure of this proposal was the inability to agree regarding the submarine.

The people of Great Britain, remembering the lessons of the World War, were desirous of abolishing the submarine. The prospect of starvation in a future war, because of the blocking of trade routes and the stoppage of food importation, had created a bitter antagonism in the British Isles against this instrument of commerce destruction. Seeking to capitalize the great moral indignation against the U-boat which continued as a hang-over from the days of the war, the British delegation asked that the submarine be abolished. Lord Lee, the principal spokesman of the delegation on the subject, advanced an elaborate argument to prove that the submarine was not of much value in coastal defense or in attack against naval vessels. The destruction of commerce was the only use to which it could be put, he alleged, and in this work it could not be employed except in violation of the rules of international law. The only solution to the problem, according to his reasoning, was to do away with the nefarious craft altogether.[1] His argument fell upon deaf ears, for all of the four other powers were able to see great possibilities for the submarine outside of the field of commerce destruction. They, accordingly, refused to agree to abolition.

Another conflict arose over the tonnage in submarines which was to be allotted under the treaty. Mr. Hughes had proposed 90,000 tons for Great Britain and the

[1] *Conference on the Limitation of Armament*, p. 474.

THE WASHINGTON CONFERENCE

United States, 54,000 tons for Japan, and it was his intention that the French and Italian submarine quotas should be fixed in accordance with their capital ship ratios, which would have given them 30,000 tons each. When the British protested that the tonnage figures were too large, Mr. Hughes suggested that the United States and Great Britain should reduce their strength to 60,000 tons and that Japan, France, and Italy should retain their existing tonnage which he understood to be 31,452 for Japan, 31,391 for France, and about 21,000 tons for Italy.

The French, who are the chief admirers of the submarine, now came forth to block further progress in this direction. They had been displeased with the low ratio awarded to them in capital ships and were not disposed to yield further ground. After receiving instruction from Paris, M. Sarraut of the French delegation announced that the cabinet and Supreme Council of National Defense had fixed 90,000 tons as the absolute minimum below which France could not go in submarines "without imperiling the vital interests of the country and of its colonies and the safety of their naval life."[1] Mr. Balfour, the cold and cynical leader of the British delegation, replied bitingly to the effect that

> this constituted a somewhat singular contribution to the labors of a conference called for the diminution of armament . . . It was perfectly obvious that the proposed 90,000 tons of submarines were intended to destroy commerce. They could not be intended for any other purpose . . . It was perfectly clear that if at Great Britain's gates a fleet of 90,000 tons of submarines (60,000 tons of which were to be of the newest type) was to be constructed, no limitation of any kind on auxiliary vessels capable of dealing with submarines could be admitted by the Government which he represented.[2]

The British thereupon refused to accept limitations as to destroyers, which are the swift surface vessels used to

[1] *Ibid.*, p. 570.
[2] *Ibid.*, pp. 574, 576.

hunt down and annihilate the submarine. The limitation of cruisers, which are the nemesis of the destroyer, was in turn impossible. Perhaps the British delegates were secretly glad that there was to be no limitation of auxiliary combat craft; but it was far better for their purposes that the breakdown should be laid to the French submarine program rather than to the needs of the British for commerce destroyers. The latter necessity might have been difficult to defend in the atmosphere of Washington. It may be that similar sentiments were held by Italy and Japan, but their delegates openly regretted that auxiliary craft were not included in the restricted classes. At any rate the failure to limit these vessels, as will be seen, left an opening for another naval race.

The conference made one final attempt to restrict the submarine. The sentiment on the part of the British delegation against that vessel was too strong to be utterly ignored. Accordingly, a draft treaty was drawn up which prohibited the employment of submarines as commerce destroyers by the five powers and invited all other nations to adhere to the prohibition. The treaty failed, however, owing to the fact that France neglected to ratify it. The French are much like other people, and when it comes to naval bickerings they are very reluctant to give up any prospective advantages. Furthermore, their moral indignation, as in other countries, runs strangely enough along the lines of self-interest. During the war the use of the submarine by the Germans against commercial vessels was widely deprecated as inhuman and barbarous. But when it came to ratifying an agreement denying themselves the right to do the same thing, the French were negligent. And so, in the final result, the submarine was not limited at Washington.

Another matter as serious as the competition in capital ships was the growing menace of fortifications in the

The Washington Conference

Pacific. The lines of attack in a conflict between the United States and Japan were gradually moving closer. Prior to the conference there had been much talk of increasing the American fortifications in Guam and the Philippines. Japan had rather hurriedly completed the naval works at the Bonin Islands and Amami-Oshima. Hector Bywater, who has studied the Far Eastern situation carefully, says that the evidence of these serious naval preparations had led many observers in the Far East to believe that Japan would have made the beginning of work on the American bases in Guam and Manila a cause for war.[1] Few people in the United States realized that American peace was thus threatened. These minor policies in the Far East which were comparatively unimportant to the American people, so far as prospective benefits were concerned, were of immense importance to Japan, who regarded her very existence as in jeopardy.

When Japan came to the conference, therefore, her delegates were firmly prepared to seek a *status quo* limitation on fortifications in the Pacific. In fact, if such limitation had not been forthcoming it is very doubtful if the Japanese would have been willing to agree to capital ship limitation on the 10:10:6 basis. On the other hand American naval officers who had long laid plans for the extension of the fortifications and fleet facilities in both Guam and the Philippines raised objections to the Japanese demand for limitation. Secretary Hughes was in a difficult situation. If he listened to the Japanese demand he would offend the American naval group. If he listened to the American naval advice he would wreck the conference. He chose to give success to the conference through an agreement to the *status quo* on naval bases.

The treaty finally provided for the maintenance of the *status quo* with regard to the following Pacific fortifications and naval bases:

[1] *Navies and Nations*, p. 149.

The United States and Disarmament

Those of the United States: The insular possessions in the Pacific except (*a*) those adjacent to the coast of the United States, Alaska, and the Panama Canal Zone (not including the Aleutian Islands), and (*b*) the Hawaiian Islands. The possessions to which the restriction applies are the Philippines, Guam, American Samoa, and the Aleutian Islands. Henceforth the United States must depend upon Hawaii for its furthest fortified western base.

Those of Great Britain: Hongkong and the insular possessions in the Pacific, east of the meridian of 110 degrees east longitude, except (*a*) those adjacent to the coast of Canada, (*b*) the Commonwealth of Australia and its territories, and (*c*) New Zealand. The line drawn at 110 degrees east longitude excluded Singapore from the operation of the treaty.

Those of Japan: The following insular possessions in the Pacific: the Kurile Islands, the Bonin Islands, Amami-Oshima, the Loochoo Islands, Formosa and the Pescadores, and any insular territories or possessions in the Pacific Ocean which Japan may hereafter acquire. This leaves the Japanese free to fortify Japan proper.

The effect of this limitation is admirably summarized by Bywater who states that before the conference the possible bases of war between Japan and the United States were about to be extended to within easy striking distance of each other. If the United States had carried out its plans to fortify Guam and the Philippines, the distance between the base at Cavite and the Japanese coast would have been 1,740 miles while the American stronghold at Guam would have been but 1,360 miles from Japan and 800 miles from the Bonin Islands. The wide waste of water which had served so well to isolate the United States in the past was to be eliminated. Now with the *status quo* decided upon at Washington the ocean barrier has been maintained. The distance from the

THE WASHINGTON CONFERENCE

Hawaiian Islands to Yokosuka, the most easterly base in Japan proper, is 3,375 miles; and thus a great stretch of ocean continues to intervene between the American base of naval operations and that of a prospective foe.[1]

The provisions of the Washington Treaty regarding fortifications are fundamental in American foreign policy and they probably mark the end of American invasion of the Far East. When in 1898 the United States had steered to the westward and planted the Stars and Stripes 7,000 miles from the shores of our Pacific coast, this country began an untimely excursion into the Asiatic sphere. For four centuries the Europeans, reversing the tendencies of previous history, had brought the oriental peoples under their economic and political influence. This had, indeed, been profitable for the merchants of Europe, and such commercial and financial centers as Lisbon, Amsterdam, and London had lolled in the prosperity of transactions conducted in the East under the guns of their fleets. The American government was partially moved by the desire to acquire similar trade using the Philippines as a commercial and naval base of operations. But the pendulum of Western influence and power had come to a stop and was about to swing the other way. In 1904, Russia, a Western power, met defeat fairly and squarely at the hands of Japan. News of Japanese victories in this war sent thrills of exultation throughout Asia. Twenty years later the awakening nationalism of China, the Philippines, and India, was to serve further notice that Western influence had passed its zenith. The propitious time for intrusion into the affairs of Asia had most definitely passed.

In acquiring the Philippines, this country found no easy road to the wealth of the East; but rather we became burdened with an expensive and thankless incumbrance. There are some persons who urge that the

[1] *Ibid.*, p. 150.

The United States and Disarmament

United States has an obligation to educate the Filipinos and to maintain for them a stable government partially at our expense. There must be, however, some definite limits to the duty of the United States to assist people who do not wish to be helped, particularly if in the performance of that duty this government throws the American people open to a tremendous liability in the matter of national defense. The Philippines are the only vulnerable spot in our otherwise easily defensible territorial system. As has been pointed out,[1] some day the United States may be confronted with the tremendously expensive task of their recapture. Who can calculate the spirit of revolt which may then arise against the governmental mismanagement which sacrifices the national interest for such emotional nonsense as is represented by the fundamentally unpatriotic sentiment "the white man's burden"?

The question which presented itself in connection with the Pacific fortifications, then, was whether the United States should entrench itself deeper as an unwelcome intruder in the Asiatic system or whether it should offer up this right in exchange for values such as the Japanese agreement to the 10:10:6 ratio and a relinquishment of the Anglo-Japanese Alliance. When the decision was made and the United States relinquished the right to push forward into the profitless zone of Asiatic politics, the action went far to reassure other nations with regard to American imperialism and to calm excitements that might easily have led to war.

One of the major results of the conference, which helped to clear the air of international suspicion, was the termination of the Anglo-Japanese Alliance. The alliance had been first formed in 1902, and in the original form it related to the questions of equal opportunity and territorial integrity in China and Korea. If either party to the

[1] See above, p. 74.

alliance should engage in war with another power regarding its interests in these questions and should be attacked by a third power, then the other party to the alliance would come to the assistance of its doubly beleaguered ally. Thus, in the Russo-Japanese War, if either France or Germany had entered the war on the side of Russia, Great Britain would have been obligated to come to the assistance of Japan. The purpose of the Japanese in entering the alliance was to secure support as against Russia, which country was at that time bearing down upon Manchuria. The Japanese also realized that an alliance with Great Britain would greatly enhance their prestige. On the part of Great Britain the alliance was intended to secure the benevolent neutrality of Japan in case of trouble with either Russia or Germany, and the assistance of Japan in case of war with both over the eastern question.

In 1905 the alliance was renewed. By that time the power of Russia had been greatly weakened in the Far East, but the rivalry between Great Britain and Germany had increased. Japan feared Russian revenge. The 1905 agreement was a stronger compact than its predecessor and bound each party to come to the assistance of the other in case of a war arising from an attack by a third power.

In 1911 the alliance was again renewed with an amendment to the effect that it should not be operative as against a third power which should conclude a general arbitration treaty with one of the parties to the alliance. By this amendment Great Britain hoped to allay the fears of the United States, for a general arbitration treaty had just been negotiated between the two Anglo-Saxon powers. Later, however, the arbitration treaty received the customary death blow in the Senate.[1]

[1] For a good sketch of the history of the Anglo-Japanese Alliance see BUELL: *The Washington Conference*, Chapter IV.

The United States and Disarmament

In 1921, the treaty, which was to run for ten years, would have been terminated if denounced by either party. If neither party took action, it was to continue indefinitely. There was at that time much speculation as to the fate of the alliance. Germany had disappeared from the scene even more completely than Russia. The only common danger which faced the two countries in the Far East was the United States with its expanding fleet. The menace of American battleships and prospective bases in the Philippines and Guam gave Japan a strong reason for desiring the continuation of the alliance. British interests were divided. A war with the United States, even with Japan as an ally, would have been exceedingly disastrous to British commerce; and it might likewise have divided the empire. The Pacific dominions regarded the United States as a lesser evil than Japan, and definitely showed their hostility to the alliance in the Imperial conference of 1921. On the other hand, a ruthless and crushing competition in shipbuilding on the part of the United States which would have compelled the British to accept naval inferiority would not have left them in a satisfactory position to terminate the alliance. Baffled for financial reasons in maintaining her position on the sea, Great Britain might conceivably have felt such indignation that she would have been moved to combine her naval strength with that of Japan. When, however, the United States at the opening of the Washington Conference showed a willingness to scrap her mammoth capital ship program, the last important reason from the standpoint of Great Britain for continuing the compact with Japan was gone. Great Britain took the initiative in the abandonment of the alliance. Mr. Balfour submitted to Mr. Hughes a tentative suggestion for a triple or quadruple entente in the Pacific. The Japanese were then bluntly told of this action which meant the passing of the alliance.[1]

[1] Ichihashi: *op. cit.*, p. 121.

The Washington Conference

In place of the alliance the Four-power Pacific Treaty was signed by the United States, Great Britain, Japan, and France. The treaty obliges the four parties to respect the rights of one another relating to their insular possessions and insular dominions in the Pacific. The obligation of consultation in a conference in case of disputes arising from any Pacific question which cannot be diplomatically adjusted is imposed. If the rights of the parties in the Pacific are threatened by the aggressive action of any outside power, the parties have agreed to communicate with one another as to the best measures to be taken.

The treaty marks a departure from the separate policy of the United States in the Pacific. If Great Britain and Japan should have a dispute over Japanese economic claims in Manchuria, the United States would be bound to meet with the treaty powers to consult as to a solution of the matter. The consultation agreement is the mildest form of joint action for the prevention of war. The slender obligations imposed upon the United States under it are, after all, to the best interests of this country, as a war in the Pacific region could not but prove a danger to all of the larger powers in that area. Furthermore, an exceedingly valuable consideration which the United States received for signing the treaty was the cancellation of the Anglo-Japanese Alliance.

The Four-power Treaty together with the other acts of the conference went far to make the great ocean off our western coast pacific in fact as well as in name. Dr. R. L. Buell admirably summarizes this aspect of the Washington treaties as follows:

As a result of the Naval Treaty, adopting the 5:5:3 ratio and the nonfortification agreement, it is now impossible for any power to intervene successfully in the Orient by force, if acting alone. By the Four-Power Treaty, it is now impossible for Great Britain and the United States to combine their fleets in order to intervene jointly. Moreover, by the Four-Power Treaty the freedom of the United States and Great Britain to bring diplomatic pressure against Japan is also probably limited. Consequently, as long as these treaties are adhered to, Japan is absolutely supreme in the eastern Pacific and over Asia.

At the same time, the Naval Treaty has made a successful Japanese attack on the Pacific Coast impossible, because Japan, as far as capital ships are concerned, will have a fleet forty per cent inferior to the American fleet; because Japan has no real bases or fortifications in the Pacific this side of the Bonins; and because the United States retains the right to increase the fortifications in Hawaii. As a result of this Treaty, it has become a physical impossibility for the United States successfully to attack Japan and Japan to attack the United States.[1]

Most academic students of international relations and most persons interested in the cause of world peace have been fairly enthusiastic over the outcome of the conference because of the check of naval competition and the removal of some formidable causes of war. Naval opinion has, however, been quite critical. The author some years ago was asked to assemble a list of periodical articles commending and condemning the work of disarmament. He was struck by the fact that most of the articles which criticised the Washington Conference adversely were written by retired naval officers. No one could expect that the abandonment of the ambitious 1916 program and the relinquishment of the right to increase fortifications in the Philippines would receive the approval of naval groups. The Washington Conference shattered a cherished dream of sea power in the western Pacific.

Representatives of high-pressure nationalism in Congress have likewise criticised the treaties. A comprehensive attack delivered in the United States Senate in 1929 by Senator McKellar is a good illustration. The substance of the Senator's objection are set forth without comment:

First. America was the only nation to sink any ships.
Second. Great Britain was given a ratio of 22 to 18, instead of 5 to 5.
Third. Great Britain was given a greater tonnage.

[1] BUELL: *op. cit.*, p. 200.

The Washington Conference

Fourth. America sank six ships of a tonnage of 43,200 tons each, leaving her with no ships of that class; and yet Great Britain was permitted to hold the *Hood*, with 41,200 tons and to build two capital ships of 35,000 tons each; and the largest ship that we had was a ship of 32,500 tons.

Fifth. America was prohibited from building any cruiser of more than 10,000 tons although we needed them because of the dearth of coaling stations.

Sixth. Merchant vessels were excluded from the terms of the agreement—and Great Britain's vessels are built so as to be convertible at a moment's notice in time of war.

Seventh. United States and Japan agreed not to build or maintain naval bases beyond what they have now—but Great Britain had already all that was necessary.

Eighth. Part 2 provides for the utter destruction of the United States vessels.

Ninth. The agreement remains in effect until December 31, 1936, and has guaranteed British superiority until that time. For all these agreements the United States received not a single benefit.[1]

Some rather enthusiastic adherents of the League of Nations have belittled the conference, working from the doctrinaire hypothesis that no good thing can be accomplished outside of the League. Salvador de Madariaga, whose book, *Disarmament*, stands high in the bibliography of the subject as to both content and literary finesse, does not share in the enthusiasm with which many Americans regard the conference. He alleges that the jealousies and irritations aroused by the bargaining at such a meeting do a great deal of harm while the reductions achieved only lead to renewed competition. The Washington Conference, according to his view, is a typical example of the inadequacy of the direct method,[2] and he feels that the only adequate manner of disarmament is through the "slow rhythm" of the League which proceeds patiently to eliminate the causes of war and thus to remove

[1] *Congressional Record*, Vol. 70, p. 2360, Jan. 28, 1929.
[2] De Madariaga, Salvador: *Disarmament*, p. 102, Coward-McCann Inc., New York, 1929.

the reasons for maintaining armaments. Senõr de Madariaga evidently failed to appreciate the great gains to peace which were achieved by reducing the causes of Anglo-American and Japanese-American friction.

The conference marks a turning point in international relations. By 1921, the western world had at last been convinced that heavy naval armaments were unprofitable and dangerous. At that point the United States, because of its wealth and on account of the building program already under way, held the key position in much the same way as did Germany in 1899. For certain understandable reasons the United States was willing to forego its leadership in naval building. These reasons were a lack of strong militarist tradition and the fact that business leaders in this country were not convinced of the economic necessity of sea supremacy. Fortunately at that moment there was in the office of Secretary of State a clear-headed man who could see with realistic vision the true self-interest of his country and who was competent to enact that interest into policy. The Washington Conference deservedly stands as one of the most commendable achievements in post-war diplomacy.

Chapter X

THE GENEVA CONFERENCE

THE Washington Conference, however, had only made a beginning in the settlement of the naval problem. The conference closed on February 6, 1922, and, with the competition in capital ships halted, some of the powers began to prepare their shipyards for a new race—this time in cruisers. In 1922 Japan laid the keels for five cruisers and France for three. In 1923 no cruisers were laid down, but in 1924 the race began in earnest. Great Britain and Japan laid down five cruisers each and France two. In 1925 Great Britain, Japan, and Italy laid down two each and France one. In 1926 the United States joined the competition with one cruiser laid down while Great Britain continued with two and France with one. For the next two years the totals were: 1927, the United States, one; Great Britain, one; Japan, two; and Italy, four; 1928, the United States, six; Great Britain, one; Japan, one; and France, one. The details of the cruiser race during this period are shown in the table on page 162. The fact that by the end of 1928 more than 48 per cent of the cruiser tonnage of the five powers built, building, or appropriated for, had been either laid down or appropriated for since the end of the Washington Conference showed that the world's strongest navies were again in a decided state of disequilibrium.

In the United States, Great Britain, and Japan a feeling of naval rivalry was revived by these programs. British writers accused the Japanese of starting a new naval race. Japanese writers replied with statistics to show that Japan was inferior in her auxiliary ship classes.

The United States and Disarmament

Cruisers Laid Down from February 6, 1922, to October 1, 1928[1]

Year	United States No.	Tons	Guns	Great Britain No.	Tons	Guns	Japan No.	Tons	Guns	France No.	Tons	Guns	Italy No.	Tons	Guns
1922	..	......	......	..	......	......	2	7,100	6—8 in.	3	7,234	8—6.1 in.			
							2	5,195	7—5.5 in.						
							1	3,100	6—5.5 in.						
1923															
1924	..	......	......	5	10,000	8—8 in.	2	10,000	10—8 in.	2	9,941	8—8 in.			
							2	7,100	6—8 in.						
							1	5,195	7—5.5 in.						
1925	..	......	......	2	10,000	8—8 in.	2	10,000	10—8 in.	1	10,000	8—8 in.	2	10,000	8—8 in.
1926	1	10,000	10—8 in.	2	10,000	8—8 in.	..	......	......	1	10,000	8—8 in.	4	5,000	
1927	1	10,000	10—8 in.	4	10,000	8—8 in.	2	10,000	10—8 in.	..	......	......			
				1	8,300	6—8 in.									
1928	6	10,000	9—8 in.	1	8,300	6—8 in.	1	10,000	10—8 in.	1	10,000	8—8 in.	6	40,000	
Total laid down....	8	80,000	......	15	146,600	......	15	117,085	......	8	71,584	......			
Appropriated for but not laid down.	..	......	......	2	16,600	......	1	10,000	......	1	6,496	......	2	20,000	
Total laid down and appropriated for...	8	80,000	......	17	163,200	......	16	127,085	......	9	78,080	......	8	60,000	

[1] The figures are taken from a Senate Committee Print, *Navies of the World*, prepared for the Senate Committee on Naval Affairs by the Chairman, Senator Frederick Hale, Government Printing Office, Washington, 1928, pp. 1 and 3.

American writers criticized the programs of both Japan and Great Britain and deplored the inferiority of this country in cruisers. They described the United States as having declined to the position of a second-class naval power.

Friends of the limitation of armaments were mildly alarmed by the fact that naval architects and builders were now bringing out a large, fast, and powerfully armed cruiser far superior to the old designs. Thus the U.S.S. *Salt Lake City*, 10,000 tons, laid down in 1926, has a speed of 32.5 knots and a main battery of ten 8-inch guns. The new type of cruiser was referred to by Commander Kenworthy as "a miniature or pocket dreadnought, miscalled a light cruiser."[1]

It was only natural that American naval sentiment should have been aroused by the cruiser-building programs of other countries. All of the competitors had been allies in a great war which professedly had been aimed against militarism. At the conclusion of their victorious fight they had forced their opponents to disarm and had solemnly signed a treaty which pledged them to the cause of disarmament. And now they were again engaged without apparent cause in costly building programs which were in direct conflict with all of their professions. At the Washington Conference the United States had taken it for granted that the principle of parity in tonnage had been established as between the British and the American fleets. But the construction program in Great Britain was placing the United States in a condition of marked inferiority as regards cruisers. This country, it is true, had no legal right to object. No treaty obligation, either express or implied, had been broken. The contention, made by navy men, that Great Britain had been pledged at the Washington Conference to the principle of parity

[1] KENWORTHY, J. M.: "The Next Conference on Disarmament," *North American Review*, p. 211, December, 1925.

in auxiliary ships is without foundation. No agreement whatever had been reached concerning such ships. But with the American belief that equality with the strongest power should be established on the sea it was not possible to feel comfortable in the face of the expanding British navy.

Although President Coolidge had adopted "economy" as the slogan of his administration, he could not indefinitely resist the pressure from naval groups for more ships. He therefore made an attempt to stop the competition before the United States would be compelled to expend larger sums of money in construction, and the Geneva Conference was called by him for that purpose.

In a memorandum of February 10, 1927, the President of the United States invited Great Britain, Japan, France, and Italy to enter direct negotiations through their delegates to the League of Nations Preparatory Commission looking toward an agreement for the limitation of classes of vessels not covered in the Washington Treaty. Mr. Coolidge's reasons for suggesting a conference between the five powers which would not be a part of the League's disarmament activities was that the League method would be too slow for his purpose. The League was engaged in attempts to settle problems which were too vast and fundamental to admit of a quick solution. But the possibility of being led into enormous and unnecessary naval expenditures was immediately threatening. The proposals for appropriations were soon to be acted upon, and speedy decision was required. Hence the method of approaching the rival naval powers directly was adopted.

In the memorandum of invitation the President said:

> The conviction that the competitive augmentation of national armaments has been one of the principal causes of international suspicion and ill-will, leading to war, is firmly held by the American Government and people. Hence the American Government has

The Geneva Conference

neglected no opportunity to lend its sympathy and support to international efforts to reduce and limit armaments.[1]

Great Britain and Japan accepted the invitation. France and Italy refused it. The French government explained that it did not desire to hinder the disarmament work of the League of Nations by entering into any outside conferences. The Italian government refused to attend because the unfavorable geographical situation of Italy made the further limitation of armaments undesirable at the time. And so the conference became a three-power affair.

The method of constituting the conference by selecting the delegations which had represented the governments at the Preparatory Commission was not fortunate. These delegations were composed of men far better fitted to wrangle over technical questions than to outline comprehensive policies of state. Particularly was this true of the American delegation, for the League Preparatory Commission had not been considered of sufficient importance by the United States to warrant the sending of outstanding public men. In the Washington Conference civilian statesmanship had risen to its zenith. At Geneva it fell to its nadir. At Washington, the United States had been represented by four delegates, Secretary Hughes, Elihu Root, and Senators Lodge and Underwood, all of whom had established reputations in domestic politics and at least two of whom were well known internationally. To this delegation there had been attached an imposing array of civilian and naval advisers. At Geneva, on the other hand, no member of the American delegation could boast of an established reputation for statesmanship. Hugh Gibson, United States Minister to Switzerland and Admiral Hilary Jones were the delegates, and up to that time neither had been extensively known as a leader in the field of public affairs. Mr. Gibson was a

[1] *Records of the Conference,* p. 6.

product of the diplomatic career service, capable and well trained in the duties of that profession. He was just beginning upon a period of activity which was to make him the outstanding American diplomatic specialist in the field of disarmament. Admiral Jones as a naval expert was thoroughly familiar with the technical aspects of the subject and entirely honest in his approach but he viewed the world through a porthole. Had the United States government been whole-heartedly enthusiastic regarding the success of the meeting it seems that a strong group of plenipotentiaries would have been sent. The strength which this country can muster for such an occasion is shown by the delegation which was sent three years later to the London Conference. But the particular strategy of choosing the delegates to the Preparatory Commission, as it turned out, placed the fate of the 1927 conference largely in the hands of experts.

Eight naval advisers, one legal adviser, one State Department adviser, a secretariat of four persons, and one archivist were attached to the American delegation. The overwhelming naval sentiment created an unfavorable situation for the civilians. The other delegations were likewise hemmed in with naval advice and showed but little eminence in their personnel. Viscount Cecil of the British delegation loomed out in the conference as the only representative possessing an outstanding reputation; but he was controlled by the cabinet in London where at least some of the ministers were under the influence of the British admiralty.

There were several other unfavorable circumstances. The problem to be dealt with, *i.e.*, the limitation of auxiliary vessels, was a difficult one. It had baffled the conferees at Washington. To the United States the question seemed simple enough. An agreement for comparatively low tonnage levels on the basis of the Washington Conference ratios would have satisfied this country. But

The Geneva Conference

for the British the problem was much more complex. The vast and scattered imperial system, the importance of sea communications, the fact that the possible naval antagonists of England were more numerous and diverse than those which confronted the United States, and the doctrine of British naval supremacy, which in 1927 was still a serious psychological obstacle, made the matter exceedingly difficult for the British delegation.

It has been pointed out that the conference was set in an environment unfavorable to the American style of open diplomacy which had proved to be so successful at Washington. Only three cut-and-dried plenary sessions were held in public and the bulk of the work was done in the privacy of technical committees.[1] The atmosphere was decidedly different from that of Washington. A comment on the theatricals of diplomacy from a stimulating book by Kenworthy and Young describes the environment necessary to the success of the American method as it is seen through liberal British eyes:

> For Americans do not yet seem to have learnt how important atmosphere is for the proper producing of their diplomacy by popular appeal. This new diplomacy of theirs with a good producer, the "star" parts well filled and featured, and the "stunts" carefully staged, will beat the old diplomacy all the time. But all diplomats know that off their own ground, in unfamiliar surroundings, Americans lose confidence in their own ways of playing the diplomatic game and are likely to copy the ways of Europe with disastrous results to themselves.[2]

Some American and British critics of the conference have furthermore commented upon the lack of preparation for the joining of issues. It has been suggested that a draft treaty should have been agreed upon in advance with blank spaces left for the filling in of the tonnage to be agreed upon. This is the sort of work which engrossed

---

[1] BAKER, P. J. NOEL: *Disarmament and the Coolidge Conference*, p. 9, The Hogarth Press, London, 1927.
[2] *Op. cit.*, pp. 168–169.

the attention of the Preparatory Commission of the League of Nations from 1926 to 1930. But the conference itself performed much of this valuable function. The reduction of the problem to simple terms and the focusing of opinion in both countries upon the vital points in dispute had to be done, and it is doubtful if a preparatory commission could have achieved the result as well or as quickly as it was accomplished at the 1927 conference. In the light of subsequent events it seems plausible that the conference, so far from being a failure, was really successful in clearing the ground for an Anglo-American agreement which was to come when the coincidence of favorable administrations in both countries should bring about a more propitious time.

At the first plenary session the American delegation submitted a plan for the limitation of auxiliary combat vessels according to the principles and ratios which had been adopted at Washington for capital ships. The limits proposed by the United States were as follows:

Cruisers: United States and Great Britain, 250,000 to 300,000 tons; Japan, 150,000 to 180,000 tons.

Destroyers: United States and Great Britain, 200,000 to 250,000 tons; Japan, 120,000 to 150,000 tons.

Submarines: United States and Great Britain, 60,000 to 90,000 tons; Japan, 36,000 to 54,000 tons.[1]

The British had two main objections to this proposal, first that the cruiser tonnage was too low, and second that cruisers should not be limited by total tonnage but that they should be divided into two classes, the 10,000-ton, 8-inch gun class and a smaller 6-inch gun class with separate limitations for each.

In support of the first objection it was claimed that the defense of the vast possessions of the British Empire and the protection of sea routes would require at least seventy cruisers. This number was arrived at as follows: On a

[1] *Records of the Conference,* p. 20.

basis of five cruisers for every three capital ships, twenty-five cruisers were to be assigned for duty with the fleet, which was ultimately to contain fifteen capital ships. Forty-five cruisers were to be used for direct trade protection. Of this number twelve would be refitting or refueling at any given moment. This would leave approximately one cruiser for every 2,500 miles of the 80,000 miles of British trade routes.[1] The figure of seventy cruisers was considered by the British delegation to be the lowest to which they could agree. The deep feeling of the Englishman as to the necessity of trade-route security was expressed by Mr. Bridgeman in a speech at the third plenary session:

> No doubt it is not easy for countries differently placed fully to realise our feelings in this matter. But no Briton who was at home during the war, at its most anxious time, will forget the feeling that the situation brought home to us. Month by month we found our rations of bread, meat, sugar and other articles being lowered, and we could see the spectre of starvation slowly approaching. Is it to be wondered at that every one of us feels that it is a duty to make what provision we can to protect ourselves and our children against a recurrence of such a danger.[2]

The tonnage which was necessary to give Great Britain the required seventy cruisers was not definitely mentioned. The American delegates interpreted the various remarks of the British delegation to point at a minimum of about 426,000 tons or 126,000 tons above the maximum in the first American proposal.[3]

The second British objection was directed against the limitation of the cruiser class as a whole. Cruisers range from 3,000 tons to 10,000 tons. It was estimated that a 10,000-ton cruiser with 8-inch guns was $2\frac{1}{2}$ times as powerful in combat as a 7,500-ton cruiser with 6-inch guns. If there was to be only a general tonnage limit for

[1] *Ibid.*, p 29.
[2] *Ibid.*, p. 37.
[3] *Ibid.*, p. 44.

the entire class, according to the British contention, the greater combat power of the 10,000-ton cruiser would bring it about that only the large cruisers would be built. The British felt that they needed a large number of smaller cruisers because of the length and intricacy of their trade routes. The number of their naval bases scattered around the world would make it possible to employ cruisers of a limited cruising radius. Accordingly, they desired that the number of larger cruisers should be strictly limited. They proposed restricting the number of cruisers of 10,000 tons mounting 8-inch guns to twelve each for the United States and Great Britain. The rest of the cruiser tonnage should be used up in smaller vessels, which should be limited to 6-inch guns. At the beginning, 7,500 tons was suggested as the limit of the smaller class, but later this figure was reduced to 6,000 tons. Thus the large number of cruisers, *i.e.*, seventy, necessary for the protection of the Empire would be twelve large and fifty-eight small cruisers and could be built within a much lower tonnage limit than if the cruiser class were not divided for purposes of restriction.

Furthermore, the British contended, if there was to be only the general tonnage limit for cruisers and if, as they predicted, all construction would be in the larger sizes of cruisers mounting main batteries of ten or twelve 8-inch guns, the net result would be a very great increase in combat power.

The discovery that the 6,000-ton cruiser was the type best fitted for the defense of imperial interests seems to have come to the British government with great suddenness. Since the Washington Conference, Great Britain had laid down no such cruiser. In the years 1922 to 1927, inclusive, that country laid down thirteen 10,000-ton cruisers and one of 8,300 tons. All had been designed to mount 8-inch guns. Under such circumstances it does seem remarkable that in the face of an American building

THE GENEVA CONFERENCE

threat the British leaders precipitately found that the small 6-inch gun cruiser was best suited to their interests.

There is some suspicion that the argument about small and large cruisers was indulged in partially to hide a more fundamental objection—an unwillingness to agree to the principle of parity in cruisers. After the Washington Conference, there had been some evidence to the effect that British naval men felt that their country should be supreme in this kind of ship. The Right Hon. E. S. Amery, formerly First Lord of the Admiralty, wrote in 1924:

> We agreed at the Washington Conference to what is in effect an equality of battle fleet strength with the United States. But obviously it would be impossible to arrive at any similar figure with regard to the strength of the cruisers required for commerce protection. For us, at any rate, a sufficiency of cruisers is a matter of life and death.[1]

This position was not openly taken at the conference. Mr. Bridegman, one of the British delegates, had accepted parity for large cruisers but had been ambiguous about the smaller ones. At another time he said: "It is not parity with America that is troubling us. We have not raised any objection to that."[2] But this remark evidently created a stir in naval circles in London and raised the ire of certain members of the British cabinet, particularly that of Winston Churchill, Chancellor of the Exchequer. A remark made by him just subsequent to the conference indicates the state of mind of this vigorous leader at that time upon the question of parity:

> Therefore we are not able now—and I hope at no future time—to embody in a solemn international agreement any words which would bind us to the principle of mathematical parity in naval strength.[3]

Meanwhile during the conference, after a period of evident dissatisfaction on the part of some members

[1] "Great Britain's Weakness in Modern Cruisers," *Current History Magazine*, Vol. 20, p. 231, May, 1924.
[2] *Records of the Conference*, p. 28.
[3] *London Times*, Aug. 8, 1927.

of the cabinet, the delegates were ordered to return to London for consultation, and, according to Viscount Cecil, they found certain ministers opposed to the acceptance of mathematical parity.[1] From that time the British delegates felt themselves muzzled on the subject.

A great deal was also said during the conference about absolute naval needs, a doctrine which is not reconcilable with the principle of parity. According to this doctrine, each country should build to meet its own special necessities without regard to the navies of others. As the British could show a much greater need of ships for defensive purposes than could the United States, the acceptance of this basis would have given them the stronger fleet. The flaw in this argument is that all of these cruisers which the British could use for empire defense could also be used for offensive purposes and for destroying the commerce of an enemy. Here is a characteristic misrepresentation or underrepresentation contained in every naval argument. Diplomats and naval officers are continually talking about plans for defending the country against some aggressor. But there is at least a 50 per cent chance that their activities will be offensive and will be aimed at the destruction of the life and property of other people. The darker and less pleasant side of military and naval power must be continually read into the official argument by those who would understand it. An exceedingly clear and commendably frank statement of this other effect of armaments was made by Rear Admiral H. E. Yarnell in his statement read before the Senate Committee on Foreign Relations in 1930:

> The real object of war of course is to make conditions so unpleasant for the enemy, by destruction of his armed forces, his commerce, blockade, invasion, starvation, that he is willing to call it off and accede to our terms.

[1] *Parliamentary Debates, House of Lords,* 69:91.

The Geneva Conference

It is customary however to avoid such a frank method of stating the case and to employ the milder term of "national security," as the measure of naval and military requirements.[1]

The British naval forces have always shown a brutal ruthlessness in the conduct of war, which is wholly in accord with the best military practice. For this reason it would be strange indeed if other governments should shed any tears over the needs of Great Britain for warships, even when the picture is made to appear as pathetic as only a British diplomat can paint it.

The American delegation was not able to agree to the British countersuggestions. The United States accepted the principle of parity as an absolute minimum and would sign no treaty which did not embody it. In addition, two points were made in rebuttal to the British proposals: The suggested figures for cruisers were too high, and the American tonnage allotment must be largely used up in the 10,000-ton cruisers which were necessary for the particular needs of the United States.

The cruiser tonnage proposed by Great Britain was, according to American interpretations, at least 426,000 tons—120,000 tons for the twelve large cruisers and 306,000 for the smaller ones. Such a tonnage would have meant a great expansion of the cruiser force of the United States and also a substantial increase in that of Great Britain. The American contention was that the conference had met to limit or reduce armaments and not to increase them. In this respect the delegation of the United States had a strong moral case.

The United States delegates insisted upon the right to use up a large part of the alloted cruiser tonnage in the construction of 10,000-ton cruisers. Admiral Jones at

---

[1] *Treaty on the Limitation of Naval Armaments*, hearings before the Senate Committee on Foreign Relations, p. 358, Government Printing Office, Washington, 1930.

one time stated that if a maximum of 400,000 tons was reached, the United States would build twenty-five of the largest permissible type, instead of the twelve proposed by Great Britain, although the number would be subject to some reduction if the total tonnage limit should be lowered.[1] It was pointed out that because of the vast distances between American naval bases, many large cruisers of long-steaming radius were needed. It was admitted that the British might find the 6,000-ton cruisers very useful on account of the fact that their bases are scattered rather thickly around the world and that on their important trade routes the interbase distances are not very great. But the situation which confronts the United States is radically different. Hawaii sets far out in the Pacific, quite remote from other American bases. From Honolulu the distances are: to Panama, 4,718 miles; to San Francisco, 2,091 miles; to Guam, 3,337 miles; and to Manila, 4,767 miles. Accordingly, American cruisers must be of the powerful long-steaming type to enable them to travel from station to station. The American delegation could see no advantage in signing a treaty which would limit construction for the most part to the smaller but nevertheless expensive vessels which, as they claimed, did not fit American needs.

Offensive power to be achieved through the batteries of 8-inch guns was even more desired than long cruising ability. Most cruisers are intended for service with the fleet. In American naval plans which were developed after the conference it was estimated that of forty-three cruisers required, twenty-eight were to serve with the fleet and fifteen were to be used for convoy and trade route protection.[2] It is to this smaller group only that the argument concerning the long-steaming radius was applied. But large guns are desirable not only in trade

[1] *Records of the Conference*, p. 64.
[2] See above, p. 88.

The Geneva Conference

route protection. They are a most important consideration in cruisers with the battle fleet. When the British proposed that the United States should be permitted to build all of its cruisers of the 10,000-ton type if it would limit most of them to 6-inch guns, the proposition was rejected by the American delegation. It was the 8-inch gun more than the cruising radius that appealed to the United States.

The desire of the American government for combat power in its cruisers was shown also by the argument that the 8-inch guns are necessary to guard against the fleet of British merchant vessels which can be converted into cruisers armed with 6-inch guns. Mr. Gibson stated that Great Britain possessed 888,000 tons of these large, fast merchant ships which were capable of conversion as compared with 188,000 tons of such ships in the American merchant marine.[1] With the 8-inch gun cruisers, the American delegation evidently felt that this country would possess an antidote to the converted merchant ships. During the conference Mr. Gibson said:

> Further we have agreed to discuss the number of 10,000-ton cruisers and to accept a secondary class of cruisers, provided that the secondary type of cruisers should not be of a maximum individual displacement which will preclude the mounting of 8-inch guns, a calibre of gun which was agreed upon by the signatories of the Washington Treaty.[2]

In the group of observers who crowded the outskirts of the conference appeared an energetic American whose activities were later to be given wide publicity. William B. Shearer had gone to Geneva in the generous pay of three large shipbuilding firms for the purpose, so the corporation officials later testified, of "observing" and "reporting" such information as could not be obtained through regular news channels. Mr. Shearer posed as a

[1] *Records of the Conference*, p. 43.
[2] *Ibid.*, pp. 42–43.

patriotic exponent of sea power. His own estimate of himself was revealed in one of his letters as follows:

> I fight internationalism, pacificism and communism. I make many enemies and many friends. I hate pink, red and yellow. Enthusiasts claim I am the best posted man in the United States on national defense. I claim nothing and expect less, but whatever I represent, it is all-American—which seems to arouse suspicion as well as curiosity.[1]

While at Geneva, Shearer mingled with newspaper men and naval advisers. Because of his forceful and evidently agreeable personality, he frequently dominated the conversation in hotel lobbies and press rooms. His knowledge of marine matters appealed to journalists in search of a lead, and he periodically handed to them mimeographed information sheets or "shots" containing facts and interpretations which were intended to be hostile to the success of the conference. It can hardly be claimed, as a news story later asserted, that he was "the man who wrecked the conference." More fundamental causes than Mr. Shearer were involved. But later, when, due to a suit against the shipbuilding companies for compensation, the facts of the employment became generally known and when a senatorial investigation revealed the character of his work at Geneva, a storm of public disapproval was aroused. The vigorous and wholesale denunciation of the Shearer activities from the American pulpit and press showed that there are vital groups in the United States which emphatically repudiate such attempts to use the mask of nationalistic patriotism to advance private interests in a manner hostile to friendly international relations. In fact, Mr. Shearer unwittingly served the cause of armament limitation, for the senatorial investigation of his activities coming in the fall of 1929 unquestionably helped to

[1] *New York Times*, Sept. 11, 1929.

The Geneva Conference

prepare a more favorable state of opinion for the London Conference.[1]

Thus far nothing has been said about the Japanese. As a matter of fact, the Geneva Conference was practically a two-power conference with the Japanese present and playing a relatively minor rôle. They were probably glad of that fact. Since the Washington Conference they had been busy laying down cruisers. They had been accused of starting the new naval competition. The condition most to be desired from their viewpoint was the maintenance of their advantage. Accordingly, the Japanese delegates contented themselves with general utterances in favor of limitation, having always in mind the retention of their existing building program. The Japanese position stated in the joint declaration made at the end of the conference was as follows:

> The Japanese delegates presented the view that low total-tonnage levels should be fixed which would effect a real limitation of auxiliary naval vessels. As for the question of the 8-inch-gun cruisers, while the Japanese Government could not agree to any restriction as a matter of principle, they had no difficulty in declaring that, provided a tonnage level of 315,000 tons for auxiliary surface vessels were fixed for Japan, they would not build any further 8-inch-gun cruisers until 1936, except those already authorised in existing programs.[2]

When the Geneva Conference was finished the public believed that it had been a complete failure. Sharp remarks had passed. The delegates had failed utterly to agree and had returned home somewhat embittered. There were, at that time, many who believed that the further limitation of naval armaments was impossible and that the matter must run the course of rivalry, militarism, and eventually war.

[1] For the investigation see *Alleged Activities at the Geneva Conference*, hearings before a sub-committee of the Senate Committee on Naval Affairs, Government Printing Office, Washington, 1930.

[2] *Records of the Conference*, p. 45.

But the Geneva Conference had not failed. It had called attention to the points of rivalry between Great Britain and the United States. Discussion and publicity had had the effect of taking the matter out of the hands of naval experts and placing it in a field where public sentiment could exert an influence. A thousand articles by trained writers approached the subject from every possible angle. And then, out of the darkness of the period of pessimism succeeding the conference, as the film editors say, "came the dawn." The slowly revolving machinery of the American government brought into the President's chair a man with a comparatively realistic attitude on world affairs gained possibly from his association with international business. And across the ocean, in the course of the political cycle, British Labor was rotated into office. A conservative, nationalistic government was replaced by one which was more flexible and more keenly aware of the possibility of using international action to promote British interests. And then it was found that the Geneva Conference had not been wasted. As a final conference, it is true, the meeting had been completely disappointing. As a preparatory body, however, it had been highly successful.

Chapter XI

THE PRELIMINARIES OF THE LONDON CONFERENCE

FOLLOWING the Geneva Conference the Anglo-Saxon world passed through a period of pessimism. The Conservative government of Great Britain, sincerely trying to solve the Anglo-French arms problem but careless of the effect upon American opinion, began secret negotiations with France. One of the striking features of the tentative agreement reached between these two governments was the incorporation of the thesis which the British had unsuccessfully advanced at Geneva and which the United States had so staunchly opposed, *i.e.*, the division of cruisers into two subcategories and a strict limitation of the larger type armed with guns of more than six inches in caliber.

On July 30, 1928, the terms of the agreement were made known to the United States. Widespread dissent and some downright indignation were expressed in this country. On September 28, 1928, the American government formally communicated its disapproval, and shortly thereafter the British and French governments dropped the matter. Meanwhile, plans for a substantial increase in cruisers had been progressing in the United States, embellished by all of the nationalistic propaganda which is necessary in the engineering of such a program. The act, providing for fifteen of the 10,000-ton cruisers with 8-inch guns, the "offensive" type toward which Great Britain had professed to entertain such grave doubts, was finally passed in February, 1929, and attracted world-wide attention. A great deal of caustic comment was occasioned by the apparent inconsistency of the cruisers with the Multilateral Treaty for the Renunciation of War which had been approved by the Senate the month previous. It seemed at this time as if the disastrous Anglo-German pre-war naval race was about to be repeated, and the question naturally arose whether Great Britain would in the course of time be prompted to make alliances against the United States as she had against Germany.

The periodical literature of the dark period during the latter part of 1928 and the early part of 1929 showed that the possibility of an Anglo-American clash over naval matters was receiving a great deal of attention in both countries. The doctrine of the freedom of the seas, so frequently sponsored by the United States, and that of expanded belligerent rights, so dear to the British admiralty, were pictured as fundamental antagonisms and as almost inevitable causes of trouble between the two nations. The subject was of warm interest and extremists in both countries were given magazine space to state their views. Thus, as an example of stimulated naval opinion in the United States, Rear Admiral Bradley A. Fiske (retired) asserted in the *Forum* for February, 1929, that the progress of civilization has always been accompanied by war and that each nation must maintain armament in proportion to its wealth—a glorious thought from the standpoint of the big-navy group. Even more reckless was an article by W. G. Carlton Hall in the *English Review* for May, 1929, which blurted out that the United States would violate a treaty whenever it suited and could manufacture evidence to support the action "as they did in 1898, when they deliberately sank the Maine in Havana Harbor to provide themselves with a *casus belli* against Spain." Great Britain should agree to no modification of sea law except to extend belligerent rights, said this patriot, and the

British government should give notice that it would not be bound by the Treaty of Washington after 1936.

Most contributors to periodicals on the subject, however, showed a genuine desire to bridge the gulf between the two nations. Proposals for far-reaching reform in sea law were made. Writing in the *Yale Review* for July, 1928, C. P. Howland outlined a plan which received wide attention. He suggested that if the United States would recognize the right of the organized world to punish an aggressor, Great Britain might be brought to agree to the freedom of the seas in private wars. Several subsequent writers of prominence approved this idea. The suggestion was, however, far too fundamental to receive immediate governmental support and it was along another line that the next step was to be taken.

The "yardstick" was to be the next important contribution to the naval solution. The plan of Charles Evans Hughes at the Washington Conference provided for a flat tonnage system of measurement. The American and British fleets were to be equal, ship for ship and ton for ton. The method was used to great advantage at Washington. But it was found to be too inflexible to meet the problem of cruiser limitation. At Geneva when the minds of the delegates were still anchored to this simple system of limitation an agreement was impossible.

Following the Geneva Conference some suggestions were openly made for a more elastic method of fleet comparison. Thus, in the American quarterly, *Foreign Affairs*, for January, 1929, Allen W. Dulles, who had been associated with the delegation at Geneva, declared that the United States should admit that the larger cruisers had a combat superiority out of proportion to their tonnage and that, therefore, the smaller cruisers could well be estimated at a discount in arriving at parity.

On March 4, 1929, Herbert Hoover became President of the United States and in his inaugural address he made a passing reference to disarmament:

The United States and Disarmament

The recent treaty for the renunciation of war as an instrument of national policy sets an advanced standard in our conception of the relations of nations. Its acceptance should pave the way to greater limitation of armament, the offer of which we sincerely extend to the world.[1]

The vagueness of this reference, however, was not to mean half-heartedness. On April 22, 1929, or seven weeks after the inauguration, the American representative on the Preparatory Commission of the League of Nations, Mr. Gibson, made a most interesting suggestion which showed the favorable attitude of the new administration. He proposed a system of equivalent naval values. Instead of a flat total tonnage for each category, he suggested that age, unit displacement, and caliber of guns should be considered in the measurement.[2] This was the yardstick formula. It permitted the comparison of two different types of fleet. Thus, the United States could have a larger number of big cruisers, Great Britain could have a larger number of small cruisers and a larger total tonnage. Each nation would then have the particular type of vessel it desired and an equality in combat power would be reached.

In the annals of naval disarmament this must be considered as an announcement of major importance. It was the blast which dislodged the key log in the jam. From that time forth it seemed that with sufficient willingness on both sides the "insoluble" Anglo-American cruiser problem would be adjusted. A new invention in the mechanics of naval limitation had been designed.

Two days later in the House of Commons, Sir Austen Chamberlain stated that:

His Majesty's Government has noted with much interest the new criteria suggested by Mr. Gibson. They attach great importance

[1] *New York Times*, March 5, 1927.
[2] *Documents of the Preparatory Commission for the Disarmament Conference. Minutes of the Sixth Session (First Part)*, pp. 56 ff., Geneva, 1929.

to the possibilities opened up by the greater elasticity given by his suggestions for the adjustment of the agreed naval strengths to the different circumstances of the two powers.[1]

A friendly attitude toward this proposal was increasingly manifest in the two countries. In his Memorial Day address, May 30, 1929, President Hoover announced himself in favor of naval reduction and said that for further progress in armament reduction a rational yardstick formula must be found. This, he thought, was by no means an impossible task.[2]

Shortly afterward, in view of the increased friendliness manifested on both sides, President Hoover postponed the construction of three cruisers. For this he was taken to task by Paul V. McNutt, National Commander of the American Legion, who contended that the United States should build up its fleet until it should regain its "lost naval parity" with Great Britain. In a letter of reply the President denounced this sort of competitive building and said:

> It creates burdensome expenditures, a constant stream of suspicion, ill-will and misunderstandings. Moreover, by constant expansion of naval strength we cannot fail to stimulate fear and ill will throughout the rest of the world toward both of us, and thus defeat the very purposes which you have so well expressed as being the object of the Legion, when you say "the Legion stands uniformly for movements which will make permanent peace more certain and assure better understanding between nations." . . . I fear that you have been misinformed as to the actual problems that lie before us if we are to succeed in such a negotiation, for they are far more intricate and far more difficult than can be solved by the simple formula which you suggest.[3]

No little favorable influence upon the movement for disarmament was exerted by the reaction from the Shearer incident in the autumn of 1929. On August

---

[1] *Parliamentary Debates, House of Commons*, 227:856, Apr. 4, 1929.
[2] *New York Times*, May 31, 1929.
[3] *New York Times*, July 31, 1929.

21, Mr. Shearer filed suit against the Bethlehem Shipbuilding Corporation, the Newport News Shipbuilding and Drydock Company, and the American Brown Boveri Electric Corporation. In his complaint Shearer asked for the sum of $257,655 which, he alleged, was the balance due him for services rendered. Part of these services were described as "the organization and conduct of a publicity campaign for the benefit of and in aid of the business and financial interests of the defendants."[1]

The fact that these three corporations had been engaged in building warships for the United States government and that their employee had been an active opponent of disarmament roused the attention of President Hoover who on September 6 issued a ringing statement calling upon the companies for an explanation, which read in part as follows:

> This propagandist has, during the past few years, organized zealous support for increased armament and has been a severe critic of all efforts of our government to secure international agreement for the reduction of naval arms, which include activities at the Geneva Conference and opposition to the movement which I have initiated in the past three months. A part of this propaganda has been directed to create international distrust and hate.
>
> . . . .
>
> I am making this statement publicly so that there can be no misapprehension of my determination that our present international negotiations shall not be interfered with from such sources and through such methods.[2]

Despite the explanation of the corporation officials that they had employed Mr. Shearer to go to Geneva for the purpose only of observing and reporting the proceedings, the publicity given by the President's statement and by the investigation subsequently carried on through a subcommittee of the Senate Committee on

---

[1] For a copy of the complaint see *Alleged Activities at the Geneva Conference*, p. 662.

[2] *New York Times*, Sept. 7, 1929.

Preliminaries of the London Conference

Naval Affairs helped to mobilize a strong public sentiment against interference with the disarmament movement by private interests.

Meanwhile across the water the naval question had been coming to a focus in British politics. In the elections of May, 1929, the Labor party won a plurality of seats. Ramsay MacDonald became Prime Minister, and the stage was set for further progress.

No sooner had Labor assumed the responsibility of government than conversations were begun with Ambassador Dawes to remove the ill will that had been created by the naval misunderstanding. From the friendly exchanges which followed, it appeared that the gulf between the two governments was not so wide as had previously appeared. The British government began with a sweeping slash in their cruiser demands. At Geneva their irreducible minimum had been placed at seventy. The number was now cut to fifty. Fifteen were to be 8-inch gun cruisers, totaling 146,800 tons, and thirty-five were to be of 6-inch guns or less, totaling 192,200 tons. In view of this concession on the part of the British, President Hoover asked the General Board of the United States Navy for its opinion as to the minimum number of 8-inch gun cruisers which this country could accept. In a memorandum of September 11, 1929, the board placed its estimate at twenty-one. The twenty-one 8-inch gun cruisers would measure 210,000 tons and in addition, the board stated, the navy would require fifteen 6-inch gun cruisers of 105,500 tons.[1]

The Labor government was unwilling to acquiesce in twenty-one 8-inch gun cruisers as compared with fifteen British vessels of this type, but signified that they could raise no objection to eighteen such vessels in the American navy. They feared that if the United States should

[1] The text of the memorandum is printed in *Treaty on the Limitation of Naval Armaments* (1930 hearings), p. 128.

go above eighteen this country would gain a superiority in combat power which would be clearly in violation of the principle of parity. Other considerations also complicated the matter. In a dispatch of August 31, 1929, Ambassador Dawes transmitted a note from Prime Minister MacDonald to the effect that the British dominions were likely to raise objections to the American demands because of the effect which a twenty-one cruiser program would have upon Japan. The Japanese were insisting upon a ratio of 70 per cent in large cruisers. If the United States should have as many as twenty such cruisers, the Japanese would demand fourteen. The British would then have but one more than the Japanese and the dominions in the Pacific would not assent to such a slender margin.[1]

The exchange thus brought out the fact that the only important difference in the whole naval problem between the United States and Great Britain was whether this country should have twenty-one 8-inch gun cruisers, as the General Board contended, or whether, as the British suggested, we should have eighteen large cruisers and an additional number of smaller cruisers to make up for the three that were thus cut off of the program.

At this point Prime Minister MacDonald crossed the ocean to pay a personal visit to the United States. His coming proved to be a splendid stroke of democratic statesmanship. On October 7 he stood before the United States Senate and delivered a stirring appeal to abandon naval rivalries. He spoke in part as follows:

> There can be no war; nay, more: it is absolutely impossible, if you and we do our duty in making the peace pact effective, that any section of our army, whether land, or sea, or air, can ever again come into hostile conflict.
>
> Think upon that when we face many of our own problems—problems of jealousy, problems of fear, problems that the young and

[1] *Ibid.*, p. 131.

rising and successful generation put into the hearts of the old generation. They all disappear, and in virtue of the fact that they have disappeared we have met together and we have said "What is all this bother about parity?"

Parity? Take it, without reserve, heaped up and flowing over. That was the only condition under which competitive armaments could be stopped, and we could create a public psychology which could pursue the fruitful and successful avenues of peaceful cooperation.[1]

Here, indeed was a great advance over the Conservative attitude as stated by such leaders as Winston Churchill.

During his visit, the Prime Minister had long and earnest conversations with President Hoover at the President's camp on the Rapidan in Virginia. The two executives agreed that the only outstanding difference between them was the question as to whether the United States should, on the one hand, have 210,000 tons of large cruisers or, on the other, 180,000 tons of such cruisers and an addition of something more than 30,000 tons to the small cruiser allotment. Such a minor matter did not appear to them to be of sufficient moment to block a general agreement. With almost certain assurance that the Anglo-American naval rivalry could be settled it was decided to call a naval conference. Accordingly, invitations were issued by the British government for a meeting to be held in London in January, 1930. The United States, Japan, France, and Italy were asked, and all of these governments accepted the invitation.

The Aims of the Powers

The United States.—An excellent psychological preparation for the conference had been made in the United States due to an interest in peace created by the Multilateral Treaty for the Renunciation of War, to the favorable attitude of the Hoover administration, and to the splendid dramatics of the MacDonald visit. The Ameri-

[1] *New York Times*, Oct. 8, 1929.

The United States and Disarmament

can government made ready for the conference with expressed expectations of substantial reductions in armament. These expectations were largely to perish as part of that excess afflatus which must accompany any progressive action.

Certain strategical considerations controlled American plans. Incomparably foremost among these was parity with Great Britain. A treaty which did not include this principle could not possibly have survived the blasts of adverse criticism which would have been awakened in certain quarters in the United States. The extension of the Washington Conference ratio with Japan of 10:6 to all classes of ships was a similar aim, although not so important or so necessary for the satisfaction of American opinion. The ratios of the United States, Great Britain, and Japan in fleets built and building at the opening of the London Conference are shown in the following table, which presents the figures as they stood on December 31, 1929:[1]

Type of vessel	United States	Great Britain	Japan	Ratios
Capital ships.................	532,400	608,650	292,400	10:11.4: 5.5
Aircraft carriers..............	76,286	115,350	68,870	10:15.1: 9
Cruisers, over 6-inch guns.....	130,000	186,226	108,400	10:14.3: 8.3
Cruisers, 6-inch guns & under..	70,500	177,685	98,415	10:25.2:13.9
Destroyers....................	290,304	184,371	122,575	10: 6.3: 4.2
Submarines...................	80,980	60,284	77,842	10: 7.4: 9.6
Total.....................	1,180,470	1,332,566	768,502	10:11.3: 6.5

From this table it will be seen that the United States entered the conference with a naval force, built and building, which was inferior to the British in capital ships, aircraft carriers, and cruisers, and superior to them in destroyers and submarines. The Japanese were above the 10:6 ratio in aircraft carriers, large cruisers,

[1] *Treaty on the Limitation of Naval Armaments* (1930 hearings), p. 23.

Preliminaries of the London Conference

and submarines, and below it in capital ships, small cruisers, and destroyers.

In addition to the general aim of reduction and the achievement of the 10:10 and 10:6 ratios, the American government was in harmony with Great Britain regarding the abolition of the submarine but did not accede to the British proposal for the abolition of the battleship. The demand for political machinery to insure security before disarmament, which was the traditional French position, was opposed by the controlling opinion in the United States. In fact, any substantial provision in the treaty which would have involved the signatories in political obligations would probably have been fatal to ratification by the American government.

The seriousness with which the United States sought to achieve its aims is shown by the remarkably able delegates who were sent to London. Not since the Conference of Ghent in 1814 had a delegation of such all-around strength and prestige gone abroad to represent the American government in an international negotiation.

Secretary of State Stimson, the head of the delegation, had seen service in a large number and variety of governmental positions. He had been United States District Attorney for the Southern District of New York, Secretary of War under President Taft, and Special Agent to Nicaragua during the troubles of 1927 where he had been connected with a different kind of disarmament, *i.e.*, the extraction of rifles from Nicaraguan rebels under threat of American marine action. He had later served as Governor-General of the Philippine Islands. He was fully in sympathy with the promotion of world peace through the reduction of armaments by agreement among the great powers.

Charles G. Dawes had established an even wider reputation, nationally and internationally. He had served as the first Director General of the Budget. As chairman of the committee of experts to solve the German reparation tangle in 1924 he had given his name to the Dawes Plan. In 1924 he had been elected Vice President, serving in that capacity until March 4, 1929, at which time he had been sent as American Ambassador to Great Britain. In London he had participated in the negotiations which paved the way for the conference.

Secretary of the Navy Adams, scion of America's best known political family, represented in a liberal way the technical views of the navy. Dwight Morrow, international banker, had just completed one of the outstanding tasks in recent American diplomacy by his brilliant adjustment of the troublous relations between this country and Mexico. Hugh Gibson, ambassador to Belgium, had represented the United States repeatedly at the Preparatory Commission and had also headed the delegation at the Geneva Conference. His experience in disarmament diplomacy was greater than that of any other American, and his ability as a conference diplomat was beginning to receive a very proper recognition.

President Hoover's desire to be successful in the approaching conference led him to include in the delegation two outstanding members of the United States Senate, David A. Reed of Pennsylvania and Joseph T. Robinson of Arkansas. The appointment of Senators on delegations to negotiate treaties is now a well recognized extra-constitutional device for making workable the very difficult treaty processes of the United States Constitution. The two-thirds rule for senatorial approval has frequently brought about a paralysis of the upper chamber in dealing with treaties, even when a large majority favor affirmative action. If the executive department and sixty-three Senators say aye and thirty-three Senators say nay, the nays have it. The appointment of Senators for the negotiation of treaties is, therefore, sometimes resorted to and has proved effective.

Preliminaries of the London Conference

In such cases when the treaty comes before the Senate it is aided by well-informed and influential advocates. The stalwart work performed by Senators Reed and Robinson in favor of the London Treaty during the special session in the hot summer of 1930 proved the wisdom of President Hoover's action.

It is difficult to resist contrasting this delegation of seven men, practically all of whom had demonstrated outstanding ability in the political field, with the delegation which had represented the United States at the ill-fated Geneva Conference. The Geneva delegation had consisted of Mr. Gibson and Admiral Jones, surrounded and almost submerged by naval experts. But at London, as at Washington, the civilian element had come into its own.

Great Britain.—Great Britain approached the conference in a realistic frame of mind. The British people had been caught between two mental forces. On the one hand were traditions handed down from the age of sea power which were voiced by the admiralty. Churchill, Bridgman, Jellicoe, and Beatty were outstanding exponents of the traditional necessity of naval supremacy. Men of this school pointed out the dependence of England upon sea trade and pictured the disaster which would engulf the country should their lines of communication be seized by an enemy. The British people, trained from their youth to view with pride the achievements of England's naval defenders, were powerfully moved by such arguments. On the other hand, the realities of the modern world had made unprofitable and impossible the old-time mastery of the sea. The international economic system, upon which British commercial greatness was based, was too delicate a mechanism to be nurtured and maintained by brute force. The World War had left Britain nominally victorious but actually in a sad plight —supreme in a naval sense but commercially desolated.

The old argument that trade is built up and maintained by sea warfare had ceased to be convincing. Airplanes were another reality which had swept away England's isolation. It had become possible for air squadrons from Europe to leap lightly over the defending fleet and scatter death and destruction in the British Isles. Safety was no longer to be sought entirely in naval defense. Finally, there was the budget problem coming up relentlessly year after year. With a heavily burdened exchequer and with a costly naval race against a rich rival in prospect, the situation was indeed gloomy.

Altogether the better arguments were against an attempt to maintain the old-time mastery of the seas in the face of the new facts. The only uncertainty was this: Did the British government have the mental elasticity to see the situation and the independent will to break with the past? These attributes were supplied by the MacDonald government. Whereas the Conservatives had hesitated and proceeded at times half-heartedly in the new direction, the Labor government sprang gladly at the opportunity to avert naval competition. The sincerity of Labor was amply demonstrated by the drastic cutting off of twenty cruisers from the naval program, the whole-hearted acceptance of the principle of parity, and the willingness to abolish the battleship.

A factor of importance in the British position was the naval rivalry between France and Italy. The all-important route to the East lies through the Mediterranean. Should France and Italy build to such a point that their combined naval strength would exceed that of the British, the situation would be regarded in England as full of danger. The British have long felt that they must have a fleet equal to the next two European powers. There are several reasons why this may not be entirely logical today. The two-power standard is derived from a period of history when a combination of French and

Spanish navies in opposition to the British was always a possibility. There is, however, no such identity of purpose between France and Italy. On the contrary, the Franco-Italian quarrel is an element of strength in the British position. With reasonable diplomatic effort the British should be able to avoid a Mediterranean combination directed against themselves. Even if such a coalition should be formed, a British fleet in the Mediterranean would under modern conditions be a questionable asset. Enemy aircraft, operating from shore bases would not only disrupt British commerce and cut the route to the East but would probably drive the British surface vessels from the Mediterranean. Nevertheless, tradition is still a powerful factor in national defense and the rise of naval strength in the Mediterranean would surely create uneasiness in Great Britain.

Japan.—Japan made ready for the conference with two partially conflicting aims, *i.e.*, security and reduction. The naval problems of Japan have become comparatively simple. No power in Asia threatens her today. China, her great competitor for the future, is too busy with domestic quarrels and too much diverted by internal confusion to count as a military rival. Russia, once a real threat, was in 1904 pushed out of Korea and away from southern Manchuria. The destruction of the Russian Far Eastern and Baltic squadrons during the Russo-Japanese War greatly simplified the Japanese problem of sea control. There are latent opportunities for conflict with Russia over Manchuria particularly as cheap Russian goods come pressing into that area. The Russian naval forces are, however, confined to the Baltic and Black seas. Japan is thus fairly secure for the present in her mastery of the narrow waters over which she must maintain her essential connections with Korea and the Chinese mainland.

The United States and Disarmament

The most serious danger which the Japanese have in mind is an attack from overseas and the specific enemies in view seem to be the United States and the British Empire. The best means to defend against these dangers is the maintenance of a fleet in accordance with an adequate ratio which will give to Japanese defending forces, operating near their own bases and in their own waters, a sufficient margin of strength to repel the invader. Altogether, the naval policy of Japan in the protection of her short trade routes and in seeking the means to repel a non-Asiatic enemy cannot be called imperialistic.

In preparing for the London Conference the Japanese evolved certain policies which were to guide their delegates. These aims may be enumerated as follows:

1. *A Desire to Reduce the World's Navies.*—Probably no nation represented at the London Conference had sounder reasons for a general reduction. The lower the strength of the great naval powers, the less danger is there that any of them can strike across the oceans at Japan. Thus mutual reductions would result in increased Japanese security. Moreover, the load of taxation caused by naval armaments is probably harder for the Japanese to bear than for the nationals of their competitors. The intelligent public official in seeking to carry out an enlightened armaments policy in Japan is, however, beset with difficulties which are not encountered in the governments of the other naval powers. There is no nation where the ancient and honorable traditions of militarism survive with greater vividness and where special patriotic groups attempt to misapply these once useful ideals to the detriment of modern life with a more reckless fanaticism than in Japan. The public-spirited and forward-looking official in seeking to adapt the policies of his country to present-day conditions is met with a fiery opposition that sometimes involves him

in personal danger.[1] Accordingly in looking forward to the conference the Japanese government was caught between a desire to serve the needs of the country, on the one hand, and a genuine apprehension of the violence of so-called patriotic groups, on the other.

2. *Opposition to the Abolition of the Submarine.*—In the Japanese plans for defense the submarine plays a very important rôle. The bays and inlets of their islands, and the uncertain channels of their innumerable sounds and straits present an ideal field for the use of the submarine in repelling an invading fleet. The Japanese were, therefore, prepared to defend their existing program of more than 70,000 tons of submarines and were certain to refuse to sign any treaty which would abolish them.

3. *A 70 Per Cent Ratio in Auxiliary Ships.*—The Japanese have often complained against the 60 per cent limitation on capital ships and aircraft carriers in the Washington Treaty and have claimed that 70 per cent is absolutely necessary for auxiliaries. As has been stated they stood ready to oppose any reduction in their large submarine program. In the matter of 8-inch gun cruisers, they were particularly insistent upon 70 per cent. In smaller cruisers and destroyers they would have been content with somewhat less, but altogether in their auxiliary tonnage as a whole, their plans called for a full 70 per cent.

France and Italy.—As the date for the London Conference drew near it was seen that probably the most difficult matter with which the conference was to deal was the Franco-Italian competition in the Mediter-

---

[1] For a violent expression of Japanese sentiment during the progress of the Washington Conference see BUELL: *The Washington Conference,* p. 158. In November, 1930, Premier Hamaguchi was shot and seriously wounded by a fanatical "patriot" on account of the London Treaty. For a serious riot in the anteroom of the Japanese House of Representatives because of opposition to the treaty, see *New York Times,* Feb. 7, 1931.

ranean. Isolated America was mildly surprised to find that her own plans for naval construction and for agreements on limitation were affected by this far-off rivalry, the causes of which were so little known or understood. The Mediterranean suddenly became excellent "news" in the United States. Columns of American newspapers were filled with it and probably more was published upon the position of France than upon that of any of the other powers.

There were many questions upon which France and Italy stood together as the conference approached. They looked upon the problem from the viewpoint of continental Europe. Naval disarmament to both of them was intimately connected with the question of land and air armaments. Disarmament was to them only one phase of the problem of peace. Both regarded security through political means as an integral part of the question. Both believed in the global tonnage method[1] of limitation. As members of the League of Nations they regarded the armaments problem as one which would eventually be solved under League auspices. It will be remembered that the reason assigned by France for failure to attend the Geneva Conference was that such a conference would interfere with the work of the League.

Upon the question of the Mediterranean, however, France and Italy parted company. Both are accustomed to use the Mediterranean routes for the transportation of their vital necessities. France lists as the most important of her naval aims the maintenance of sea communications with her African possessions. The Napoleonic expedition to Egypt which was completely demoralized by the victory of the British fleet at the mouth of the Nile is a sad memory in French military and naval circles. When Napoleon's communications with his base in France were cut, the expedition was doomed to defeat and the

[1] See below, p. 293.

Preliminaries of the London Conference

French expeditionary army was placed in peril. Today France has an African empire of enormous size, containing food resources and man power which would be needed in time of war. The foremost task of the French navy, then, is to maintain connections with French Africa. The principal naval port is Toulon, where the Mediterranean fleet, the most important part of the French navy, is based. Bizerte in Tunisia is also maintained as a base of considerable strategic importance because of its proximity to Italy.

The Italian government has aims which conflict with those of the French. The important route from Italy through the Strait of Gibraltar to the Atlantic cuts directly across the Franco-African route. Like France, Italy has possessions in Africa. The communications with Africa are doubly important due to the fact that there are causes for dispute between the two countries arising from African possessions and spheres of interest. These disputes concern the southern frontier of Libya, the position of the Italians in Tunis, and the influence of the two countries in Abyssinia.[1] It is perfectly obvious that Italy cannot have a fleet which will guarantee her an outlet to the Atlantic and communications with Tripoli and Suez if France is to be assured of an open route to Tunis, Morocco, and Algeria.

In preparing for the London Conference the two nations announced their naval aims with much emphasis and it was found that they were decidedly irreconcilable. Italy's demand was for parity with France in naval power. France answered that she would agree to parity in the Mediterranean only. In addition to the Mediterranean fleet, however, the French would maintain squadrons outside the Mediterranean. It was emphasized

[1] DEAN, VERA MICHELES: "France and Italy in the Mediterranean," Foreign Policy Association *Information Service*, Vol. VI, No. 1, March 19, 1930.

that France has coast-lines to guard on three seas and also possesses territories in the Far East. The Italians were not satisfied with parity in the Mediterranean only, for, they reasoned, in case of war France could bring in her outside naval forces and would establish a marked superiority in the Mediterranean. Italy stated that she would not be satisfied with anything less than parity with the whole French fleet.

There seemed to be no solution for this problem in naval bargaining alone. In an effort to remove the feeling of rivalry over the Mediterranean, the French were prepared at London to suggest a security agreement in that sea which would bind the important Mediterranean powers to keep the peace and to take joint action to settle any disagreements which might arise in that area.

Because of the Franco-Italian problem it was difficult to see in advance how any final agreement could come out of the London Conference. As has been stated, any refusal to agree to limitation by France and Italy would make the situation very uncertain for Great Britain and would thus render difficult an agreement between Great Britain, the United States, and Japan. At the opening of the conference it seemed, therefore, that the greatest threat to the plans for limitation and reduction lay in this insoluble Mediterranean dispute.

Chapter XII

THE LONDON TREATY

Crises and Compromises at the Conference

THE London Conference began on January 21, 1930, with a short address by the British King which was broadcast to the world. The opening ceremonies were completed by responses from the delegations expressing the usual preliminary sentiments of good will. At the second plenary session two days later, an opportunity was given to the heads of the delegations to state the naval needs of their various governments. The most significant declarations were those of France and Italy. M. Tardieu, speaking for France, stressed the need for the protection of coast lines, colonies, and commerce. He reminded the conference that the coast lines and ports of France proper are distributed on three seas. The oversea territories cover 12,000,000 square kilometers and are inhabited by 60,000,000 people. The length of the coast lines of the home country and the colonies is 18,109 nautical miles, and the lines of communication are 33,850 miles in length. The ocean commerce of France and her territories amounts to 83,200,000,000 French francs and constitutes 66 per cent of the total trade.[1] The statistical evidence of M. Tardieu showed that French officials had been exceedingly busy preparing the case for a large French navy. The tonnage requirements for naval vessels were, however, not definitely stated at this time.

Signor Grandi responded for Italy with similar arguments based on national necessities. The mountainous

---

[1] *Documents of the London Naval Conference*, 1930, pp. 103 ff., His Majesty's Stationery Office, London, 1930.

character of the Italian land frontier on the north and the limited capacity of the Alpine passes which supply only one-fourth of the annual imports make it necessary that Italy must be served from the sea. Italy, he asserted, is much like an island and depends upon ocean communications through Gibraltar and Suez for the food and raw material so essential to the life of her people. Signor Grandi stated that his country stood willing to reduce her navy along with other countries, but, whatever the level of armaments, she expected to keep her right to a one-power standard in Europe, that is, to maintain the Italian fleet on a par with that of any other European Continental power.[1]

These opening statements placed the Franco-Italian rivalry before the conference. After three weeks of comparative quiet in which the rival delegates sparred for an opening, the French delegation emphasized the vital relation of Mediterranean competition to the world problem by releasing to the press on February 13, a definite statement of their naval requirements. The announcement began with a claim that France had greatly reduced her navy. The existing naval forces of 681,808 tons built, building, and authorized, showed a reduction of 452,192 tons from the 1,134,000 tons of the 1914 fleet. The 1929 French budget for naval defense represented a decrease of approximately 18 per cent over the pre-war budget. The memorandum then proceeded to outline a program which by December 31, 1936, would raise the navy to 724, 479 tons.

The statement concluded with a declaration that the French delegation was ready to examine favorably any formula for mutual guarantees which would permit of further reductions.[2] This offer is typical of the French in the years since the war during which time they have

[1] *Ibid.*, pp. 109 ff.
[2] *Ibid.*, p. 519.

frequently reminded the world of their great military needs. They have also, however, consistently suggested that if a reasonable security should be established they would be willing to join in a reduction of armaments.

The French announcement of February 13 seemed in the minds of some observers to spell the doom of disarmament. The demand for approximately 725,000 tons, together with the Italian claim to parity with France, would have brought the authorized limits of the combined fleets of the two Mediterranean powers up to 1,450,000 tons. As has been stated, the British policy contemplates maintaining a fleet equal to these two. The British tonnage built and building was 1,332,566. If the conference was to be successful, this tonnage must be reduced by from 100,000 to 200,000 tons. Yet the French program, accompanied by the well-known claim of Italy to equality with France, pointed to the necessity of substantial increase on the part of the British. Accordingly, some of the London newspapers greeted the French announcement with pessimism. The rock upon which it had been predicted the conference would be wrecked was now clearly visible above the water.

At this point the Tardieu cabinet in France fell, the French delegation was called home, and the conference adjourned for two weeks. During the adjournment the delegations busied themselves with desperate attempts to hit upon some plan that would prevent the failure of the conference.

After the conference had reassembled the first effort to save the situation was an attempt to obtain a suitable security pact which would permit a reduction of the French figures. The proposed pact, it was recognized, must meet two tests. In the first place it must provide such security as would reassure the French and in the second place it must be mild enough not to offend the United States. The American delegates soon made it clear that they would not sign a pact which would bind this country to take military action against an aggressor. An effort was then made to determine whether an agreement could be reached which, while binding Great Britain, France, and Italy to a strong program to maintain the peace, would obligate the United States to do no more than consult with the other countries in time of an international crisis after the manner of the four-power consultation pact signed at Washington. At first the American delegation refused to consider a consultation treaty. Press dispatches of March 11 reported that "the American delegation has reached the unanimous opinion that the United States will not take part in any consultative pact in connection with the proposed London Treaty."[1] The delegation defended its position by asserting that if France should reduce her fleet in return for an American promise to consult in time of crisis, this country might feel obliged to go to the defense of France, as did England in 1914. Later, on March 26, the delegation, evidently moved by the prospects of a break-up of the conference, announced its willingness to consider such an agreement.[2] This declaration was highly important and evidently came upon the initiative of the delegation without instructions from Washington. For a time the American concession regarding consultation seemed to revive the hopes of the conference.

Negotiations between France and Great Britain were carried on for a security compact centering around Article XVI of the Covenant of the League of Nations. Eventually the security plans failed of result because of the fact that a general treaty to satisfy Italian sentiment would still have had to embody the principle of parity as between France and Italy, a situation to which the French would not agree. The conference leaders then

[1] *New York Times*, Mar. 12, 1930.
[2] *Ibid.*, Mar. 27, 1930.

The London Treaty

determined that the only alternative was to resort to a three-power agreement between the United States, Great Britain, and Japan with regard to the limitation of auxiliary vessels and to secure the agreement of France and Italy to certain more general principles.

In order to make it possible for Great Britain to sign a treaty limiting her auxiliary ships without at the same time limiting those of France or Italy, a practical measure of statesmanship was resorted to and embodied in what is known as the "escalator" clause. This clause would permit Great Britain to increase her naval strength in case of an emergency caused by the naval expansion of France or Italy. It was the formula which saved the conference from failure.

While the British and French were debating the possibility of a security agreement and related questions, the American delegation was negotiating with the Japanese regarding the question of the naval ratio which was to exist between them. Senator Reed conducted the negotiations for the United States. The Japanese had come to London with the determination to insist upon their program of 77,842 tons in submarines and a 10:7 ratio in 8-inch gun cruisers. They stated that they would be willing to accept smaller ratios in 6-inch gun cruisers and destroyers, but that the ratio in all auxiliary combat ships should be 70 per cent. Thus, the Japanese ratio program was composed of these main demands: no reduction in submarines, 10:7 in 8-inch gun cruisers, and 10:7 in all auxiliary classes. These claims were difficult for the American delegates to admit in the light of the 10:6 ratio established at Washington for capital ships and aircraft carriers. In resisting the 70 per cent demand in 8-inch gun cruisers the Americans had the support of the British dominions which objected to thirteen large cruisers in the Japanese navy as compared with fifteen British cruisers of the same sub-category. They insisted

The United States and Disarmament

that the Japanese allotment be not larger than twelve. It soon became fairly clear to the Japanese that no treaty embodying the ratio of 10:7 in large cruisers could be signed. By a demonstration of good will on both sides a compromise was reached. Japan was given twelve large cruisers as contrasted with eighteen for the United States. The Japanese cruisers were to total 108,400 tons as contrasted with 180,000 for the United States, making a tonnage ratio of 10:6. Two of the American cruisers, however, were not to be finished until after the year 1936. Of these two, one could be finished in 1937 and the other in 1938. The Japanese were given a larger ratio than 60 per cent in some of the other categories, going as high as 100 per cent in submarines. By this splendid spirit of compromise on both sides the "irreducible" demands of each were modified and an agreement between the two countries was made possible.

The Terms of the Treaty—Battleships

At the beginning of 1930 the powers were confronted with the prospect of enormous expenditures to carry out the capital ship replacement program outlined at Wash-

Year	United States	Great Britain	Japan	France[1]	Italy[1]
1931	2	2	1	1	1
1932	2	2	1	1	1
1933	1	1	1	1	1
1934	2	2	1		
1935	1	1	1		
1936	2	2	1		
1937	1	1	1		
1938	2	2	1		
1939	2	2	1		

[1] France and Italy were permitted by the treaty to lay down one capital ship each in 1927 and 1929, but neither had yet exercised the right thus conferred.

ington in 1922. The Washington treaty had postponed capital ship replacements until 1931 and had provided that thereafter the signatories might begin to lay them down at the rates specified in the foregoing table.

The cost of a modern capital ship is at least $40,000,-000. The construction of fifteen capital ships would have meant an expenditure by the United States of $600,000,-000 during the next twelve years, and the charges upon the treasuries of the other naval powers, while not so great in amount, would have been probably more burdensome.[1] Many naval experts had questioned the value of the capital ship. Admiral Sims, for example, had said that in case of war in which an enemy fleet approached our shores the safest place for the American battleships would be up the Mississippi River. While this was not the orthodox naval view, it was nevertheless sufficiently widespread to prevent any united demand for the preservation of the battleship. And it made any considerable expenditures by the war-torn world for such ships a very questionable matter, to say the least.

Prior to the conference the British government had publicly advocated abolishing capital ships or reducing their effectiveness. At Geneva, in 1927, the British delegation proposed the extension of the life of the capital ship from twenty to twenty-six years, limiting its size from 35,000 to something under 30,000 tons, and reducing the limit on guns from 16 inches to 13.5 inches.[2] On January 14, 1930, a little more than a week before the opening of the London Conference, a circular, signed by seventy-seven Labor members of the British Parliament, called upon the British delegation to support the abolition of all warships of more than 10,000 tons.[3] On the following day, Prime Minister MacDonald announced that he

[1] Great Britain would have constructed the same number of ships but the building costs are somewhat less in that country than in the United States.
[2] *Records of the Conference*, p. 22.
[3] *New York Times*, Jan. 15, 1930.

desired the eventual abolition of the capital ship and that in the meantime he wished to bring about an agreement to postpone replacements. If replacements should come, however, he hoped that they would be limited in size.[1]

The British suggestions were taken up by the conference and the result was a provision for another holiday in capital ship construction which must be regarded as one of the most important clauses of the treaty. The five powers agreed not to lay down any capital ship replacement tonnage until after 1936, although this was not to affect the right of the French and Italian governments to start construction of the capital ships which each could have laid down under the Washington Treaty in 1927 and 1929.[2] A reference to the table on p. 204 will show that the powers thus agreed to postpone the laying down of the following numbers of ships: United States, ten; Great Britain, ten; Japan, six; France, three; and Italy, three.

Aside from the saving of huge expenditures, these provisions mean the weakening of the capital ship strength of the five powers. Accepting the figure of twenty years as the effective life of the capital ship, by the end of 1936 the United States will have eight such ships under age, Great Britain will have four, and Japan will have five. Unless France and Italy exercise the right to build the two vessels which under the Washington Treaty each could have laid down in 1927 and 1929, neither country will have a capital ship of the first line by the end of 1936. Thus, the effective capital ship strength of the powers will have been more than cut in half. Perhaps it can be said that the great mammoths of the sea, like the monsters of the dinosaur age, are rapidly becoming extinct through failure to reproduce.

[1] *Ibid.*, Jan. 16, 1930.
[2] Article I. For this and other clauses see the text of the treaty, Appendix II.

The London Treaty

In addition to the agreement not to lay down new capital ships during the life of the treaty, an arrangement was concluded to make some immediate reductions by scrapping existing ships. Five British capital ships, three American, and one Japanese were offered up in the name of reduction. The ships to be scrapped were as follows:

United States: *Florida, Utah,* and *Arkansas* or *Wyoming.* These ships totaled 70,000 tons and were armed with 12-inch guns. The first two were nineteen years old and the second two eighteen years.

Great Britain: *Benbow, Iron Duke, Marlborough, Emperor of India,* and *Tiger.* These ships totaled 133,900 tons and were armed with 13.5-inch guns. They were all sixteen years old.

Japan: *Hiyei,* a ship of 26,330 tons which carried 14-inch guns and was sixteen years old.

Of these ships the following may be retained for training purposes: by the United States, *Arkansas* or *Wyoming;* by Great Britain, *Iron Duke;* and by Japan, *Hiyei.*

The following table shows the effect of this provision upon the relative standing of the capital ships of the three fleets:

Country	Capital ships before London Treaty		Capital ships after the disposition of vessels under London Treaty	
	No.	Tonnage	No.	Tonnage
United States....................	18	532,400	15	462,400
Great Britain....................	20	608,650	15	474,750
Japan...........................	10	292,400	9	266,070

The effect of the scrapping of these ships was to give the United States immediate parity with Great Britain in numbers of capital ships, each retaining fifteen. Under the Washington Treaty this parity in numbers was to be achieved in 1936 and parity in tonnage was to be arrived at in 1942. A great deal of argument has been indulged in to prove that this provision does or does not give the United States immediate equality in capital ship combat power with Great Britain, or, in other words, that the fifteen American ships to be retained are or are not as good as the fifteen British ships. American naval officers who are critical of the treaty have denied that the American capital ships are the equal of the British. They have showed that the fifteen British vessels possess a total tonnage of 474,750 as compared with 462,400 tons for those of the United States. They have also pointed out that the British *Nelson* and *Rodney* are newer, faster, and more powerfully armed than any in the American navy. Each possesses nine 16-inch guns. On the other hand, the defenders of the treaty have called attention to the fact that the United States has three battleships almost as good as the *Nelson* and *Rodney*. The three are the *West Virginia, Colorado,* and *Maryland*. Each has eight 16-inch guns. Thus, the United States can boast of twenty-four 16-inch guns as compared with eighteen in the British navy. The following table shows the total number of large guns in both fleets:

Country	16-inch	15-inch	14-inch	12-inch	Total
United States.......	24	...	124	12	160
Great Britain.......	18	100	...	..	118

Whether the slight edge of the United States in 16-inch guns coupled with its 12-inch and 14-inch guns and superiority in total number of large guns is to be considered as offsetting the British supremacy in 15-inch guns and their slightly larger total tonnage is no question for a layman. In the face of such confused statistics of armaments even the naval experts are bewildered and seem to be able to render opinions in favor of either fleet as political reasons may dictate. It may be concluded with a fair amount of confidence that there is no great disparity of strength on either side and that the treaty makers did about as good a job of achieving equality as is possible in the case of two such dissimilar fleets. It is certain at any rate that the capital ships are much more nearly equal than they were before the conference. Furthermore, as the situation set up is only a temporary one and will be changed by the passage of a few years, if any errors in computation of fleet strength were committed in favor of either side, the mistakes are only of slight and temporary significance, and are not to be compared in importance with the magnificent political results derived from the treaty.

The fate of the capital ship still remains an interesting matter for speculation. One of the naval questions for the future is: What will be the attitude of the United States at the conference in 1935 toward a renewal of capital ship construction? The great wealth of this country and the comparative ease with which the naval burden has been carried explain the absence of an active movement among Americans to abolish the capital ships. What has appeared to the financially distressed countries of Europe as a striking piece of folly has been regarded here with indifference. One of the trump cards possessed by the United States in naval conferences has been the potential threat to resume capital ship construction. American naval men in general, including all the members of the United States Naval Board, favor the capital ship. American experts were reported as "cold" to the Labor government's suggestion for abolition at London. A member of the American delegation is reported to have said that the large ships are the backbone of the navy, the "infantry of the sea."[1] Senator Hale, Chairman of the Senate Committee on Naval Affairs and congressional spokesman of naval opinion, voiced the sentiment

[1] *New York Times,* Jan. 17, 1930.

of the navy group as follows: "If the battleships are to be later replaced, and God forbid that statesman diplomacy should ever bring about such a calamity over the heads of naval opinion as not to replace them, the postponement or replacement is analogous to the postponement of the payment of a note and nothing more."[1] However, the enormous expenditures that will be necessary to rehabilitate the waning capital ship contingents will be a most formidable obstacle to the resumption of building in this field, and the advocates of capital ship construction will be at a most decided disadvantage when the next naval conference assembles.

Aircraft Carriers

The Washington Treaty had provided for tonnage limits in aircraft carriers, but by 1930 none of the powers had built up to its permitted strength. There was, consequently, no demand for revision of this part of the Washington Treaty. Some need for greater clarity in the definition of a carrier did, however, exist. The Washington Treaty defined an aircraft carrier as a war vessel of more than 10,000 tons, specially fitted for carrying aircraft. Accordingly, craft of 10,000 tons or less, although fitted to carry planes, did not strictly come within the definition. Under literal interpretation, the treaty did not limit such vessels at all. The evident defect of language seemingly permitted the unrestricted building of smaller vessels, and might have given rise to serious competition coupled with accusations of bad faith.

The London Treaty remedied this situation by redefining the aircraft carrier as any surface vessel of war, *whatever its displacement*, specially designed for carrying aircraft. Such ships of 10,000 tons or less were forbidden to carry guns of more than 6.1 inches in caliber. Carriers of more than 10,000 tons can under the Washington

[1] *Congressional Record*, Vol 73, p. 96, July 11, 1930.

The London Treaty

Treaty carry as many as ten 8-inch guns. The limit imposed upon aircraft carriers at Washington was 27,000 tons, except that each power was permitted to build two larger carriers of not more than 33,000 tons. These could be armed with not more than eight 8-inch guns.[1] The United States ships, *Lexington* and *Saratoga*, are of this larger type, but none of the other powers has a carrier of more than 27,000 tons.

The Washington Treaty had set forth no clear rule as to whether capital ships, cruisers, and destroyers could be fitted with landing-on and flying-off platforms or decks. The London Treaty expressly authorizes the fitting of such platforms on decks excepting that no existing capital ship shall be fitted with a landing-on platform and that such platforms can be fitted on not more than 25 per cent of the total tonnage in the cruiser category.[2]

The United States General Board has under consideration the building of cruisers in accordance with this last provision. Twenty-five per cent or 80,875 tons of American cruisers can be built with landing-on platforms. As all of the 180,000 tons of 8-inch cruisers have been provided for, the naval authorities hope to experiment in the new landing-on type by building a 10,000-ton cruiser with 6-inch guns. The ship would carry about twenty-five planes. Perhaps this is but one step in the process of the changing naval warfare which will ultimately result in making the plane carrier the supreme fighter on the sea.[3]

Cruisers

In the matter of auxiliary combat ships, only the United States, Great Britain, and Japan were willing to

[1] Articles IX and X of the Washington Treaty and Articles III and IV of the London Treaty, Appendices I and II.

[2] Article III, Clause 3 and Article XVI, Clause 5.

[3] Thus far Congress has not appropriated the money for such a ship, although a request for an appropriation has been submitted.

sign a limitation agreement. Accordingly, the tonnage limits placed upon cruisers, destroyers, and submarines apply to these three and not to France and Italy.

The primary purpose of the London Conference was to settle the cruiser rivalry between the United States and Great Britain. Preliminary negotiations between the two governments had greatly simplified the originally complicated problem and, as has been previously pointed out, the only important question which remained at the opening of the conference was whether the United States should have twenty-one 8-inch gun cruisers or should be limited to eighteen with a suitable compensation in 6-inch gun vessels. The treaty finally fixed the numbers of 8-inch gun cruisers as eighteen for the United States, fifteen for Great Britain, and twelve for Japan. The cruiser tonnage limits were adopted as follows:

Cruiser Sub-categories	United States	Great Britain	Japan
Sub-category *a* with guns of more than 6.1 inches (155 mm.) caliber..............	180,000	146,800	108,400
Sub-category *b* with guns of 6.1 inches (155 mm.) caliber or less................	143,500	192,200	100,450
Total...........................	323,500	339,000	208,850

Should the United States desire, it may duplicate the British cruiser tonnage by limiting itself to fifteen cruisers of sub-category *a*. In place of each of the three large cruisers which it fails to build, it will be entitled to construct 15,166 tons in sub-category *b*. This would give the United States the same total cruiser tonnage as Great Britain. However, the present plans of the United States are based on the construction of 18 cruisers in sub-category *a*.

Certain naval men have attacked the treaty as sacrificing the interests of the United States in thus limiting

The London Treaty

the large cruisers in our navy to eighteen. To analyze this sacrifice let us compare the "irreducible minimum" of the General Board of September 11, 1929, with the figures of the treaty.

Cruiser Sub-categories	General Board's minimum tonnage	Treaty provisions	Changes made by treaty
Sub-category a..............	210,000	180,000	−30,000
Sub-category b..............	105,500	143,500	+38,000
Total.....................	315,500	323,500	+ 8,000

The alleged sacrifice of American interests consisted in exchanging 30,000 tons of 8-inch gun cruisers for 38,000 tons of 6-inch gun cruisers. The difference would not appear to be of much importance either way. Nevertheless, most of the naval experts called to testify before the Senate Foreign Relations Committee in the summer of 1930 criticised this deviation from the plans of the General Board in an emphatic manner. The explanation of this criticism lies partly in the fact that the cruiser clause of the London Treaty was a blow dealt by civilians to the pride of the General Board. For several years the board had carefully planned a program of 8-inch gun cruisers and much effort had been spent in designing this type of vessel. At Geneva in 1927, the American delegation, at the behest of their naval advisers, had fought against dividing cruisers into sub-categories. They had contended for the right to build any kind of cruiser up to the limit of total cruiser tonnage, and had specifically named the 8-inch gun cruiser as best adapted to American needs. Accordingly, the London Treaty by limiting the United States to eighteen of these cruisers violated a principle of the General Board and was attacked by practically all of the officers on the board. It seems that in the spirit of competition engendered by striving to achieve a certain fixed program, the naval experts of the United States have shown little adaptability and have attached a fictitious importance to the replacement of 30,000 tons of 8-inch gun cruisers by 38,000 tons of 6-inch gun cruisers.

In the rather heated debate which took place in the United States following the conference, both before the Senate Foreign Relations Committee and on the floor of the Senate, the merits of the 6-inch and 8-inch gun cruisers were thoroughly aired. From the arguments presented by technicians it seems that the 6-inch gun cruisers have a valuable part to play in fleet action, particularly in close-up work in the inner screen. They are well suited to perform such tasks as repelling destroyer and submarine attacks at night. The speed of fire of the 6-inch guns is greater than that of the larger guns. When operated on the open deck the 6-inch guns can fire ten or twelve times per minute. The projectile which weighs 100 pounds can be inserted rapidly by hand. When mounted in turrets these guns can fire five or six times per minute. The 8-inch projectile weighs 250 pounds and is loaded by machinery. The rate of fire is about half that of the 6-inch gun. Also the 6-inch gun cruiser can carry twelve guns, which is two or three more than are mounted on 8-inch gun cruisers. Accordingly, in short range work or under conditions of poor visibility the 6-inch gun cruiser is more valuable because of its rapidity of fire and its larger number of guns.

On the other hand, for combat under conditions of good visibility the 8-inch gun has the advantage of longer range. The effective range for these guns is about 30,000 yards as compared with a range of 20,000 yards for the 6-inch gun. Thus, at 25,000 yards an 8-inch gun can fire effectively on a 6-inch gun cruiser but the latter cannot reply. In the Senate debates, Senator Reed stated that there had never been a shot fired in a naval combat

The London Treaty

at a greater range than 20,000 yards.[1] However, the use of airplanes in spotting shots at long distances is expected to increase this range in future wars.

On detached missions the 8-inch gun cruiser would be superior. The advantage is not necessarily in the size of the ship, for under the London Treaty the 6-inch gun cruisers can be built up to 10,000 tons. If, however, the 8-inch gun cruiser should encounter raiders or merchant ships armed with only 6-inch guns it would be able to proceed to the attack in cases when the 6-inch gun cruiser would find it advisable to retire. This superiority for cruising in distant waters appeals to the naval officer who emphasizes the rôle of the navy in the defense of commerce.

Summing up the matter it seems that the 8-inch gun cruiser has greater combat power than the 6-inch gun cruiser and the advantage is especially marked if airplane observation is available for spotting shots beyond a range of 20,000 yards. Both types are necessary in the fleet. The difference between 30,000 tons of 8-inch gun cruisers and 38,000 tons of 6-inch gun cruisers is of little consequence as compared with the greater values obtained by the treaty. Furthermore, it must be remembered that Great Britain is to have but fifteen of the 8-inch gun cruisers and in so far as the arguments of the General Board members are true, the United States, with eighteen, has a superiority in cruiser combat power over the British fleet. This position has been obtained without a costly armaments race.

Destroyers

The destroyer class presented less difficulty than any other in the matter of limitation. During the World War the United States had been assigned the task of providing large numbers of destroyers to drive the sub-

[1] *Congressional Record*, Vol. 73, p. 105, July 11, 1930.

marine from the sea, and, accordingly, this country had proceeded with rapidity to build up a great superiority in the destroyer class. These ships, which had practically all been laid down in the years from 1917 to 1920, would, with the exception of 14,000 tons, have reached the age limit of sixteen years by 1936.[1] It would have been unwise for the United States to have replaced this tonnage, which was well in excess of that necessary in a well-balanced fleet. The American government was, therefore, willing to relinquish its superiority in destroyers and to cut its tonnage almost in half, reducing it from 290,304 tons to 150,000 tons. The figures fixed in the treaty were as follows:

	United States	Great Britain	Japan
Tons	150,000	150,000	105,500
Ratio	10:	10:	7.03

The destroyer was limited in size to 1,500 tons but an additional provision was inserted to permit as much as 16 per cent of the total tonnage to be used in vessels above that figure. The present American destroyers are of about 1,300 tons' displacement. The exception in the treaty permitting the building of a limited number of larger destroyers was added for the purpose of providing destroyer leaders. Such vessels may be built up to 1,850 tons according to the treaty. The leaders will direct the course of the destroyer flotillas and provide the proper information for setting the torpedo tubes. They have better sea-keeping qualities, have steadier observation platforms, and contain more space for the housing of various kinds of radio, signaling, range-finding, and plotting equipment than the smaller vessels. The additional personnel necessary to perform these various functions can also be accommodated. The destroyer leader

---

[1] *Treaty on the Limitation of Naval Armaments* (1930 hearings), p. 18.

will have the same speed in smooth seas as the other destroyers, but due to its greater steadiness it will be faster in heavy seas.

As a concession to the global method of naval limitation[1] a provision was incorporated in Article XVII of the treaty permitting certain transfers between the destroyer class and cruisers of sub-category *b*. The transfer cannot exceed 10 per cent of the total allowed tonnage of the category or sub-category into which the transfer is to be made. Thus, the United States might transfer 15,000 tons of small cruiser tonnage into the destroyer class or 14,350 tons of the destroyer tonnage into the cruisers of sub-category *b*.

Submarines

The British government previous to the London Conference had been persistent in the attempt to obtain an agreement abolishing the submarine. The ocean trade routes over which the British Isles are supplied with food and raw materials and which have been well guarded with surface vessels will in case of war under modern conditions be threatened by enemy submarines. At the Washington Conference the British delegates had waged an earnest but unsuccessful battle to bring about submarine abolition.[2] This battle was renewed at London.

Mr. Alexander, First Lord of the Admiralty, presented the British arguments. He contended that the submarine is not a defensive vessel, because the modern naval attack against a coast consists as a rule of "a sudden raid, probably under cover of darkness, or of a bombardment at dusk or dawn by a vessel approaching at high speed." To meet this attack the slow-moving submarine with its limited vision is comparatively ineffectual.

[1] See below, p. 292.
[2] See above, p. 148.

The principal use of the submarine is as an offensive weapon. Is it not difficult, he asked, to use the submarine in offensive operations without resorting to methods which the civilized nations regard with horror? Abolition of the submarine would bring about economies in construction and maintenance, and would eliminate the necessity of compelling men to endure the bad living conditions of submarine life. It would also remove the dangers of peace-time catastrophes which have so frequently shocked the world. The British dominions' spokesmen and Mr. Stimson of the American delegation supported Mr. Alexander in his demands.

In reply M. Leygues, the French Minister of Marine, avowed that the submarine has other uses than the destruction of merchant ships. During the war 312,860 tons of allied warships were sunk by submarines. They are, he said, the defensive weapon of the lesser naval powers. In the French naval system the submarine serves to protect the coastal population against naval attack, to escort and protect convoys between the mother country and the colonies, to guard the lines of communications, and to serve as a scout and protector of the high seas fleet. Admiral Takarabe of the Japanese delegation also defended the submarine as "an appropriate medium of defense, as a scout and as an instrument to ward off an enemy attack in the adjacent waters of a country."[1] Because of this opposition the attempt at abolition failed.

As a concession to the British, however, the conference adopted a clause which, like the ill-fated submarine treaty signed at Washington, was intended to eliminate the barbarity of submarine warfare. This clause is contained in Article XXII of the treaty which reads as follows:

---

[1] The debates on this subject are found in *Documents of the London Naval Conference*, 1930, pp. 187–202.

The London Treaty

Article XXII. The following are accepted as established rules of international law:

1. In their action with regard to merchant ships, submarines must conform to the rules of international law to which surface vessels are subject.

2. In particular, except in case of persistent refusal to stop on being duly summoned, or of active resistance to visit and search, a warship, whether surface vessel or submarine boat, may not sink or render incapable of navigation a merchant vessel without having first placed passengers, crew and ship's papers in a place of safety. For this purpose the ship's boats are not regarded as a place of safety unless the safety of the passengers and crew is assured, in the existing sea and weather conditions, by the proximity of land, or the presence of another vessel which is in a position to take them on board.

The high contracting parties invite all other powers to express their assent to the above rules.

This article is stronger than the unratified treaty of the Washington Conference in that it makes more specific the obligations of the submarine commander. The sinking of a surface ship is unlawful except in case of "persistent" refusal to stop or of "active" resistance to visit and search. The words "persistent" and "active" raise the obligations of the commander above those ordinarily regarded as fixed by international law. The article goes beyond the treaty drawn up at Washington by providing that the placing of passengers in the ship's boats shall not be regarded as depositing them at a place of safety excepting under certain conditions.

Many international lawyers regard the attempt to humanize the laws of war as a futile gesture. A nation, with its existence at stake, will frequently violate legal rules which interfere with the success of its operations. The provisions of the London Treaty, would, however, be of some effect in arousing neutral sentiment against a belligerent which should flaunt the above-quoted provision to the detriment of neutral commerce. The fear of such neutral opposition might under certain conditions constrain a belligerent to observe the provisions of the treaty.

After refusing to abolish the submarine, the conference turned its attention to the reduction of tonnage in this class of vessels, and a submarine provision was incorporated in the limitation agreement as between the United States, Great Britain, and Japan. In bringing about this limitation Japan held the key position. The Japanese entered the conference with 77,842 tons of submarines built and building which they claimed to be a necessary part of their war plans; and they came prepared to resist any reduction of that force. They informed the American delegates that if they were permitted to retain their existing strength they would have no objection to any tonnage which the United States might desire, even if it were double the Japanese tonnage.[1]

The United States and Great Britain opposed the maintenance of submarine strength at this high level. The two governments suggested the reduction of the Japanese submarine strength to 52,700 tons, which was what the Japanese would possess by the end of 1936 if they should make no replacements and should permit their over-age vessels to be retired. To secure Japanese assent, the United States and Great Britain were willing to reduce their tonnage to the same figure and to agree to equality as between the three powers. This proposition was finally adopted. Japan reduced her submarine tonnage but received a 10:10:10 ratio.

The size of the submarine was limited to 2,000 tons for all five of the conference powers. Each of the powers was given the right to three submarines of not more than 2,800 tons with 6.1-inch guns, and, as one of these, France was permitted to retain a submarine of 2,880 tons with 8-inch guns. Aside from this no submarine is to be constructed above 2,000 tons and the guns are to be limited

[1] *Congressional Record*, Vol. 73, p. 162, July 15, 1930.

The London Treaty

to 5.1 inches, except that those possessed on April 1, 1930 under 2,000 tons, but with guns in excess of 5.1 inches, may be retained.

The success of the London Conference in reaching an agreement upon auxiliary ships can be best understood by comparing the results with the aims which were sought at previous conferences. The following table sets forth the limits on tonnage of auxiliary combat craft proposed by the United States at Washington and Geneva and the maximum decided upon at London:

Country	Mr. Hughes' Proposal at Washington, 1921	Mr. Gibson's Proposal at Geneva, 1927	The London Treaty, 1930
United States.........	540,000	510,000 to 640,000	526,200
Great Britain.........	540,000	510,000 to 640,000	541,700
Japan................	324,000	306,000 to 384,000	367,000

Had Mr. Hughes or Mr. Gibson been successful, the achievement would have been regarded as a great stroke of statesmanship. From the above comparison it would appear that the London Treaty has secured stabilization at figures, which, except in the case of Japan, are not higher than we have considered desirable in the past. The Japanese figures, moreover, are substantially below the maximum proposed by Mr. Gibson at Geneva.

The British government was able to sign the agreement to limit the tonnage of auxiliary ships in spite of the public uneasiness over the unstable naval situation in the Mediterranean because of the reassurance given by a diplomatic device before alluded to—the escalator clause. Article XXI of the treaty, which contains this provision, reads as follows:

Article XXI. If, during the term of the present Treaty, the requirements of the national security of any High Contracting Party in respect of vessels of war limited by Part III of the present Treaty are in the opinion of that Party materially affected by new construction of any Power other than those who have joined in Part III of this Treaty, that High Contracting Party will notify the other Parties to Part III as to the increase required to be made in its own tonnages within one or more of the categories of such vessels of war, specifying particularly the proposed increases and the reasons therefor, and shall be entitled to make such increase. Thereupon the other Parties to Part III of this Treaty shall be entitled to make a proportionate increase in the category or categories specified; and the said other Parties shall promptly advise with each other through diplomatic channels as to the situation thus presented.

The treaty thus leaves an opening for naval increases, although the probabilities are that such increases will not be made. If French and Italian naval rivalries can be fortunately settled without an increase in construction there will be no occasion to invoke the escalator clause. If the two Mediterranean powers cannot adjust their disputes and one or both of them proceed to additional construction, the worst that will probably result will be some additional building of destroyers and 6-inch gun cruisers by Great Britain. This, in turn, may conceivably lead to some minor increases in American and Japanese tonnage. Conceding the possibility but not the probability of such expansion, the treaty can nevertheless be regarded as bringing about a condition of practical stability as between the three larger naval powers. By making this possible despite the Franco-Italian controversy, the escalator clause plays an exceedingly useful part in the London Treaty.

The Unlimited Classes

Certain classes of naval vessels upon which no limits are imposed are described in Article VIII of the treaty. These vessels, which can be built in any numbers, fall into three classes:

1. Surface combatant vessels of 600 tons or less.
2. Surface combatant vessels of more than 600 tons but not more than 2,000 tons, providing they conform to certain limitations. They

The London Treaty

are not to mount guns of more than 6.1 inches; and not over four guns of more than 3 inches can be installed. They must not be designed or fitted to launch torpedoes. They cannot be designed for speeds greater than 20 knots.

3. Naval vessels which are not built as fighting ships, such as troop transports. There are no tonnage limits on these ships but they must observe the same limits as to guns, torpedoes, and speed as those just described. Furthermore, they must not be protected by armor plate. They must not be designed or fitted to launch mines. They must not have landing-on facilities for airplanes. If fitted for launching airplanes, they are confined to one apparatus on the center line or two on the sides (one on each broadside), and they must not be designed or adapted to operate more than three planes at sea.

It has been suggested that the vessels permitted in Class 2 above could be made superior to the ordinary armed merchant ship, and that they might be used by the United States to overcome the superiority of Great Britain's merchant marine. Most merchant vessels are slower than 20 knots, and, accordingly, a 20-knot war vessel of 2,000 tons with four 6.1-inch guns operated by a well-trained crew could be used to raid enemy commerce. Such vessels because of their slowness as compared with high-speed cruisers would probably operate most effectively in the vicinity of their own coast lines or bases.

Results of the London Treaty

The hopes that the London Conference would result in drastic disarmament and an immediate reduction in the naval budget were not realized. The naval forces of the United States were brought to a stabilized condition at or somewhat under the existing level. Before the conference the total American vessels, built and building, amounted to 1,180,470 tons, of which 120,000 tons were under construction. The authorized strength under the treaty by the end of 1936 will be 1,103,600 tons built. In addition, two cruisers provided for by the treaty, totaling 20,000 tons, will be building. Other tonnage of an indefinite amount will be under construction for replacement purposes, and this replacement tonnage may include two capital ships. Accordingly, if Congress builds up to the treaty limits and there are no further reductions at the 1935 conference, we may assume that the fleet in 1936 will be slightly greater than it was at the beginning of 1930. However, it is probable that Congress will decide not to construct the entire tonnage permitted in all classes of ships. Taking all contingencies into consideration, it seems fair to say that the London Treaty has stabilized the United States navy at about its existing strength or something less.

The agreements of the conference will not necessarily result in a reduction of appropriations below previous levels. In fact, under the treaty the expenditures for naval construction may show a substantial increase. Since the Washington Conference the United States has not been building ships on a large scale. Destroyers, submarines, and battleships have been approaching the age of obsolescence and no replacements have been in process of construction. The necessity of replacements during the next few years would have led to an increase in building appropriations regardless of the London Conference. Accordingly, the fact that the naval construction costs, which have been less than $50,000,000 per year, may be raised to something above $100,000,000 per year cannot be charged against the treaty. It is probable that if the treaty had not been signed the costs for construction would have been raised even to higher levels.

The great gain from the London Treaty is not in the certainty of an immediate naval reduction or in the lowering of costs during the next few years. It lies in the outstanding demonstration that the limitation of all classes of naval ships is possible. London added evidence to the proposition that had been substantially proved at Washington, that the rivalries of the naval powers can be diminished by conference diplomacy. When the Washington and London Conferences are compared with those at The Hague before the war, a very gratifying progress in the direction of international limitation is shown. The gains of the Washington and London Conferences include the following principal points:

1. The abrogation of the Anglo-Japanese alliance and a decided improvement in the relations of the United States and Japan.
2. The lessening of tension in the Anglo-American rivalry.
3. A demonstration that the construction of huge armaments is a matter of international concern which can be dealt with by treaty.

Chapter XIII

THE RATIOS

THE United States has consistently held to the relativity theory in fixing the limits of naval strength. The needs of the American navy, according to this view, vary with the strength of our naval competitors. A different doctrine, that of absolute naval needs, has sometimes been put forward. Thus at Geneva the British delegation contended that they required a minimum of seventy cruisers for the security of the empire, and at London the Japanese stated at one time that their existing strength of 77,842 tons in submarines was necessary for national defense, regardless of the submarine tonnage of other powers.

Perhaps there is an absolute minimum below which a maritime power cannot go for reasons of sea police. But except in the case of Germany such a minimum has not been reached by any of the great powers, and it will probably not be reached by them in this generation. Under present conditions there appears to be little logic in the contention that an adequate naval defense is an absolute matter and can be determined without regard for the naval strength of rival nations. A navy which would be adequate under present conditions would be much more than adequate if the tonnage of competitors should be abolished or drastically reduced. Accordingly, it seems that the United States approached the subject in the correct way at Geneva in 1927 when Mr. Gibson announced: "It is our belief that naval needs are rela-

The Ratios

tive."[1] In fact, this doctrine is absolutely essential to any progress in the reduction of armaments.

Working upon this theory the American government has sought to secure treaty restrictions on naval armaments according to certain definite ratios with Great Britain and Japan. These are parity with Great Britain and a 10:6 ratio with Japan.

Probably the most important guiding principle in the whole disarmament activities of the American government is the achievement of parity with Great Britain. The demand for parity may lack logic. There may be nothing in the necessities of national defense or offense which actually calls for exact equality between the two fleets. But from the standpoint of public psychology there are very practical reasons why the point we call parity is the most convenient one at which the two navies can be brought to a point of equilibrium. A commercially expanding and nationalistic country such as the United States, which can build its fleets without great effort, will hardly be satisfied with a position of inferiority. Great Britain, with her embarrassed treasury can afford to concede this point for by so doing she gains respite from a costly competition. But with her splendid naval traditions she cannot be expected to submit to more without going the limit of competition, alliances, and the whole gamut of bitter retortion. Parity then is the ultimate concession of both parties. The United States will not be content with less and Great Britain will not concede more. Each can accept this status and still retain its national dignity. For psychological reasons, therefore, parity is the most practical place at which the two navies can be brought to a position of rest.

At Washington, the British agreed to parity with regard to capital ships and aircraft carriers. At Geneva, while not openly denying the principle of parity in auxil-

[1] *Records of the Conference*, p. 33.

iaries, the British delegation inspired by instructions from London acted in a manner which convinced many observers that they were seeking to prevent the establishment of parity. The MacDonald government which came into power in 1929, however, freely admitted the principle.

Even after the principle of parity is agreed to there is still room for controversy over the meaning of the word. By parity, as the term was accepted at London, is meant equality in vessels of war, as measured by their tonnage and gun calibers.[1] There are many critics of the London Treaty who point out that such a limited use of the term does not give equality in the ultimate strength that can be exerted in a naval war. They insist that there are certain other factors than warships which count heavily in favor of Great Britain, such as the greater size of the British merchant marine and the large number of widely distributed British naval bases. Parity in naval vessels only, according to the critics, will mean inferiority on the seas for the United States.[2] They contend particularly that the United States navy would be at a disadvantage in capacity for commerce protection as distinguished from combat power. There are, however, other factors of equal or greater importance which weigh in favor of the United States, such as the larger population and resources of this country and the more easily defensible lines of internal and external trade. There are, likewise, political factors, such as the capacity of a nation for alliance diplomacy, which would be of vast importance in time of war. Thus, a multitude of considerations may throw the balance of strength to one of two opponents which are exactly equal in tonnage and gun power. But it is manifestly impossible to estimate all of these factors accurately or to bring them within

[1] *Treaty on the Limitation of Naval Armaments* (1930 hearings) pp. 10, 29, 65.
[2] *Ibid.*, pp. 96, 115, 121.

The Ratios

the scope of an agreement, even if they could be computed. For these reasons, parity in combat power as measured by naval vessels remains the most convenient formula and perhaps the only practical one for adjusting the rivalries of the two great Anglo-Saxon competitors.

The ratios of the tonnage measurements of the different classes of naval vessels as fixed at the end of the London Conference are as follows:

	United States		Great Britain
Capital ships	10	:	10.3
Aircraft carriers	10	:	10
Cruisers, sub-category *a*	10	:	8.1
Cruisers, sub-category *b*	10	:	13.4
Destroyers	10	:	10
Submarines	10	:	10
Total	10	:	10.2

While the British fleet as fixed in the treaty still has a slight advantage over the American treaty fleet in tonnage, the fact that the United States has an advantage in the number of large guns mounted on capital ships and in 8-inch gun cruisers probably equalizes the situation. American naval experts at London were of the opinion that after the modernization of American battleships, which was agreed to by the British, the American fleet would be at least the equal of that of Great Britain in combat strength.[1]

The ratio with Japan is not so simple a matter as that with Great Britain, but neither is it considered to be of such importance. At Washington the proportion of 10:6 was established between the two countries with regard to capital ships and aircraft carriers. No agreement was entered into concerning the other categories. Since the conference, certain advocates of a larger American navy have complained regarding the good faith of Japan

[1] *Ibid.*, pp. 16, 17, 39.

in observing the 10:6 ratio. It is pointed out that after the conference Japan began to build cruisers until her tonnage in that category was considerably in excess of 60 per cent of the American cruiser tonnage. It is alleged that although Japan was not legally bound to observe the ratio in auxiliary vessels she was, nevertheless, morally obligated to do so. There is no evidence of this in the records of the conference. The Hughes proposal of a 10:6 ratio for all combatant ships was accepted by the Japanese as a basis for discussion; but nothing was said and certainly no document was signed which in any way bound the Japanese to the details of the Hughes plan beyond the provisions which were later written into the treaty regarding capital ships and aircraft carriers.

A shifting of emphasis in naval opinion as to what constitutes the measure of a fleet's strength may have had something to do with the allegations of bad faith made against Japan. At the time of the Washington Conference, with the lessons of the Battle of Jutland in mind, the opinion was widespread that the limitation of capital ships would automatically fix the combat strength of the respective fleets. Smaller vessels, or "auxiliaries," so-called, were not regarded as of primary importance, and there was a common belief that they would naturally conform to the capital ship strength. Following the Washington Conference, when competition began anew, the strategy of commerce protection by units cruising independently from the fleet was emphasized; and the idea was revived that a considerable part of naval strength exists in smaller vessels which may bear no necessary relation to the number of capital ships. There is no reasonable foundation for the claim that Japan was limited in auxiliaries at Washington further than this evidently mistaken opinion that the 60 per cent in capital ships had fixed the combat power of the Japanese navy. There was no lack of good faith on the part of

The Ratios

Japan, so far as the treaty was concerned, although the Japanese must, of course, bear no small blame for commencing competition in the building of warships, wholly aside from the obligations of the treaty.

As the London Conference approached, the problem of the ratios to be applied to auxiliaries became important. The United States contended that the Washington ratios should be extended to the other classes of ships, while the Japanese aspired to a 10:7 ratio. This claim for a 70 per cent strength went back as far as the Washington Conference. When Mr. Hughes proposed the 10:6 ratio at Washington it was with the idea that it represented something like the existing proportion in capital ships and that capital ships represented the best measure of naval strength. This seemed to be a good, practical rule for achieving results. The Japanese protested that 70 per cent was the minimum necessary for their national security. After the non-fortification agreement was reached they acquiesced in the 60 per cent limit for capital ships and aircraft carriers. But with the coming of the London Conference the former figure of 70 per cent, which seemed to have a certain magic in Japanese naval circles, was revived. The Japanese delegates were unsuccessful in securing a 70 per cent agreement, and the result was a compromise which has been described above.

The ratios between the two countries resulting from the London Treaty are as follows:

	United States		Japan
Capital ships	10	:	5.8
Aircraft carriers	10	:	6
Cruisers, sub-category *a*	10	:	6
Cruisers, sub-category *b*	10	:	7
Destroyers	10	:	7
Submarines	10	:	10
Total	10	:	6.3

The United States and Disarmament

American naval critics of the London Treaty have objected to the raising of the Japanese ratio above 60 per cent because of the adverse effect which it may have should the United States and Japan engage in a war in far eastern waters. At the time of the Washington Conference many Americans were convinced that a 10:6 ratio was not sufficient to enable the United States to operate in the Far East against Japan. Strong naval opinion still seems to support this view. However, in the 1930 hearings on the London Treaty before the Foreign Relations Committee of the United States Senate, a number of naval officers ventured the opinion that under the 10:6 ratio the United States would still have a bare chance against Japan in Asiatic waters. Any increase in the Japanese ratio, they claimed, would make American operations against Japan a hazardous matter, and accordingly they condemned the ratios established in the London Treaty.[1]

For reasons set forth elsewhere it is believed that a policy of securing a ratio which will enable the United States to defeat Japan in the Far East is worth very little from the standpoint of essential American interests. The extension of American power in the western Pacific will create liabilities for which there can be no adequate recompense. Any attempt by a western power to conquer a strong Asiatic nation can no longer be profitable and cannot be defended from either the financial or ethical standpoint. Commercial reasons which have been set forth for the maintenance of the 10:6 ratio are also open to criticism. It has been pointed out that the United States has nearly $2,500,000,000 in annual commerce in the oceans from China and Australia to Suez.[2] But a 10:6 ratio could not possibly protect American Asiatic trade in case of war with Japan. It is idle to talk of pro-

[1] *Ibid.*, pp. 116, 178, 274, 277, 283, 287, 324.
[2] *Congressional Record*, Vol. 73, p. 257, July 18, 1930.

THE RATIOS

tecting and fostering commerce in war-time in those waters which are even approximately near to the bases of a strong enemy.

On the other hand from a practical standpoint, there must be some point of naval inferiority at which the Japanese shall be limited if there is to be any settlement of the question. For reasons of the most practical character, *i.e.*, those of finance, Japan cannot aspire to equality in a naval race with the United States or Great Britain. Tradition is likewise against equality, and any attempt to upset tradition by building a powerful Japanese fleet must be productive of anarchical competition in which the nation with the longest purse or the most adroit alliance diplomacy will win, and in which the blame must be largely thrown upon that government which upsets the equilibrium. It would not appear to be wise statesmanship for Japan to attempt uncompromisingly to raise her naval ratio. After all, in a war with the United States which might some day be precipitated over the naval dispute, a few Japanese cruisers more or less could not save that country from a crushing disaster which in the long run would be inescapable on account of the overwhelming economic power of the United States.

Because of the most practical considerations it does not appear that the ratio of about 10:6.3 as fixed in the London Treaty should be regarded as unfair by either party. Neither would be justified in attempting to revise it in a radical manner.

PART IV
COÖPERATING WITH THE LEAGUE OF NATIONS

Chapter XIV

THE LEAGUE APPROACH TO DISARMAMENT

THE direct naval conferences at Washington, Geneva, and London have captured the attention of the people of the United States in a dramatic way and have ranked as distinctly major events in American political life. These, of course, have been wholly aside from the work of the League of Nations. As preparations for the World Disarmament Conference of 1932 move forward, the importance of the relationship of this country to the work of the League becomes apparent. Up to this time, however, the rôle which the United States has been forced to assume in connection with the League movement has been carried on in the less advertised preparatory discussions and has occasioned but relatively little publicity.

Since the formation of the League of Nations Preparatory Commission in 1926, the meetings of that body have been regularly and officially attended by American representatives. This country has participated actively and with no little influence in the persistent attempts of the commission to set the stage for the world conference. Our association with the commission has brought the efforts of the League into the American diplomatic program in a formal way. It has introduced us officially to all the ramifications of the world military system and to the efforts which are being made to lessen the burden of armaments and to soften the sharpness of nationalistic rivalry on the over-militarized continent of Europe. Our interest in these oversea negotiations has been amply justified by the prospect of reducing our own colossal military expenditures and by the hope of averting another world conflagration, the burning brands of which would be certain to fall in the midst of the American economic system.

From the beginning, one of the chief purposes of the League has been to reduce armaments.[1] The idea of a league was born during the days when the Allied populations were being urged to continue the "war to end wars" and to put a stop for all time to the curse of militarism. Naturally enough, the plans for a league hatched at such a moment carried provisions for drastic disarmament. President Wilson proclaimed in the fourth of his "fourteen points" that the United States would demand, as a condition of the final settlement of the war, "Adequate guarantees given and taken that national armaments will be reduced to the lowest point consistent with domestic safety." The words "consistent with domestic safety" seemed to mean that the military system must be limited to that force which was necessary to maintain order at home; and they would have required sweeping reductions by all the principal governments. As a practical matter such a formula would have necessitated reduction to a point which would have jeopardized the maintenance of order in a troubled world for it would have left out of consideration the necessities of international police. Accordingly, in his first draft of the Covenant of the League of Nations, President Wilson revised his aims to provide for the needs of international order by placing the standard at "the lowest point consistent with domestic safety and the enforcement by common action of international obligations."[2]

When the powers assembled in Paris in 1919 they were relieved of the fear of Germany. The necessity of appealing to popular idealism against an allegedly wicked foe no

[1] For a general discussion of the disarmament efforts of the League see League of Nations, *Ten Years of World Coöperation*, Chapter II.

[2] MILLER, DAVID HUNTER: *The Drafting of the Covenant*, Vol. II, p. 14, G. P. Putnam's Sons, New York, 1928.

longer existed, and the former good intentions of the Allies began to disappear. When President Wilson's proposal came before the commission on the League of Nations at the Paris Conference, the expression "domestic safety" was struck out and the term "national safety" was put in its place.[1]

The change removed any definite standard of limitation. The words "national safety" and similar expressions have long been used to justify almost any naval building program or increase of land armaments which the most militaristic mind can devise. They may be interpreted as leaving all the nations free to maintain their forces practically intact for defense or offense against dangers real and imaginary. While there is an undoubted pledge of reduction, as will be seen in Article VIII of the Covenant, the amount of reduction demanded is so vague as to give ample opportunity for procrastination.

The aims of the League were finally expressed in Article VIII of the Covenant which reads as follows:

Article VIII. The Members of the League recognize that the maintenance of peace requires the reduction of national armaments to the lowest point consistent with national safety, and the enforcement by common action of international obligations.

The Council, taking account of the geographical situation and circumstances of each State, shall formulate plans for such reduction for the consideration and action of the several governments.

Such plans shall be subject to reconsideration and revision at least every ten years.

After these plans shall have been adopted by the several governments, the limits of armaments therein fixed shall not be exceeded without the concurrence of the Council.

The Members of the League agree that the manufacture by private enterprise of munitions and implements of war is open to grave objections. The Council shall advise how the evil effects attendant upon such manufacture can be prevented, due regard being had to the necessities of those Members of the League which are not able to

[1] *Ibid.*, pp. 264-265.

manufacture the munitions and implements of war necessary for their safety.

The Members of the League undertake to interchange full and frank information as to the scale of their armaments, their military, naval and air programmes and the condition of such of their industries as are adaptable to warlike purposes.

The need of an international army and navy to be mobilized on occasion to maintain the provisions of the Covenant was discussed at Paris. The French delegates, whose principal demand was for security and whose minds were troubled by the vivid memories of the advance upon Paris in 1914, were the chief advocates of an international military force. They proposed that the Council of the League should prepare to mobilize with great rapidity the air, land, and sea units contributed by the member states to enforce the obligations of the League in times of crisis. This has frequently been referred to as a plan for general staff. The proposal was promptly vetoed by other powers whose independent nationalism would not permit the formation of a militaristic superstate.[1] All that finally remained of the French proposal was a provision for a permanent commission to render advice on military matters. This is contained in Article IX which reads as follows:

Article IX. A permanent Commission shall be constituted to advise the Council on the execution of the provisions of Articles 1 and 8 and on military, naval, and air questions generally.

In addition to the above-quoted Articles VIII and IX, it was provided in Article I that any state to be admitted to membership in the League "shall accept such regulations as may be prescribed by the League in regard to its military, naval and air forces and armaments." These three parts of the Covenant, Articles I, VIII and IX, contain the authorization and obligation of the League in the matter of disarmament.

[1] *Ibid.*, Vol. I, pp. 207, 260.

The League Approach to Disarmament

One kind of disarmament was actually achieved at the Peace Conference, that is, the disarmament of the defeated states. The German army was limited to 100,000 men. The navy was reduced to six small battleships, six light cruisers, twelve destroyers, and twelve torpedo boats. Submarines were prohibited. Military and naval air forces were abolished.[1] Thus the Germans were placed upon a basis which was practically that recommended for all nations by President Wilson, the lowest point consistent with domestic safety. The armies of other of the enemy countries were limited to the following numbers: Austria, 30,000; Hungary, 35,000; and Bulgaria, 20,000. The Allies were not so conscientious in fulfilling their own pledges. In fact, the French desired to enhance their armaments by taking a generous share of the German battleships and cruisers. The German sailors, who were manning the fleet, finally scuttled and sank the ships at Scapa Flow. In doing so they performed one of the most practical feats on record in behalf of disarmament.

The disarmament of Germany has placed an undoubted obligation upon the Allied countries to make large reductions in their own armaments. The Germans were led into the armistice partly, at least, on the basis of President Wilson's "Fourteen Points." They and the Allies are parties to the Treaty of Versailles which carries the uncertain pledge of general reduction mentioned in Article 8 of the Covenant. The fact that a decade has passed and no substantial action has thus far been taken seems to the Germans not unnaturally like a breach of faith. On the other hand it must be remembered that the League is here dealing with one of the most difficult problems in international relations. Probably all that can be reasonably expected is a genuine and persistent

[1] Treaty of Peace between the Allied and Associated Powers and Germany, Part V.

effort to carry out the pledges of the treaty. It may be questioned whether any such sufficiently sincere attempt has thus far been made. The growing resentment of Germans against the slowness of the League constitutes a pressing reminder of the disarmament obligation in the Covenant, and likewise a threat that if action is not taken Germany will consider herself relieved of the armament restrictions placed upon her.

The first agency created by the Council to consider the questions of armaments was the Permanent Advisory Commission, hereafter referred to as the P.A.C., which was specifically provided for in Article IX of the Covenant. There are three functions of the commission as set forth in the article: (1) to advise with regard to the condition of armaments of any country applying for admission to the League and as to any regulations which may be prescribed by the League under Article I of the Covenant; (2) to advise regarding the reduction of armaments as set forth in Article VIII; and (3) to advise the Council concerning any military, naval, or air questions upon which it may need technical advice and information.

The P.A.C. was constituted by act of the Council on which the powerful military states are heavily represented. The commission consists of military, naval, and air experts. Each country represented on the Council sends three technical advisers, one from each main branch of the service. Three subcommittees have been created for military, naval, and air matters respectively and each member country is represented on each subcommittee by one delegate from the appropriate branch of the service.

The matter of advice regarding disarmament was thus entrusted to military technicians and the P.A.C. gave forth but little hope of any actual reduction. According to the observations of Salvador de Madariaga:

The League Approach to Disarmament

It was as foolish to expect a disarmament convention from such a commission as a declaration of atheism from a commission of clergymen . . . When the first Assembly of the League of Nations met in November, 1920, it found that the Commission had reported negatively on practically every point of the program submitted to it by the Council. What else could be expected?[1]

This was exactly what had happened in the subcommittees of the First Hague Conference, when bodies of military and naval men reported adversely on the Russian proposals for armament limitation.

The first Assembly of the League, meeting in 1920, was not satisfied with the character of the P.A.C. and recommended to the Council that the problem should be entrusted to a body which would have the civilian element in the majority. After some modification the Council approved the proposal and the T.M.C. (Temporary Mixed Commission) was created. The new commission was composed of six civilians of standing, six experts from the P.A.C., four from the Economic and Financial Committee of the League, and six chosen from the International Labor Office. The armaments question was thus removed, in part at least, from the military forum and given to a body under civilian control.

The secretariat of the T.M.C. and that of the P.A.C. were made parts of the Disarmament Section of the Secretariat of the League of Nations, at the head of which was placed a Director of Disarmament. De Madariaga remarks that the secretariat of the T.M.C. was listed in the League records as the disarmament section while that of the P.A.C. was called the armaments section[2].

One important development inaugurated by the T.M.C. was the publication in 1922 and 1923 of statistical information. The publication was based on the last paragraph of Article VIII above quoted. On the basis of this work, the Council authorized the Secretariat to

[1] *Disarmament,* p. 92.
[2] *Ibid.,* p. 94.

publish a yearly volume containing detailed information as to the organization of the armed forces of each country, the budget expenditures for national defense, and the industries capable of being used in case of war. The annual publication, *Armaments Year-Book: General and Statistical Information,* is a source of outstanding importance regarding the world's armaments.

Two proposals for direct disarmament were considered by the League during the first two years. The first was Lord Esher's plan for reducing land forces by adjusting their size according to national needs. A unit of thirty thousand men was proposed as the basis of the plan and each country was to have as many units as were justified by its resources and by its position with relation to its neighbors. The scheme was rejected. The nations were not yet ready to reduce their land forces.

The T.M.C. then recommended that the principles of the Washington Conference Treaty should be extended to non-signatory powers. A conference was called of all such powers possessing capital ships. Members of the P.A.C. were likewise represented. The sessions were held in Rome in February, 1924; but the conference was unable to accomplish anything. The problem of limiting the navies of nations from every part of the globe was too complex to be solved in one conference.

During the next two years the League devoted its primary attention to the limiting of armaments by what is called the "indirect" method, *i.e.,* the removal of the causes of armaments by removing the causes of war. This has thus far been a distinguishing feature of the efforts of the League. According to the League view the main obstacle to the lowering of armaments is the dread of insecurity. If fear can be removed, the principal objection to reduction of armaments will be gone.

Americans who live in a country which is practically immune from attack may not always be able to grasp or

The League Approach to Disarmament

appreciate the importance of security in the discussions of European nations. Let us consider the position of France as typical. The author remembers mentioning the Franco-Prussian War once to an elderly French lady whose memory extended back to the days of 1870. The bare allusion to that conflict brought forth such a rapid torrent of emotional language as to baffle completely the writer's meager understanding of the French tongue. The fears and humiliation of that invasion are like live coals in the Gallic memory. Even more burning in the French mind is the invasion of 1914. There were days in that year when the nation seemed to totter on the verge of destruction. These fears of national annihilation are unforgettable—veritable nightmares to the French people. How difficult then is it to bring the French statesmen to an agreement to disarm so long as there is danger of the repetition of these former disasters. Security before disarmament is not only the demand of France, but also of practically all of the European nations, excepting, of course, those that have already been disarmed.

With a view to relieving the fear of insecurity which made the work of arms reduction almost impossible, the Third Assembly in 1922 passed Resolution XIV which advised that:

In the present state of the world many Governments would be unable to accept the responsibility for a serious reduction of armaments unless they received in exchange a satisfactory guarantee of the safety of their country.

The question of providing the means of guarantee was referred to the T.M.C., which after examining several proposals, particularly one prepared by Lord Robert Cecil of Great Britain, drew up a draft treaty and submitted it to the Assembly. When some modifications had been introduced by the Assembly the document became the Draft Treaty of Mutual Assistance.

The United States and Disarmament

The treaty proclaimed aggressive war to be an international crime. Within four days of the outbreak of war the Council should decide which country was the aggressor and should determine the methods by which the other parties to the treaty on the same continent would come to the aid of the victim of the aggression. The draft also authorized special regional agreements or defensive alliances for the same purpose of mutual protection against aggressor nations. Each state was then to make an estimate of the reduction which it could bring about in armaments in view of this increased security, and on the basis of these estimates the Council was to draw up plans for a general reduction.

The treaty failed of acceptance. The criticism was advanced that it provided no compulsory method of settling disputes. It was pointed out that the determination of the aggressor was to be made by a political body, the Council, and that the Council's decision evidently required a unanimous vote. The obligations imposed upon the signatories were looked at with suspicion. Ramsay MacDonald, who succeeded to the premiership shortly after the treaty was drafted, opposed ratification by Great Britain, and contended that the security offered was not sufficient to bring about a reduction in armaments. He alleged that if the obligations to supply force under the treaty were to be scrupulously observed an actual increase in armaments would result.

In the Fifth Assembly of 1924 a thoroughgoing effort was made to construct a security compact which would permit the nations to reduce armaments. The committees of the Assembly, after laboriously working on the idea, brought forth the Geneva Protocol. Three principles were incorporated in it. *Disarmament* necessitated *security*, but there could be no real security until an air-tight method of settling disputes by *arbitration* could be found. And thus Arbitration, Security, and Disarmament

THE LEAGUE APPROACH TO DISARMAMENT

became the three principles upon which the protocol was based, the famous "trilogy," as it has been so frequently referred to in League circles.

Arbitration.—Every signatory of the protocol was to be required to accept the optional clause of the World Court Statute and thus to agree to compulsory arbitration of the four classes of disputes mentioned in that clause. In any case outside of these four classes the signatories agreed to apply the methods of the League Covenant and to submit the matter to the Council. Decisions of the Council made by unanimous vote are binding under the Covenant to the extent that the parties agree not to go to war with any party to the dispute which complies with the recommendations of Council; but if the Council cannot render a unanimous report the parties retain their freedom of action. This is the "loophole" in the Covenant and the protocol now attempted to close it by providing that:

1. If either party wished arbitration the Council should arrange for the arbitration committee, the decision of which should be binding.
2. If neither party wished arbitration the Council should again consider the matter and endeavor to settle it by unanimous vote.
3. If the Council should for the second time fail to arrive at a unanimous decision it should set up a committee of arbitration which should have power to settle the dispute.

These provisions all but closed the loophole. There were, however, several classes of cases which could not be settled by this machinery. These were disputes arising out of the measures of force taken by a League member acting by authority of the Council or Assembly, those arising out of domestic questions, and certain international disputes which for some reason could not be submitted to compulsory arbitration, the principal class here being disputes under the peace treaties.

Security.—The security provisions were devoted to defining and outlawing aggressive wars and providing sanctions against them. "Private" hostilities waged for national gain were abolished leaving to signatory nations only two kinds of war, those conducted in resistance to aggression and those conducted under authorization of the Council or the Assembly.

The method of defining the aggressor was carefully worked out as follows:

1. The state which should go to war should automatically be presumed to be the aggressor if:
   a. It should refuse to accept the provisions for pacific settlement,
   b. It should refuse to accept the methods set down by the Council for limiting hostilities after the outbreak of war, or, in other words, if it should refuse to obey the "stop-fighting" order of the Council, or
   c. In those disputes which were decided to have arisen out of domestic questions, if it should start hostilities without first submitting the matter to the Council or the Assembly for conciliation.
2. If none of these conditions should exist the Council should attempt to decide which was the aggressor, the decision requiring a unanimous vote.
3. In case the Council should not be unanimous in its vote, it must by a two-thirds vote require an armistice, and if either party should refuse to respect the truce it should automatically be considered the aggressor.

After the aggressor should be determined by the Council the signatories to the protocol were to carry out their obligations under Article XVI of the Covenant loyally and effectively and to come to the assistance of the attacked state. In doing so they were to be entitled to exercise the rights of belligerents against the aggressor.

Disarmament.—Upon the ratification of the protocol by May 1, 1925, by a majority of the Council members and ten other parties (a condition which was never fulfilled) a conference for the reduction of armaments was to be held. This conference was to work out a plan for the reduction of arms and to fix a period during which the plan should be carried into effect. If at the expiration of that period the plan was still not carried out, the whole protocol should be declared null and void.

The protocol was not ratified chiefly because of the failure of the government of Great Britain to approve it. The Labor government, which had been in power during the drafting of the protocol, went out of office and the Conservative government refused to accept the plan. One of the reasons for the British refusal was fear of conflict with the United States. The American government was not a signatory and it was apprehended that the execution of the security provisions in the protocol might bring the British navy into conflict with that of the United States. This might happen if the United States should be deemed to be an aggressor in some dispute or, what was more likely, if the United States should try to maintain economic relations with a country designated as an aggressor and blockaded by the other powers signatory to the protocol.

The protocol did not entirely fail. It remains as a foundation upon which future movements for arbitration and security will probably be based. Some of its spirit was carried over into the Locarno Treaty of Mutual Guarantee of 1925 which constitutes a pact for regional security along the Belgian-German and Franco-German frontiers. Furthermore, member after member of the League has accepted the optional clause of the World Court Statute until thirty-four states or members of the League are now so obligated.[1] The Kellogg Pact, to which all nations but two have adhered or announced intentions of adherence, has given moral support to the European movement for security. The question naturally arises if,

---

[1] HUDSON, MANLEY O.: "The Ninth Year of the Permanent Court of International Justice," *American Journal of International Law*, Vol. 25, p. 13, January, 1931.

with this progress in arbitration and security, the world is not now ready for substantial achievements in armament reductions.

The T.M.C. went out of existence following the Assembly of 1924. Its place has been partially taken by a Coördination Commission which consists of the members of the Council and representatives from several other League organizations. This commission has worked quietly in drawing together the various agencies for disarmament and has not played any conspicuous part in the movement.

In 1925 the Preparatory Commission for a Disarmament Conference was established by the Council. One might think from the name of the body that it was created to fulfill a comparatively minor function but for a period of five years it overshadowed all other League institutions in dealing with the disarmament problem. The Preparatory Commission consisted of the representatives of the principal members of the League including the governments represented in the Council and other governments affected by the problem. Some of the outstanding nations which did not have League membership were also invited to send delegates, and accordingly, the United States (from the beginning), Russia (from 1927), and Turkey (from 1928) were represented at meetings of the commission.

The function of the Preparatory Commission was to resolve into simple terms in a provisional draft treaty the principal outstanding questions of disarmament. The ultimate goal was a general conference which, because of the preparatory discussions, definitions, and concessions on all sides, could have some hope of adopting a general world-wide treaty.

At the beginning of its labors the Preparatory Commission, or P.C. as we shall call it, was greatly assisted by the two subcommissions: Subcommission A, which dealt with the military side of disarmament, and Subcommission B, which dealt with economic and political questions. Of these the more important in its contribution to the discussions of the main commission was Subcommission A. This subcommission was the old P.A.C. revised, and thereby hangs a short tale which throws some light upon the American attitude toward the League. The Preparatory Commission desired at the outset to use the technical advices of the P.A.C. The United States government did not desire to be represented on a League agency. Accordingly, the P.A.C. was rechristened Subcommission A, an American military and naval delegation was added, and the uniformed group continued to function under another name.[1] American pride was saved and no harm was done.

During 1926 this subcommission assembled for three sessions at Geneva and in these sessions altogether eighty-six meetings were held. The personnel of the commission was made up of fifteen generals, twenty-six colonels and lieutenant colonels, eleven majors, nine captains, 4 lieutenants, nine admirals and rear admirals, fifteen commanders and lieutenant commanders, one squadron leader, and five civilians.

This subcommission largely set the standard of work and the method of approach which were to dominate the discussions of the P.C. Each delegation brought to the subcommission the views of its own country regarding military necessities. It would be a mistake to think that because the subcommission was overwhelmingly "expert" in its composition it was animated by a desire to prevent the limitation or reduction of armaments as a general principle. On the other hand much excellent preparation was done. But each delegate was willing and determined to oppose any movement which ran counter to the military and naval policies of his own government.

[1] DE MADARIAGA: *op. cit.*, p. 155.

Accordingly, there was a well-defined conflict on almost every major issue.

The disagreements brought out in Subcommission A made clear the nature of the problems to be solved and these problems were attacked with vigor in the third session of the P.C., which met in 1927. At this session two draft conventions were submitted, one by the British and one by the French. As these two countries were representative of opposing opinions on most of the issues raised, the two drafts were combined for the sake of simplicity to set forth the divergent views in parallel columns. The task of the P.C. from that time forth centered around the attempt to arrive at acceptable compromises on these opposing provisions and to bring them together in a skeleton protocol to be placed before the Disarmament Conference.

Altogether six sessions of the P.C. were held. At times a spirit of pessimism prevailed. On one occasion in the third session the able Belgian delegate, M. de Brouckère, who had fought vainly for an agreement to limit military budgets, threw up his hands in despair.

> We began with that celebrated trilogy, which has aroused such enthusiasm: Arbitration, Security and Disarmament. We then said: "We are not concerned with disarmament but with reduction." Then in a subsequent stage of our work it was pointed out that it would perhaps be too ambitious to attempt reduction, and that we should have to content ourselves with limitation. Well, we have now reached a point when we may even have to erase this last word.

Events of 1930, however, hastened the work of the P.C. The London Treaty, which was signed in that year, proved to be something of a triumph for direct disarmament and simplified the problem of competition between the larger naval powers. The German elections of September 14 increased the number of seats of the National Socialists or Hitlerites in the Reichstag from 12 to 107 and gave warning of a significant revival of German nationalistic spirit. Following the election the government of the Reich took a much firmer position on foreign questions. Large and responsible elements of the German public demanded that the disarmament provisions of the League of Nations Covenant must be carried out, or that otherwise Germany should insist upon the right to increase her own armaments. This sentiment was too strong to be ignored without causing an impossible European situation.

At the meeting of the League Assembly in September, an increased interest in a disarmament conference was manifested. Arthur Henderson, British foreign minister, took the position that disarmament must precede security. Reminding the Assembly of the pledge of the Covenant regarding disarmament, he said, "that obligation forms part of the treaties of peace, and it is no less sacred than any other obligation which those treaties contain."[1] A week later, Hugh Dalton, British undersecretary for foreign affairs, in discussing the League appropriation for the reduction of armaments, emphasized his hope that the conference would meet in 1931.[2] When, however, Count von Bernstorff, representing Germany, moved in the Third Committee (on disarmament) to convene the conference as early as possible in 1931, the motion failed. The committee approved a draft resolution, which was then adopted by the Assembly, expressing a conviction that the Preparatory Commission would be able to finish the draft convention at its November session and would thus enable the Council to convene the general conference "as soon as possible."[3]

[1] League of Nations, *Verbatim Record of the Eleventh Ordinary Session of the Assembly, Fourth Plenary Meeting*, p. 3.
[2] League of Nations, *Official Journal*, Special Supplement 88, pp. 41, 42.
[3] League of Nations, *Official Journal*, Special Supplement 87, p. 101, and *Verbatim Record of the Eleventh Ordinary Session of the Assembly, Nineteenth Plenary Meeting*, pp. 4–9.

The Assembly adjourned without recommending a definite date.

The second part of the sixth session of the P.C. met on November 6. Fully aware that a failure to make way for a conference would give rise to acute dissatisfaction in Europe, the commission hastened its labors to complete the skeleton protocol. Blank spaces were left for the insertion of armament figures by the conference. Reservations were made by different powers to practically all of the principal clauses. Finally on December 9 the draft was finished and the P.C. was permanently dissolved. A parting recommendation was made that the Council should call the general conference early in 1932. The Council met in January, 1931, and fixed the opening of the conference for February 2, 1932. The friends of disarmament have since that time turned their attention toward the 1932 conference which promises to be an outstanding event in the field of post-war diplomacy.

Chapter XV

THE WORLD CONFERENCE: GENERAL PROBLEMS, BUDGETS, AND SUPERVISION

IN FORECASTING the disarmament conference it is possible to outline to some extent the questions that will present themselves and also to indicate the attitude which the United States has thus far taken toward these problems. At the meetings of the Preparatory Commission the United States has not been a silent observer but has stood out as one of the most active and influential members of the commission. In the interchange of opinion and clash of debate, the contentions of this country have represented a fairly cohesive policy and our relations to the various European cliques and factions are roughly understood.

In the politics of League disarmament the most fundamental line of cleavage lies between the defeated and disarmed powers of Central Europe and the victorious Allies of the Continent. In the bloc of disinherited governments are counted Germany, Austria, Hungary, and Bulgaria. These can expect support from Russia in opposing the system of militarism that now dominates Europe and in demanding a radical reduction of armaments. On the other side are France and her allies, Belgium, Czechoslovakia, Poland, Rumania, and Yugoslavia. The French group is heavily overarmed. To the German and Russian demand for drastic reduction the Allied bloc replies like a well-disciplined chorus, "Security first."

Whether Italy can be counted in this group is one of the riddles of current politics. For decades Italy has acted an uncertain rôle, playing with the affections of one *entente* and then another. In the fall of 1930 it appeared as if the Italian government had joined forces with Germany for the revision of the peace treaties. As this book goes to press the possibility of a Franco-Italian naval agreement is frequently interpreted as signalling an inclination on the part of Italy to return to a political understanding with France. The web of financial control which France has been weaving around her political supporters may yet catch Italy in its meshes. What the Italian position at the World Conference will be, however, none but the most foolhardy would attempt to predict.

The position of the United States with regard to these factions would appear to be one of independence. At times this country has stood against the proposals of Germany and Russia. Thus, when the Russian delegation set forth its plan for drastic disarmament, the United States joined with the French group in cold opposition. The United States also opposed the proposal of Germany to prohibit the dropping of explosives and gas bombs from airplanes. When the bitter controversy arose over reaffirming the armament limitations of the peace treaties the United States undertook to occupy a middle ground. Finally, many of the other activities of the United States in the P.C. have been in opposition to the disarmament views of the French group. In these efforts the United States has frequently been associated with Great Britain.

American and British coöperation in opposing the policies of France and her allies requires some explanation. These two Anglo-Saxon countries do not have the tradition of compulsory military service. Neither has attempted to build up reserves by the conscript system. This fact, in the beginning at least, inclined both countries to sympathize with the German demand for a limitation of trained reserves. Both the United States and Great Britain emphasize naval defense and both have felt that the problems which affect the fleet can be separated to a large extent from those which concern the land and air forces. In taking this attitude they have come into conflict with the big-army countries of Europe. Similar opposition has arisen when these two naval powers have desired to stereotype their maritime supremacy by limiting the world's navies according to well-defined categories of ships. As strong producing countries the two possess an enormous war potential in their peace-time industries which they have desired should not be counted in the general scheme of limitation. Here again has been a reason for differing with the heavily armed Allied countries of Europe, some of which are industrially very weak, and here also has been a cause for coöperating with Germany which has a small army but great industrial strength.

As the discussions in the P.C. progressed, the gulf which separated the two Anglo-Saxon nations from the big-army countries of Continental Europe was appreciably narrowed. Compromise after compromise removed causes of dispute between them. It seems, however, because of the similarity of the positions of the United States and Great Britain and because of the differences between their armaments systems and those of the great land powers, that these two will frequently find themselves working together in opposition to the views of the Continental Allies.

In the following pages more specific consideration will be given to the principal problems of world disarmament and a summary will be attempted of the views of the United States expressed upon each of them in the Preparatory Commission.

General and Drastic Disarmament.—The most far-reaching of all the issues which will probably arise at the conference is that of drastic disarmament. The disinherited nations of Europe, squirming under the unequal restrictions of the peace treaties, will ask that the war victors fulfill their pledges of arms reduction. They will have a formidable ally in the Russian delegation, for the U.S.S.R. also seeks to disarm the capitalist nations and thus to deprive them of their power to crush the Soviet system by force. Perhaps the Russians see in the horoscope a great inter-systemic war between capitalism and communism of which the present commercial complaints against Russian exports coming from a score of fronts indicate the preliminary economic skirmishes. Furthermore, that part of Russian communism which clings to the hope of an approaching world revolution would prefer to see armaments generally abolished so that the great international uprising which they have in mind can proceed unhampered by armed opposition.

One of the most dramatic episodes in the life of the P.C. occurred during the fifth session when the Russian delegate, M. Litvinoff, presented the Soviet proposal for immediate, complete, and general disarmament. In supporting his proposal, M. Litvinoff criticised the League of Nations for its do-nothing policy. He said:

Mere theoretical discussions and arguments about disarmament no longer meet the case—it is time to take practical steps toward the realisation of disarmament. It seems to me there has been more than enough of discussion of disarmament. I shall venture to furnish members of the Commission with a few data (Annex 4) from which it will be seen that, as well as the general Assemblies of the League of Nations and the Council of the League, the thirty-eight sessions of which occupied themselves with the question of disarmament, no fewer than fourteen different commissions and other League organs devoted over a hundred and twenty *sessions*—not sittings, mark you, but sessions—to this question of disarmament, on which one hundred and eleven resolutions have been passed by general Assemblies of the League and the Council of the League alone. Turning to the results of this vast quantity of work, the documentation of which has taken reams of paper, we are forced to the conclusion that not a single step of real importance has been taken towards the realisation of disarmament.[1]

Litvinoff proposed that all military units and formations, as well as effectives of the land, naval, and air forces, whether of the home country or its oversea possessions, should be disbanded within four years. A police service was to be permitted in each country for internal protection, the numbers to be in proportion to the population of the several contracting States, the length of the means of communication, the existence of objects deemed by the state to require protection, the development of forestry, etc. A naval police service was to be organized regionally for the suppression of piracy and the general maintenance of maritime order. Police vessels were not to exceed 3,000 tons or to have more than two guns and these should not exceed 50 millimeters in caliber. The carrying out of the convention was to be under the supervision of a Permanent International Commission of Control.[2]

The proposal precipitated a lively debate. Count Bernstorff of Germany spoke sympathetically of the plan. A few delegates felt that it presented difficulties which should be discussed further. But the great majority were hostile to the suggestion. The French bloc presented an unshakeable front in opposition. The point that complete disarmament was to be undertaken without some guarantee of security brought forth the greatest objection, for here the Soviet project ran counter to the trilogy of Arbitration, Security, and Disarmament which had come to be the accepted mode of attack upon the problem at Geneva. Some delegates feared that brigandage, piracy, and revolution would result from such sweeping

[1] League of Nations, *Documents of the Preparatory Commission for the Disarmament Conference, Minutes of the Fifth Session*, p. 240, Geneva, 1928
[2] *Ibid.*, p. 324.

disarmament. States without industries would be left at the mercy of states with industries. The members of the League would not have the means with which to fulfill their obligations to that body when called upon to join together in opposing an aggressor. In short, the plan was directly opposed to the notion of the correct approach to disarmament which had gained ascendency in orthodox League circles.

Particularly aggressive in his attacks upon the scheme was the British delegate, Lord Cushendun, whose political associates in the Conservative government had been nursing a special grievance against Russia. Lord Cushendun cited the persistent and tedious labors that had been performed by the League of Nations for seven years and accused the U.S.S.R. of doing nothing to assist and much to obstruct this work. He quoted a translated extract from the *Izvestia*, the official organ of the Soviet government, to show that the purpose of the Litvinoff proposal was not a sincere desire to have the plan adopted but rather an intention "to disclose the sabotage of the Soviet proposals for disarmament," which was to be expected from the capitalist states. He attacked the Soviet government for its program of world revolution and for its influence in stirring up disorders in other countries. These propagandist activities were, he alleged, the greatest obstacle to disarmament. He likewise intimated that the standards which were suggested to determine the size of the protective police bodies were loaded in favor of a large Russian force. Undoubtedly Lord Cushendun and some of the other delegates suspected Russia of desiring to disarm the nations in order to make way for a general uprising of the proletariat.

Mr. Gibson of the United States might well have wished to remain silent during this discussion, for the main objection to the Soviet proposal, *i.e.*, that it provided no adequate machinery for security, was one in which the United States, because of its independent and isolationist attitude, could not logically join. At the third session of the P.C., in opposing the jurisdiction of the League over disarmament administration and in refusing to subscribe to any agreement based on supervision and control, Mr. Gibson had said: "We cannot divest ourselves of the idea that the only practical way to disarm is actually to disarm." Accordingly, Mr. Gibson probably wished to keep his seat during this debate. He was, however, moved to offer some remarks by a passage in M. Litvinoff's speech which had been directed at the United States. The Russian delegate had said that the Soviet government counted particularly upon the support of the United States because of the Kellogg proposals for the renunciation of war. Adherence by the United States to the Soviet disarmament plan, he contended, was a good test of the sincerity of the peace pact. Since the sole purpose of armed forces is the conduct of war, and since the prohibition of war would make such forces entirely superfluous, he suggested, perhaps sardonically, that consistency and logic on the part of the United States would compel support of the Russian proposals.

Having been specially called upon, Mr. Gibson could hardly avoid making an explanation of the attitude of the United States. He was therefore moved to attempt a most difficult feat, *i.e.*, to explain how opposition to the Soviet proposal was not logically at variance with the Kellogg Pact but actually consistent with it. It is no criticism of the ability of Mr. Gibson that he was not particularly successful in this task.

The reasons why the United States, while upholding the Kellogg Pact, must still oppose the Russian plan for radical disarmament seem to be about as follows: (1) that we have not that confidence in the Kellogg Pact which we have been compelled by circumstances to assert in public; (2) that governments are dual or rather plural in their nature and, therefore, it is perfectly possible and entirely in accord with the frailities of human nature for a government to avow the renunciation of war and to prepare for a coming conflict at the same time; (3) that there are powerful forces in American society working for larger armaments and these are strong enough to block completely any such plan as that of general disarmament; (4) that the Senate of the United States could not be expected to give a two-thirds vote in favor of a program which would so completely circumscribe the functions of Congress regarding national defense; and (5) that it would not be good diplomacy from the point of view of the United States government to side with communist Russia against the protests of the greater part of the capitalist world.

These or similar reasons could not have been openly avowed without giving a considerable shock to a gathering of diplomats even under the new diplomacy. Accordingly Mr. Gibson announced as follows:

··· it is precisely on grounds of sincerity, consistency and logic that my Government supports the idea of a multilateral pact renouncing war as an instrument of national policy, and at the same time finds itself unable to support drastic proposals for immediate and complete disarmament which we do not believe are calculated to achieve their avowed purpose. Any other attitude on the part of my Government, Mr. President, would be lacking in sincerity, consistency and logic, for my Government believes in the one project and disbelieves in the other. We believe that the idea behind the proposal of a pact for renouncing war can be made effective as an articulate expression of an almost universal will for peace. We believe that such an expression is more effective at this time than any scheme, however drastic, for doing away with weapons. We have always stated our conviction that, as we build up the will for peace and confidence in peaceful methods for settling international disputes, through regional agreements or otherwise, our need for armaments will automatically decrease. We have never believed that the converse was true and that the suppression of armaments would alone and by itself have the effect of creating that confidence which is essential to the successful conclusion of our task.[1]

[1] *Ibid.*, p. 258.

The World Conference

Thus the American government, which is not even a member of the World Court, was made to talk the language of the League of Nations and to advocate the building up of peaceful methods of settling disputes as a condition precedent to reduction in armaments.

Following the defeat of the proposal for complete disarmament, the Soviet delegation introduced a second plan for incomplete but drastic reduction. The principal feature of this plan was that disarmament should be according to a progressively graduated scale, which would reduce the armaments of the strong powers in greater proportion than those of the weaker powers. Thus the reduction of land effectives would be in accordance with the following schedule:

A. States with 200,000 troops in active service or with 10,000 regular officers in the *cadres* of the armed land forces, or with more than 60 regiments of infantry should reduce by one-half.

B. States with 40,000 troops in active service or with 2,000 regular officers in the *cadres* of the armed land forces, or with more than 20 regiments of infantry should reduce by one-third.

C. All other states maintaining armed forces inferior in number and composition to the figures for Group B should reduce by one-fourth.[1]

This plan likewise failed of acceptance. At the final session of the P.C., however, M. Litvinoff gave notice that the Soviet government would continue the advocacy of its proposals before the world conference.[2]

The attitude of Russia toward the coming conference, as expressed by M. Litvinoff, is not one of faith or hope. In an interview given during the final session of the P.C., the Russian representative declared that if the dele-

---

[1] *Ibid.*, p. 347.
[2] *Minutes of the Sixth Session (Second Part)*, p. 403.

gates to the world conference should come with the same instructions as guided the delegations at the P.C. there would be no reduction of armaments. He continued:

> The general impression the Soviet delegation received from the discussions of the preparatory committee is that certain countries who, thanks to the numerical and qualitative superiority of their armaments, hold the ruling position in the world, which they endeavor to expand and maintain, are determined to resist reduction of their military power.[1]

Germany, because of her disarmed condition, has expressed sympathy for the Russian proposals. The swelling sentiment of Teutonic nationalism demands in no uncertain terms that the victorious Allies shall fulfill their pledges of disarmament contained in the peace treaty. The Germans are convinced that if such action is not taken their own government will be at least morally released from the disarmament provisions of the Treaty of Versailles. This attitude has been made clear in the German press in recent months and it was also signified in the debates of the last session of the P.C. The matter came to a climax during the discussion of the binding effect of previous disarmament treaties. On November 27, 1930, the commission debated a British proposal that the general disarmament convention should in no way diminish the obligations of the parties under previous treaties. The intent of the British was to protect the Washington and London naval treaties. To this was attached a French amendment permitting the signatories of the world treaty to declare that the limits accepted by them under the convention are dependent upon the observance of previous armament limitation treaties. The purpose of the French amendment was particularly to reaffirm the military prohibitions placed upon the defeated powers by the peace treaties and to make the observance of such prohibitions an essential con-

[1] *New York Times*, Nov. 28, 1930.

dition to the carrying out of the general disarmament convention.

Count Bernstorff, the German delegate, objected in no uncertain terms to the French amendment as a measure which would permanently exclude Germany from the disarmament system. He said:

> It may be that some delegates here are under the impression that my Government might be induced to accede to a Convention which, instead of leading to genuine disarmanent, would merely serve as a cloak for the actual state of the world's land armaments, or—even worse—would make it possible to increase those armaments. That, in my opinion, would be tantamount to renewing the German signature to the Disarmament clauses of the Treaty of Versailles.
>
> I beg of you, Gentlemen, to renounce any such illusions.[1]

The delegate of Bulgaria, another disarmed power, moved that the matter be postponed until the general conference. The Bulgarian motion was lost by a vote of five to twelve, the affirmative votes being cast by Germany, Russia, Bulgaria, Turkey, and Italy. The Anglo-French proposal was then carried by a vote of fourteen to nothing, the five above-mentioned nations abstaining. Mr. Gibson, in supporting the Anglo-French plan pointed out that he was merely seeking a reaffirmation of the obligations under the Washington and London naval treaties and that his vote had no connection with the question of the peace treaties.

The issue raised by the French amendment regarding the previous disarmament treaties is of paramount importance and may easily wreck the final conference. It is impossible to conceive of a permanent continuance of the present system of a heavily armed French *entente* in Europe and an unarmed group of defeated countries. If the coming conference seeks to continue armaments at existing levels and at the same time to bind the disarmed countries permanently to the restrictions of the peace

[1] *Minutes of the Sixth Session (Second Part)*, p. 262.

treaties it will be attempting the impossible. For these reasons Count Bernstorff at the final meeting of the sixth session, in surveying the tentative convention drawn up by the commission, stated that "the German Government must reject the draft, which, in its opinion, is full of the most serious and fundamental defects and omissions."[1]

The Limitation of Budgets.—Limitation of military budgets has been frequently suggested as the simplest and easiest method of preventing arms competition. The restriction of expenditures for both armies and navies was proposed by Russia at the First Hague Conference. Before the war a plan was discussed at meetings of the Inter-Parliamentary Union for disarmament founded on the sole principle of the reduction of the total military budgets of the contracting states.[2] Following the war the Assembly of the League of Nations has considered a similar plan.

During the sessions of the P.C. the French delegation energetically and consistently moved for budgetary limitation as an auxiliary method of arms reduction, and to this movement the Continental Allies have given their solid support. Perhaps a reason for this can be found in the fact that the defeated powers are severely limited both as to numbers of men and as to war materials but their budgets are unrestricted. By spending a large amount of money upon a small number of men it is possible under modern mechanized and chemicalized methods of warfare for a numerically weak army to become highly effective. Budgetary limitation would cut the Central Powers off from their one remaining chance of attaining military strength.

---

[1] *Ibid.*, p. 409.
[2] BAKER, P. J. NOEL: *Disarmament*, p. 66, The Hogarth Press, London, 1926.

The World Conference

Furthermore, the Continental Allies have the system of compulsory military service by which their citizens are conscripted at comparatively small rates of pay. On a given budget they can provide a more powerful military force than can other countries with voluntary enlistments and higher rates of pay. This reason is not all-impelling, for some states with the draft system have at times opposed budgetary limitation. But the matter of conscription is a factor which helps to explain why the restriction of expenditures was so enthusiastically embraced by the French group.

Some of the arguments which have been made before the P.C. in favor of budgetary limitation are as follows: The restriction of expenditures would reduce the burden of the taxpayer and would produce favorable psychological effects upon the masses, thus giving encouragement to the work of reconstruction. The world is confronted by the possibility of huge outlays of money because of the expensive mechanization of warfare. The richer a country becomes, the more it tends to spend for military preparation and, therefore, the more it prepares to bankrupt itself. The restriction of budgets is a supplementary method of reduction which will round out a system of direct armament limitation. It furnishes a device by which non-comparable items in the military establishments of various countries can be mutually limited on an equitable basis.

Particular measures have been advocated for the limitation of expenditures for land material and for naval material. The specific argument for checking the expenditures for land material is that such armaments cannot be directly limited without a system of supervision to see that the agreement is observed. Land material consists of widely scattered rifles, machine guns, field pieces, tanks, armored cars, and stocks of munitions. It would be a matter of guesswork at any time as to whether treaty limitations regarding such weapons were being observed unless there were some method of careful inspection by an international body. Many of the governments are not willing to submit to such inspection, and claim that the only method by which such materials can be limited is by the indirect system of budget restriction. It is alleged that without budgetary limitation, a government can, by expanding its appropriations for material, greatly increase the power and effectiveness of its land forces. French military officers have shown some signs of anxiety in recent years because the Germans, with an army limited to 100,000 men and with their war material directly restricted, have been spending each year sums for army maintenance which are much greater in proportion to the number of troops than they disbursed before the war. For these reasons the advocates of budgetary restriction allege that the system is particularly necessary with relation to land material.

The special motive for placing limits on the expenditures for naval material is that the direct method of limiting the number of tons and the number and caliber of guns has proved to be insufficient. A government which may be restricted in tonnage and guns may nevertheless increase its appropriations to add to the effectiveness of its ships by improving its engines and installing additional costly devices. The modern German armored ships of the type of the *Deutschland* will be considerably more expensive and more powerful than former vessels of the same tonnage. Limited by the Treaty of Versailles to a maximum of 10,000 tons, the Germans nevertheless by careful designing and by raising the cost of such ships to about $20,000,000, have been able to create a most formidable type of war vessel.

The program submitted to Congress in December, 1930, likewise illustrates the rising unit cost of warships. The growing expensiveness and effectiveness of aircraft carriers are particularly interesting features of this program. A 13,800-ton carrier, which in 1928 had been estimated to cost $19,000,000, was included in the 1930 program at $27,650,000. Allowing for the fact that the new figure included $4,000,000 for airplanes, which item was not considered in the 1928 calculation, there has evidently been a substantial increase in the cost of these ships. The effectiveness of the carrier as represented in the new design is in some ways greatly improved. The proportionate numbers of men and planes are much larger than on existing carriers. The present carriers *Lexington* and *Saratoga* are 33,000-ton ships, and at the time of their construction they were considered enormously expensive, costing about $45,000,000 apiece. Each has a complement of 106 planes and 1,934 men of whom 158 are officers. The new ship of 13,800 tons will carry 80 planes and 1,434 men of whom 151 will be officers. Allowing for the fact that the *Lexington* and *Saratoga* were not originally designed to be carriers but were begun as battle cruisers, it is still clear that in this important class of warship the effectiveness and cost per ton are decidedly on the increase. A flying-deck cruiser of 10,000 tons was included in the 1930 program at $20,780,000 and, of this sum, $1,180,000 was represented by the cost of planes. Previous estimates of 10,000-ton cruisers, not of the flying-deck type, had been about $17,000,000. Likewise other cruisers, destroyers, and submarines have shown a decided rise in the cost per ton in recent years.[1] When we consider the requests made to Congress for large appropriations to meet the increased costs of construction it is not strange that the British government has viewed these requests with concern and has become a most decided convert to the budgetary limitation of naval material.

[1] Items regarding costs in the 1930 program are discussed in *Hearing before the House Committee on Naval Affairs on H. R.* 14688, Government Printing Office, Washington, 1931.

The United States and Disarmament

Some of the arguments against general budgetary limitation which have been advanced during the last few years by various delegations to the P.C. are as follows: Costs of armaments differ greatly in different countries and therefore cannot be compared as between nations. Increases in expenditures do not always measure increases in armament. The sending of the fleet into colonial waters, for example, involves an increase in expense but does not add to armaments. Likewise fluctuations in rates of pay and rates of exchange may raise costs without affecting armaments. If budgetary limitation should be adopted, each country would try to take care of these unforeseen contingencies by obtaining for itself a high budget limit. Instead of reduction the result would be an actual rise in expenditures. Furthermore, the military, naval, and air services are in process of change due to increasing mechanization. The nations cannot, therefore, keep in step with military progress if they agree to limit expenditures. Simple publicity of expenditures has at times been declared to be preferable to limitation.

The United States, which possesses the longest purse among the nations, which annually spends the largest sums for armaments, and whose soldiers and sailors are paid at a comparatively high rate has been the strongest opponent of budgetary limitation. At the third session of the P.C. the American delegate, Mr. Gibson, voiced his objections as follows:

> My Government is strongly of the opinion that monetary expenditure for the creation and maintenance of armaments does not afford either a true measure of armaments or a fair basis for the limitation of armaments. It holds this opinion for the following reasons.
>
> First, the direct and indirect costs of personnel under the conscription and voluntary systems are so variable in different countries and in their overseas possessions, and are influenced by so many different factors, that these costs are practically impossible of simple and equitable conversion to a common basis.

The World Conference

Second, due to differences in rates of pay, in production costs, in maintenance charges, in costs of labour and material; due also to varying standards of living and to variations in rates of exchange and to lack of uniformity in the preparation of budgets, any attempt to apply this method of limitation would, in our opinion, be unfair and inequitable.

Third, the method of limitation of expenditure is an indirect method of obtaining a limitation or reduction of armaments. My Government is of the opinion that armaments may be limited effectively by direct methods, and, in consequence, the application of an indirect method seems highly undesirable as a means of accomplishing what might better be accomplished by direct methods.

For these reasons, my Government is firmly of the opinion that any method of limitation of armaments based upon the limitation of budgetary expenditure is impracticable, inequitable and hence inadmissible.[1]

An American objection which was given publicity during the last session of the P.C. is that budgetary limitation would conflict with the constitutional authority of Congress over appropriations.[2] This argument is open to serious question. Similar constitutional protests could be urged against a large number of existing treaties. Thus the Multilateral Treaty for the Renunciation of War could be said to conflict with the power of Congress to declare war, and it might be claimed that the Washington and London naval treaties illegally restrict the power of Congress to provide and maintain a navy. To admit the soundness of such reasoning would be to concede that the Constitution of the United States blocks the participation of this country in any general agreement looking toward peace or, in other words, is a serious obstruction in the path of world progress.

More technically, it is pointed out that the draft convention looks forward to restricting expenditures and not appropriations. Expenditures are made under the supervision of the executive who can, and sometimes does,

[1] *Minutes of the Third Session*, p. 178.
[2] *New York Times*, Nov. 22, 1930.

limit them to sums less than those appropriated. In making expenditures for armaments the President could be guided by the provisions of an international convention except, of course, that he could not exceed Congressional appropriations. Congress could, at the same time, be left free to make whatever appropriations it might desire.

Other objections to budgetary limitation on the part of the United States, but ones which cannot well be aired in public, are that this country does not desire to restrict expenditures at the beginning of what appears to be a period of rapidly expanding naval costs[1] and that this country desires to use its wealth and potential as a diplomatic weapon in any naval disputes that may arise with Great Britain and Japan.

Probably the strongest point raised by the United States against a general system of budgetary limitation at the outset was that the costs in the different countries vary widely and that, accordingly, the amount spent by each government affords no true basis for judging the extent of military preparedness. The argument was, however, rendered inapplicable when the commission decided that the expenditures of different countries were not to be contrasted but that the sums spent by one country were to be compared with those of the same country in previous years. Thus the expenditures of the United States would not be compared with those of France or Great Britain but only with former American figures. This would operate to prevent increases in armament costs, and might bring about reductions. The committee of experts on budgetary questions recommends

[1] For a discussion of budgetary restriction and other points of the draft treaty see the very useful study, WILLIAM T. STONE: "The Draft Treaty for the World Disarmament Conference," Foreign Policy Association, *Information Service*, Vol. VI, No. 25, Feb. 18, 1931. The numerous excellent reports by the Foreign Policy Association on the various phases of disarmament have been a most valuable aid to the public understanding of the question in the United States.

that the average expenditures for the previous four years be taken as the standard of measurement in order to avoid comparison with the requirements of a peak year.[1]

Despite the decision not to contrast budgets as between countries the United States still remains firm in its opposition to the limitation of expenditures. At the last session of the P.C., Mr. Gibson stated that the United States was unlikely to accept a convention which contained this feature. He declared, however, that, if other countries should accept a sufficiently detailed system of budgetary limitation to constitute a real restriction, the United States would be willing to apply to itself a direct limitation of material together with the obligation of full publicity.[2]

Aside from the United States, every government represented at the P.C. came finally to accept budgetary limitation in some form or other. The final ballot on budgetary limitation found only the United States and Japan voting in the negative. Japan had already accepted the plan for land material but objected to it for naval and air material. There is some hope that the Japanese will reconsider their position before the world conference. It may thus occur that the United States will be the only country to stand in the way of the plan, for it is unlikely that all of the other countries will be willing to accept it if the United States is not included. If this contingency should arise, the spirit of compromise, already manifested by the American government, will, it is hoped, lead to an abandonment of our position. For certainly the serious consequences of a failure of the conference would be vastly more detrimental to the

[1] The committee of experts was formed at the last session of the P. C. to work out the details of budgetary limitation. For their report made after the dissolution of the P. C. see League of Nations, Preparatory Commission for the Disarmament Conference, *Report by the Committee of Experts on Budgetary Questions*, Geneva, 1931.

[2] *Minutes of the Sixth Session (Second Part)*, p. 72.

United States than the inconvenience of budgetary limitation.

The draft convention contains a clause providing for a general restriction of total expeditures and also for separate restrictions on expenditures for land material and for naval material[1] because of the rapid development of military aviation. Viscount Cecil argued before the P.C. that a separate limitation upon the expenditures for each of the three branches of the service should be provided for. He argued that if the limitation applied only to the entire defense budget it would be possible to shift funds from land or naval defense into the air service. The whole international situation might be changed if some power would suddenly divert £10,000,000, £20,000,000, or £30,000,000 into military aviation.[2]

The commission refused to include this feature in the draft convention, but agreed to ask the committee of experts on budgetary limitation to examine the possibility of separate restriction for land, sea, and air forces. The budgetary experts, after the final adjournment of the P.C., drew up a plan for the limitation of expenditures. They declared that separate restriction could be set up for the land, sea, and air forces and that expenditures in each of the three branches could be limited according to the following four classifications: (1) effectives, (2) transport, (3) buildings, and (4) war materials. From this recommendation it appears that the question of the separate limitation of budgets for aviation will come before the world conference.[3]

Publicity.—To the uninformed novice it would seem to be an easy matter for nations which sincerely desire

[1] For a copy of the convention see League of Nations, Preparatory Commission for the Disarmament Conference, *Draft Convention*, and Annex 20 of Preparatory Commission, *Minutes of the Sixth Session (Second Part)*, p. 597. For a summary of the convention see Appendix III.

[2] *Minutes of the Sixth Session (Second Part)*, p. 203.

[3] *Report by the Committee of Experts on Budgetary Questions.*

THE WORLD CONFERENCE

a reduction of the military establishment to agree at least to the principle of full publicity regarding their armaments. In fact, all members of the League of Nations are already pledged to such publicity. The closing paragraph of Article VIII of the Covenant binds the members to exchange "full and frank information as to the scale of their armaments, their military, naval and air programs and the condition of such of their industries as are adaptable to warlike purposes." The Secretariat of the League gathers statistics in accordance with this clause and publishes the annual *Armaments Year Book* which is mentioned in the previous chapter.

Full information has not, however, been submitted to the Secretariat by the various governments. Thus the figures for land material have been quite incomplete. Reports on such equipment as rifles, machine-guns, and tanks in service are rarely given and statistics regarding stocks in reserve have not been given at all.[1] It is with regard to land material that the warmest contest over publicity has waged in the P.C., for here the friends of disarmament have attempted to draw back the veil of secrecy hiding the elaborate equipment in possession of the great conscript armies and also to expose the immense stocks that are kept ready to arm at a moment's notice the mammoth trained reserves of the Continental Allies.

At the third session of the P.C., M. Rutgers of the Dutch delegation proposed that full information according to a well-classified schedule should be submitted for land material both in service and in reserve.[2] The Japanese delegate, M. Sato, objected that "secrecy must be maintained in the case of measures taken with a view to a defensive war." The French delegate, Count Clauzel, felt that the Dutch plan would require international supervision, which made it unacceptable to him. Italy

[1] STONE: *loc. cit.*, p. 482.
[2] *Minutes of the Third Session*, p. 302.

and Yugoslavia likewise indicated that they could not agree with the Dutch proposal.

At the second part of the Sixth Session the plan was again brought before the commission and was definitely rejected. Instead the commission inserted in the final draft a clause requiring that publicity should be given to *expenditures* for the upkeep, purchase, and manufacture of material for the land and sea forces. Such statistics of expenditure will not, however, reveal the exact details of equipment nor will they show existing stocks.[1] They will not apply to air material.

There are many other items concerning which the draft treaty provides for exchange of information. The parties are to send to the Secretary-general of the League annual statistics regarding the number of men in the armed forces and formations organized on a military basis; the number of youths who have compulsorily received preparatory military training; the number of days' service required of conscripts in the different periods of training and reserve; statistics concerning war vessels laid down and completed; the names and tonnage of any merchant ships whose decks have been stiffened for the mounting of guns;[2] the number and total horsepower of military aircraft and also the total volume in the case of dirigibles; the number and total horsepower of civil aircraft; the sums expended by the government and local authorities on civil aviation; and, finally, the total annual expenditures on land, sea, and air armaments.[3]

The United States has warmly favored the general principle of publicity. At the last session of the P.C., Mr. Gibson stated:

We consider that full and frank exchange of information and publicity are essential to the success of any Treaty—that they are essen-

[1] STONE: *loc. cit.*, p. 482.
[2] The maximum caliber of such guns is to be fixed at 6.1 inches, Draft Convention, Article 19.
[3] Draft Convention, Part IV.

THE WORLD CONFERENCE

tial to the building up of that common confidence and goodwill without which no treaty will constitute a great forward step.

When, however, the French group advocated publicity for civil aviation, Mr. Gibson felt that the commission was getting on "dangerous ground." He was willing that the United States should give full information regarding such matters but contended that a treaty for the limitation of arms and materials of war should not concern itself with civil aviation or any form of war potential. He felt that this information should be dealt with outside the treaty.[1]

International Supervision.—In order to put into operation a practical plan for limiting or reducing armaments some method of supervision must be agreed to. It is impossible to expect that a thoroughgoing convention which touches national policies at so many points and which comes into direct conflict with militaristic interests in every country would be fully and conscientiously carried out by the parties without some form of administrative or judicial machinery. The system of enforcement may provide for international inspection or it may set up an investigatory tribunal which will act only upon the complaints and accusations which are certain to arise regarding alleged violations of the convention. There are, however, strong objections which have been urged against supervision. In the first place most governments are reluctant to submit for international investigation such matters as the state of their armaments which have heretofore been regarded as strictly domestic affairs of an inviolable character. In the second place, any system of supervision can hardly ignore the League of Nations which has become so identified with the idea of world organization that many nations are unable to think of international action disassociated from the League. But certain other governments are exceedingly wary of

[1] *Minutes of the Sixth Session (Second Part)*, p. 232.

the League. The United States, because of isolationist reasons, is particularly shy of League associations. Soviet Russia also opposes such coöperation for she regards the League as something in the nature of a conspiracy of capitalist nations to control the world.

Until the last session of the P.C., the United States had repeatedly voiced its opposition to international control. In the proceedings of Subcommission A, the American representatives joined with Great Britain, Chile, Italy, Japan, and Sweden in declaring that any form of supervision or control of armaments by an international body would be more calculated to foment ill will and suspicion than to foster confidence. Belgium, Czechoslovakia, Finland, France, the Netherlands, Poland, Rumania, and Yugoslavia, on the other hand, favored a commission which would work in coöperation with the Secretariat of the League in issuing reports regarding the application of a disarmament convention.

The French delegation in the third session of the P.C. proposed a Permanent Disarmament Commission which in its composition was to be connected with the League. The commission was to consist of (1) those members of the League Council which should sign the treaty; (2) the United States and Russia, and (3) other nations to be selected by the disarmament conference. The commission would be set up at the seat of the League and would be summoned by the Secretary General. Its functions would be to study the data submitted by the parties to the disarmament convention and to make reports as to the progress of disarmament.

In the Third Session, Mr. Gibson set forth the attitude of the United States as unmistakably opposed to a commission under the League and also to any form of international supervision. He said:

During the general discussion it was clearly the obvious conviction of many delegations that the solution of the armaments problem

THE WORLD CONFERENCE

can best be found through utilising in full measure the machinery and authority of the League of Nations. My Government, however, is deeply and genuinely sensible of the friendliness and good will which was shown throughout the general discussion in an effort to deal in a practical manner with the problem created by the fact that the United States is not a Member of the League of Nations. As was brought out in the discussion, this fact constitutes a difficult problem. I am confident, however, that if it cannot be it will be through no lack of careful study and good will. There are other Governments which are not Members of the League, but the American Government is the only one of them which is represented here [1927]. The fact that my Goverment is not a Member imposes certain very definite limitations as to the undertakings which it is in a position to give in connection with a convention of this sort. In the course of the discussions in the Preparatory Commission and its Sub-Commissions, it has repeatedly been made clear that any Convention, in order to be acceptable to my Government, must take full account of the fact that it cannot accept the jurisdiction of the League, and, further, that it is not in a position to subscribe to international agreements based on supervision and control.[1]

He indicated, however, that if the other governments insisted upon international control and were willing to apply it to themselves while eliminating it for the United States, the American government would make no objection.

In the first part of the sixth session, the French delegate, M. Massigli, took note of the difference between the apparently opposite points of view. He therefore announced that the French government was willing to submit a compromise plan of "certain simpler and more general proposals."

In the final part of the sixth session, accordingly, a modified plan for a Permanent Disarmament Commission was drawn up which happily proved to be acceptable to the United States. In providing for the constitution of the new commission the plan does not mention the League of Nations but states the membership shall consist of x members (the number to be fixed by the con-

[1] *Minutes of the Third Session*, p. 273.

ference) which members are to be appointed by the governments . . . (the list of states to be drawn up by the conference). The members are to be individuals which do not represent their governments.

The commission in its operations is to have some connections with the League. It is to be set up at the seat of the League. It shall be summoned for its first meeting by the Secretary General of the League. The powers of the commission are to receive the information which the signatories are to supply to the Secretary General of the League. It shall make one report per year. In case a party to the treaty complains that another party is exceeding its fixed quota of armaments or is in any other way violating the convention, the matter may through the Secretary General be laid before the commission. After a hearing the commission may report on the matter to the parties to the convention and to the Council of the League. Only in case the parties in the dispute are members of the League will the Council take action.[1]

Thus, while the Permanent Disarmament Commission will in some respects take advantage of the assistance of the League Secretariat, yet the membership of the commission is not to be fixed by membership in the League and has nominally nothing to do with it. Furthermore, a non-member of the League is not to be brought under the jurisdiction of the League Council. These may not be important deviations from the French plan of the third session. But changes in language are very important in dealing with questions which are affected by traditional prejudices. Altogether the decision of the United States to concur in the plan for the commission has substantially added to the prospects for the success of the conference and indicates that the American aversion to contact with the League is gradually giving way before the necessities of world affairs and the practical demands of the peace movement.

[1] Draft Convention, Part VI, Chapter A.

Chapter XVI

LIMITATION OF PERSONNEL AND MATERIAL

Land Effectives (Numbers of Men).—The huge armies still maintained by the victorious Allies of the World War must be counted as among the most serious obstacles to the advancement and recovery of Europe. The dizzy state of unbalance of European armed forces has an all-pervading effect upon Continental psychology, creating a condition of nervousness which may some day lead to another rampage of madmen and the overthrow of the political structure of Europe. The armament question in Europe is, to a large extent, the question of the size of armies. For this reason it may be predicted that one of the severest tests of the disarmament movement at the world conference will be presented by the proposition for reducing land effectives.[1]

From the standpoint of land forces the Continental nations can be divided into three main groups. First, there are France and her allies, which are Belgium, Czechoslovakia, Poland, Rumania, and Yugoslavia. Whether Italy can be counted on to adhere to this group is an open question which has been previously referred to. All of these nations are heavily overarmed. Following their victory in the World War, they imposed upon their enemies a crushing peace which cannot be supported except by force, and for this reason the victors now fear to carry out their own pledges to reduce armaments.

The second group is that of the defeated Central Powers, and consists of Germany, Austria, Hungary, and

[1] For a good review of the situation regarding land forces see WOODWARD: "Limitation of Land Armaments," Foreign Policy Association, *Information Service*, Vol. VI, No. 2, Apr. 2, 1930.

Bulgaria. Drastically reduced in armaments by the peace treaties these nations constitute a military vacuum surrounded by crowding armed forces. It is impossible to believe that such a condition will permit of permanent equilibrium and peace.

The third factor in the European situation is Russia with her changing economic and military status. The sympathies of Russia are with the defeated central powers and her most fundamental clashes in armament policy have come with the French bloc, although the most dramatic single conflict was with the British Conservative government represented in the person of Lord Cushendun. For the purpose of strengthening her own security and particularly because of what she considers to be the menace of large armies in capitalistic countries, Russia joins with the defeated powers in asking for a drastic reduction in armaments.

The great discrepancy in military strength between the victorious Allies and the defeated powers as seen in the table on page 283 is one of the factors which makes the future of Europe a matter of uncertainty. The reduction of these unbalanced land armaments to a reasonable and stable footing is a principal aim of the disarmament movement. For this purpose the draft convention provides skeleton tables with blank spaces to be filled in at the conference in order to fix in each country the maximum strength of land forces and land formations organized upon a military basis.

If the final treaty contains only an agreement not to increase present forces it will be utterly unsatisfactory to the German group. Substantial reduction is necessary for the achievement of real success at the conference. There would seem to be three possible ways of reduction: a simple percentage reduction which would bear with the same proportion upon all countries; a graduated percentage reduction, similar to the second Russian proposal,

Limitation of Personnel and Material

Armies of Rival European Powers

Country	Population	Effectives	Reserves
The French Bloc:			
France....................	41,020,000	522,737	5,676,000
Poland....................	30,408,000	265,871	1,974,000
Rumania...................	17,694,000	186,143	1,671,000
Czechoslovakia..............	14,535,000	130,134	1,489,000
Yugoslavia.................	13,290,000	110,445	1,240,000
Belgium....................	7,996,000	67,086	495,000
Total....................	124,943,000	1,282,416	12,545,000
Italy.......................	41,169,000	360,505	5,695,000
The Defeated Powers:			
Germany...................	63,319,000	99,191	
Austria....................	6,687,000	20,930	165,000
Hungary...................	8,604,000	35,033	
Bulgaria...................	5,707,000	19,956	
Total....................	84,317,000	175,110	165,000
Russia.....................	153,956,000	562,000	4,528,000

Estimates of the numbers of troops vary widely. The above figures are taken from *Armaments Year Book*, 1929–1930, except the number of reserves which are taken from the *World Almanac*, 1931. With regard to the number of reserves which can actually be used during the early weeks of a war, see note 1 on p. 285.

which would reduce the more strongly armed countries by a greater coefficient than the weaker countries; and an arbitrary system which would arrive at the strength of the different countries by a process of bargaining depending upon political strength, finesse in conference diplomacy, and the uncertain currents of emotion which happen to be moving through Europe at the time. This latter process would pretend to proceed from fixed principles, such as relation to population, frontiers, etc., but in the last analysis it would be a matter of bargaining.

Trained Reserves.—The trained reserves are made up of those individuals who, having passed through a term of active military service have retired to private life. They are under obligation to be called back to the colors in times of need. The question of counting reservists in determining military strength for purposes of reduction has been a cause of dispute from the first technical discussions in Subcommission A to the present time.[1] The victorious Allies, fearful of their defeated opponents and seeking to protect themselves by large citizen armies, combined in the subcommission to declare that reserves must not be counted. France, Italy, Belgium, Poland, Czechoslovakia, Rumania, and Yugoslavia were united in this stand. These countries have given instruction in the art of warfare to millions of their people who stand ready at a moment's notice to take their places in vast conscript armies, the skeleton organization and *cadres* of which are already prepared. The representatives of these countries have pointed out that reserves are not to be mobilized until after war has begun. This fact, they have claimed, proves that they are not an offensive weapon, but a shield for defense. As M. Sokal of Poland put the argument in the third session of the P.C., reserves "are necessary for the maintenance of our independence, and we cannot accept a Convention providing for their limitation."[2] If this is true, however, the defeated countries which cannot build up trained reserves are deprived of an instrument which is necessary to the maintenance of their independence. They cannot be expected to feel happy in this situation.

Germany has been the foremost advocate of the limitation of trained reserves. Her civilian soldiers are gradually being eliminated as the generation of the World War slowly passes out of the age of military service. It is impossible for the Reich to instruct new reserves because

[1] For the position of the technical experts see League of Nations, Preparatory Commission for the Disarmament Conference, *Report of Subcommission A*, Geneva, 1926.

[2] *Minutes of the Third Session*, p. 65.

LIMITATION OF PERSONNEL AND MATERIAL

of the requirement of the Versailles Treaty that enlistments in the army must be for a term of twelve consecutive years. The German delegation has, therefore, demanded that the reserves be limited and to achieve this has proposed that the size of the annual contingents shall be cut down. Other countries which are weak from a military standpoint, as Finland, the Netherlands, Spain, and Sweden have, in the past, taken a similar position. The United States and Great Britain, which have traditional objections to conscription, have been counted on the side of reserve limitation. Likewise Russia, viewing the 18,000,000 reservists of the French bloc (including Italy) has contended that reserves should be limited.

In supporting the British proposal for the limitation of reserves at the third session of the P.C., Mr. Gibson, the American delegate, called attention to the great importance of reservists. He alleged that in a number of countries they constitute the bulk of the fighting strength, in some instances ranging as high as 90 per cent of the military establishment.[1] It seemed unfair to him that these forces should be left outside of the restrictions of the disarmament convention.

At the sixth session in 1929, during a time of compromise when it was believed that Great Britain had yielded to the French view in this matter, Mr. Gibson announced that the United States would withdraw its insistence upon the limitation of trained reserves. He said:

> I am able to declare that the United States Government, as a practical matter, is disposed to defer to the views of the majority of those countries whose land forces constitute their chief military interest, and in the draft Convention before us to accept their ideas in the matter of trained reserves.[2]

[1] Of course, no such high percentage of reserves could be made immediately available on the outbreak of war. Military experts have estimated on the basis of World War experience that in the first weeks of mobilization the armies can be expanded to about $2\frac{1}{2}$ or $2\frac{3}{4}$ times the number of troops maintained in times of peace. BAKER: *Disarmament*, p. 77.

[2] *Minutes of the Sixth Session (First Part)*, p. 114.

The United States and Disarmament

This statement, taken together with the concession on the limitation of ships by categories and with the yardstick principle of naval limitation which came at about the same time and within a few weeks of Mr. Hoover's accession to the Presidency, was doubtless a result of the new President's interest in the reduction of armaments. These concessions were generally regarded as showing that admirable spirit of compromise which is so necessary to any progress in international legislation. The compromise on reserves, however, had the effect of moving the United States substantially nearer to the position of the French bloc and away from that of Germany and her associates.

Great Britain, in the negotiation of the ill-fated naval agreement with France in 1928, intimated that her insistence upon the limitation of reserves would be withdrawn. Later, at the sixth session in 1929, Lord Cushendun announced in behalf of the Baldwin government that Great Britain was willing to yield in the matter of reserves. The Labor party on returning to power in 1929 gave evidence of some dissatisfaction with this concession to the French view. In the latter part of the sixth session (1930) Viscount Cecil announced that he favored a proposal of Germany to limit the number of annual conscripts, but he abstained from voting as did Mr. Gibson when the matter was put to a ballot.

Despite the protests of Germany and Russia, the draft convention has no provision for the restriction of the number of reserves and does not limit the size of the annual contingent. It does contain a provision by which limits on the length of conscript service may be written into the treaty for each country, and also a provision for a maximum length of service which will be binding upon all countries. It is predicted, however, that such a clause is not likely to affect the present situation as a maximum limit will likely be placed sufficiently high to legalize the existing terms of service in the various countries.

LIMITATION OF PERSONNEL AND MATERIAL

Indirectly, the present draft may result in the limitation of reserves. If the numbers of effectives in active service are reduced the result will necessarily be that smaller annual contingents will be called. This might be compensated for, should the nations unexpectedly agree to do so, by reducing the term of active service and thus permitting a larger number of men to pass through the training period. A shortening of the term would, however, reduce the quality of reserves. It may thus result that a reduction in the number of military effectives will cut down either the quantity or the quality of the trained reserves.

Land Material.—In an age of mechanized warfare, weapons have become increasingly important in comparison with personnel. As has been stated, the First Hague Conference was called by the Czar because the rapid growth of industrialized militarism was robbing him of the advantage of the numbers of men enrolled in his vast Slav armies. This development has continued since the war. Artillery, machine guns, tanks, airplanes and chemical equipment multiply the destructive powers of a given number of men. As Count Bernstorff stated in the third session of the P.C.:

> The technique of modern weapons increases the fighting power of a man. The fighting power of a machine-gunner represents many times that of a man handling a single rifle. A heavy gun has a greater range and greater destructive power than a light field-gun, although the number of men serving them may be the same. A tank manned by a few men can go through and destroy whole battalions which are not armed with anti-tank weapons. It follows that a reduction in effectives can be compensated to a very large extent by material factors. Accordingly, a system of disarmament which only covered effectives without at the same time covering material would not be worthy of the name of disarmament.[1]

In the preparation of the draft convention in the P.C. the conflict over the direct limitation of land material

[1] *Minutes of the Third Session*, p. 213.

has, in the main, followed the general lines of opposition between the French bloc and the German-Russian combination. The Treaty of Versailles sets forth definite tables of limitation of German material in service and in reserve. Accordingly, Germany has a strong motive for applying similar restrictions to the armaments of her neighbors. The countries of the French bloc are, however, decidedly opposed to the direct limitation of such material. They possess large trained reserves which would be of little use without adequate stocks of material. Japan, also possessing compulsory military service, has joined these countries in opposing direct limitation. Italy, however, finally voted for direct limitation of land material at the second part of the sixth session, probably for the same political reasons which cause her to adhere to the German-Russian group on a number of points.

Some of the various objections to the direct limitation of land material as brought out in the debates of the P.C. have been as follows: Such a plan could not be enforced without a system of international inspection which would be highly objectionable. Countries without resources and with no war industries would be at a disadvantage as compared with strong industrialized nations unless they could maintain large reserve stocks of war materials. Limitation of reserve materials might compel the poorer countries to create war industries to supply the materials in case of need. No accurate standards of materials can be established during times of rapidly changing methods of warfare.

In the sixth session of the P.C. the Russian delegate, M. Litvinoff, proposed schedules for direct limitation[1] which were accepted by Count Bernstorff in lieu of a plan previously placed before the commission by Germany. The Russian schedules aimed to limit land materials according to the following classifications:

[1] *Minutes of the Sixth Session (First Part)*, p. 161.

LIMITATION OF PERSONNEL AND MATERIAL

1. Rifles, carbines, and pistols
    a. Automatic
    b. Non-automatic
2. Machine guns
    a. Heavy
    b. Light
3. Artillery
    a. Light field guns
    b. Heavy field guns (not more than 107 mm. and howitzers up to 155 mm.)
    c. Heavy, of a caliber up to 204 mm.
    d. Heavy, of a caliber above 204 mm.
    e. Very long range of all calibers
    f. Mortars of all kinds
    g. Guns accompanying infantry
        aa. Guns and howitzers
        bb. Mine-throwers, grenade-throwers, and bomb-throwers
4. Tanks
5. Armored cars
6. Grenades, hand and rifle
7. *Armes blanches*

The plan of direct limitation was rejected by the commission and instead the provision for budgetary limitation of land materials mentioned in the previous chapter was included in the draft convention. The draft provides that the expenditures of each party for the upkeep, purchase, and manufacture of land materials are to be limited according to figures to be decided upon at the conference. This provision, if adopted, will not affect the large stocks of materials now in existence. It is, however, practically certain that the question of the direct limitation of land materials will be reopened by Germany and Russia in the world conference.

The position of the United States with regard to land materials has shifted. Originally the American delegation stood for direct limitation. This conviction was not strongly held and in the first part of the sixth session Mr. Gibson declared that the United States was willing to defer to the desires of the majority of powers whose defense is primarily military,[1] meaning France and her allies. In the final session, the United States voted with the minority for direct limitation of land armaments[2] but abstained from voting on the successful proposal for budgetary limitation.

Naval Effectives.—The question as to whether the numbers of men in the various navies should be limited was the subject of considerable debate in the P.C. The stronger naval powers, the United States, Great Britain, and Japan, favored only the limitation of naval material, *i.e.*, ships and guns. In this they were joined by Argentina and Chile. They argued that the limitation of ships, and hence of accommodations aboardship, would automatically limit the number of men who could be employed. In the third session Mr. Gibson made the point that if a ship is sunk and the crew saved, the seamen are of no combatant value until another ship is procured. Accordingly, he contended, the restriction of material places a limit upon the personnel.

The Continental states felt that this argument was not convincing. They argued that a large and well-trained naval force might be of value without naval material. The sailors could, for example, be used to supplement the land forces in the form of landing parties and expeditionary forces. Thus the land forces would have an unexpected strength not shown in the tables of land effectives.

Eventually the United States and Great Britain modified their position to accept the principle of the limitation of naval effectives with the understanding that such restriction was to be generally accepted and also that a satisfactory agreement should be reached respecting warships. The draft treaty contains a table in which is to

[1] *Ibid.*, p. 162.
[2] *Minutes of the Sixth Session (Second Part)*, p. 108.

LIMITATION OF PERSONNEL AND MATERIAL

be inserted the maximum number of effectives for the sea forces of the naval powers.

Naval Material: The Separability of Naval Material from the General Disarmament Problem.—The United States has shown special interest in that part of the commission's discussions which has dealt with naval armaments. This country has frequently joined with Great Britain and Japan in expressing views which have been designated as the contentions of the greater naval powers and which have differed from the theories of the Continental states. The three larger naval powers have been inclined to seek quick results in settling their own rivalries by dealing directly and separately with the problem of naval material. The pressing need for immediate action has been brought home each year by the urgent problem of naval appropriations. Furthermore, the race in warship construction has been a continually moving matter which has constantly given rise to dangerous situations. Attention to this bitter competition could hardly have been postponed until the slow routine of the League had been able to effect a general world reduction in all kinds of armaments. These are the considerations which have moved the three larger naval powers to deal directly and separately with the problem of naval material and, as has been shown, a great deal of progress has been made by the direct method in the Washington, Geneva, and London Conferences.

On the other hand the countries of Continental Europe have viewed naval armaments as only one phase of the larger problem. They have been constantly confronted with the possibilities of a war which would be waged simultaneously by land, water, and air. Each of the three major branches of the service has seemed to them, therefore, to be an integral part of the whole which could not be detached for separate treatment.

In Subcommission A, the entire French bloc, including Italy, combined to declare: "Any method which arbitrarily separated the three categories of armaments on the combination of which the security of a country depends would be going beyond the degree of simplification which can be accepted."[1] The following year France and Italy refused to participate in the Geneva Conference called by President Coolidge for the separate treatment of naval material. Both of these nations were represented at the London Conference of 1930, however, and since then the two have dealt directly with one another in long and arduous negotiations concerning the naval problem. Nevertheless, they still maintain the inseparability of the three branches of the service and look upon the direct naval negotiations as preliminary efforts to clear the way for the main settlement which is expected to come in the world conference.

The Category and Global Dispute.—One of the most persistent conflicts regarding the method of restricting naval material has arisen over the question as to whether limitation shall be by the category or global method. Limitation by the global method means fixing a total tonnage figure for each navy and permitting each power to build the kinds of ships which it may desire within the limits assigned to it. Limitation by categories means that certain well-defined categories or classes of ships (capital ships, cruisers, destroyers, etc.) shall be established and that the tonnage of each power shall be fixed for each category. The Continental states have preferred the former method and the three larger naval powers joined by Argentina and Chile have preferred the latter.

The case for the global method was presented before Subcommission A and the various sessions of the P.C. by Belgium, Finland, France, Italy, the Netherlands, Poland, Rumania, Spain, Sweden, and Yugoslavia.

[1] *Report of Subcommission A*, p. 26.

LIMITATION OF PERSONNEL AND MATERIAL

These countries have not been willing to compete with the three larger naval powers in the building of big ships. Specialization in such craft as submarines will, according to their naval strategists, offset to a considerable extent the capital-ship superiority of the larger naval powers. The Continental countries have, therefore, contended that each nation should be permitted to arrange its tonnage to fit its own needs and that this can best be done by the flexible global method. So whole-heartedly did their experts hold to this view in the naval subcommittee of Subcommission A that they concurred in a most remarkable vote to the effect that it is not possible to create classes of ships even roughly so as to "convey to a technical mind the distinction between them."[1]

The advocates of the category method claimed that the global tonnage limitation would place no restriction upon the number of ships, and that numbers of ships are important in determining the strength of navies. Simple global limitation would keep the door open for sudden shifts in the character of navies, for under such a system one or more categories could be abandoned and the tonnage concentrated in the construction of a particular type of ship. Limitation by categories has appealed to the larger naval powers as offering greater security by prohibiting quick changes of this sort. Great Britain has been particularly interested in maintaining the naval *status quo*. In the third session, Lord Cecil stressed the British desire for static security and emphasized that sea-borne commerce is the lifeblood of Great Britain. "My country," he said, "cannot afford to run the risk of a sudden development of even, it may be, not a very powerful navy, a sudden development directed entirely at this vulnerable spot in our system."[2]

[1] *Ibid*, p. 53.
[2] *Minutes of the Third Session*, p. 173.

In the third session of the P. C., M. Paul-Boncour, representing France, offered a compromise to the effect that fleets should be limited by total tonnage and also according to four defined classes. Each power would be permitted to alter the division of its tonnage from class to class subject to the requirement that it should inform the Secretariat of the League at least one year before laying down the portion of the tonnage to be transferred.[1] This suggestion was evidently accompanied by informal intimations that the increases in any category would be limited to a certain percentage of that category. In the first part of the sixth session, Mr. Gibson agreed to accept this proposal as the basis for discussion. The compromise was incorporated to a limited extent in Article XVII of the London Naval Treaty which provides that concerning the United States, Great Britain, and Japan a transfer can be made as between cruisers of sub-category *b* and destroyers up to 10 per cent of the permissible tonnage of the category or sub-category into which the transfer is to be made.

In the draft convention the compromise method is provided for with rather striking modifications to suit the smaller naval powers. The parties are to agree to limit their global tonnage according to figures to be inserted in Table I annexed to the chapter. In Table II they are to indicate how they intend to distribute this tonnage among the main classes of warships, *i.e.*, capital ships, aircraft carriers, cruisers of sub-category *a*, cruisers of sub-category *b*, destroyers, and submarines. Transfers are to be allowed from this distribution, however, up to certain maximum figures to be inserted in Table III. Rules are included for working out the amount of transfers thus permitted. The lesser naval powers whose total tonnage does not exceed a certain amount, 100,000 tons being inserted as a suggestion, will have full freedom

[1] *Ibid.*, p. 225.

LIMITATION OF PERSONNEL AND MATERIAL

of transfer in surface ships. As regards other naval powers, the amount of transfers to be permitted is to vary in inverse ratio to the amount of the total tonnage of each.[1] Doubtless this part of the treaty will call for much further negotiation at the conference.

Maximum Specifications of Warships.—One part of the draft convention which has special interest for the United States is that which deals with the maximum tonnage of capital ships. The Washington Treaty restricts such ships to 35,000 tons and the maximum caliber of guns permitted is 16 inches. American naval men take the position that the United States requires large ships for defensive purposes, particularly in the area of the Panama Canal. They also argue that, because of the lack of bases, this country must continue to build huge vessels of long cruising radius. All of the other naval powers are either anxious or willing to reduce the limit on capital ships. At the Geneva and London naval conferences such reductions have been proposed. In the P.C., also, various plans for reduction have been considered. The Soviet delegation asked that the maximum size be placed at 10,000 tons and that the guns be limited to a caliber of 12 inches. At the last session of the P.C. it appeared that the United States was all but isolated in its stand against a radical reduction of capital-ship specifications. Rather than precipitate a conflict which might block the formulation of the draft treaty, the commission inserted the figures of the Washington Treaty, *i.e.*, 35,000 tons and 16-inch guns. The Washington and London figures were likewise followed as to other classes of ships. A note appended to the chapter on naval material, however, states that such figures and dates as appear in this chapter are only given for purposes of illustration. The contest has thus been transferred to the 1932 conference.

[1] Draft Convention, Part II, Chapter B, Table 3.

"As a supplementary method of naval limitation the draft convention provides that the annual expenditures of each party on the upkeep, purchase, and manufacture of war material for naval armaments shall be limited. This question has been considered in the previous chapter.

Air Effectives.—A skeleton table is included in the draft convention for the limitation of the personnel of air armed forces and air formations organized on a military basis. Such a provision, of course, will not affect the numbers of men trained in commercial flying and ground work, and these will constitute a most valuable aviation reserve.

Air Material.—Plans for attack and defense now being developed by general staffs give increasing prominence to the airplane. The growing use of aircraft and anti-aircraft equipment in war problems the world over is evidence of this tendency. The airship has had a conspicuous place in the execution of American maneuvers at the Panama Canal, around the Hawaiian Islands, and in continental coast defense. In Europe the matter of aërial warfare is far more important than it is here. The European city dweller would in case of war be immediately exposed to the danger of destruction by bombardment from aircraft. In a recent address, Arthur Henderson, the British Foreign Secretary, said:

> Every year our air forces carry out maneuvers over London. Have you ever thought what those maneuvers mean? They mean that our staff, like every other staff, is now expecting that the operations of the next war will be air attacks against great centers of industry and civilian populations.[1]

If airplanes are the great menace of future war they also represent a new, vital, and rapidly growing method of operation in both military and civil affairs. An attempt

[1] *New York Times*, Feb. 10, 1931. See also DAVID WOODWARD: "Limitation of Air Armaments," Foreign Policy Association, *Information Service*, Vol. VI, No. 17, p. 297, Oct. 29, 1930.

to abolish the military plane would at present be as futile as the protest against firearms in the waning days of chivalry. The limitation of this arm of the service will likewise be a difficult matter.

Dealing with the problem of air material, the draft convention contains a skeleton table for the limitation of the number and total horsepower of airplanes in commission and in immediate reserve in the land, sea, and air armed forces and formations organized on a military basis. A similar table is included to limit the number, total horsepower, and total volume of dirigibles in commission. Dirigibles in reserve are not mentioned and the phrase "in immediate reserve" as applied to airplanes evidently does not include stocks of unassembled planes. It would, therefore, be possible for the various nations to increase their air material to a very great extent despite such limitations as are contemplated in the draft convention.

A plan for the limitation of expenditures for air material was not included in the convention, but was discussed by a committee of budgetary experts following the dissolution of the P.C. The committee reported favorably upon the practicability of such restriction, and the matter will undoubtedly be considered in the conference.

Civil Aviation.—A special phase of the question of aërial armaments arises in the consideration of civil aviation. The American government has strongly opposed the restriction of this activity in any limitations that may be placed upon air strength. The United States has a rapidly expanding civil aviation industry. The growth of this new enterprise is annually made manifest in the increasing figures of the production of aircraft, aircraft engines and parts, the lengthening of airway mileage, the additions of new municipal and commercial ports, and the increased number of miles flown. The most natural ally of the United States in asking that civil aviation be disregarded in the treaty has been Germany, a country without military strength but with a strong commercial aviation industry. According to recent figures, the United States and Germany lead the world in air transportation. The United States stands in first place in the mileage of air lines, the number of miles flown, and weight of mail carried. Germany stands first in the number of passengers carried and freight transported.[1]

In the third session of the P.C., Mr. Gibson explained why the United States cannot accept a disarmament plan which includes civil aviation. He said:

> My Government does not believe in the efficacy of any method proposed for the reduction or limitation of air armaments which takes into account either the personnel or *matériel* of civil aviation. Any method of limitation or reduction whose application extends beyond dealing with visible and tangible air armaments is not acceptable to my Government.[2]

On the other hand it is well recognized that commercial planes can be used for bombing purposes. They have speed, carrying capacity, and radius of action. "These," says Professor Baker, "are precisely the qualities which a bomber needs."[3] Those countries which stand to suffer from aërial bombardment and those whose aviation industries are not developed have, accordingly, demanded that civil aviation shall be considered in any scheme of general limitation. Belgium, Chile, Czechoslovakia, France, Italy, Poland, Rumania, and Yugoslavia have belonged to this group. The views of these countries were well expressed in the debates of the third session. M. de Brouckère of Belgium, whose countrymen had so often heard the hum of enemy motors above their heads, felt that civil aviation should be included in the general

---

[1] COLEGROVE, KENNETH W.: *International Control of Aviation*, p. 13, World Peace Foundation, Boston, 1930.
[2] *Minutes of the Third Session*, p. 110.
[3] *Disarmament*, p. 220.

LIMITATION OF PERSONNEL AND MATERIAL

scheme of limitation, and he supported his remarks with a story:

> May I remind you of the well-known case of the thin man who was fighting a duel with a fat man, and who, with a laudable desire to be perfectly fair, marked out a circle on the big man's stomach and said: "If I touch you outside this circle, it won't count." Unfortunately it did count, as the fat man felt it.
>
> To suggest a parallel, then: The bombs that destroy our towns, the bombs dropped from civil aircraft, will not count? I should be quite satisfied but that will not prevent them from destroying our houses.[1]

M. Yovanovitch of Yugoslavia explained that his country had no civil aviation industries and no factories for the manufacture of aircraft. Yugoslavia was, therefore, at a great disadvantage as compared with those countries in which reserves of air material and personnel could be built up from the civilian industry. He announced that his government would raise the question whenever the disarmament conference should be convened.

The P.C. in the third session did not provide for any limitation upon civil aviation or that it should be considered in arriving at limitations upon military aviation. It did, however, adopt a plan to prevent the civil industry from being controlled for military ends. This plan was substantially incorporated in the draft convention as ultimately drawn up, and provides:

1. The parties shall not prescribe the embodiment of military features in the construction of civil aircraft or make preparations in time of peace for the installation of warlike armament for the purpose of converting civil aircraft into military aircraft.

2. The parties shall not require civil aviation enterprises to employ personnel specially trained for military purposes.

[1] *Minutes of the Third Session*, pp. 113–114.

3. They shall not subsidize airlines principally established for military ends instead of for economic, administrative, or social purposes.

4. They will undertake to encourage economic agreements between civil aviation in the different countries.

War Potential.—Closely connected with the problems of material and personnel is that of war potential, a term which includes the population and peace-time resources which may be conscripted in time of war for national use. In plans for the wars of the future these human, natural, industrial, commercial, and financial resources are to be used without stint to enlarge and equip the land, sea, and air forces. Nations which are plentifully endowed with war potential or "invisible armaments" and whose standing armies are not relatively large have felt that the peace-time establishment should be left out of account in framing a disarmament convention. The United States, as the world's leading producer of foods, fuels, iron and steel products, chemicals, and other commodities that will feed the war machine in times of conflict, is a natural opponent of the consideration of potential. Great Britain, Germany, Chile, Finland, the Netherlands, Spain, and Sweden have taken the same position. Their view as stated in Subcommission A was that "ultimate war armaments cannot themselves be used for direct comparison since they do not exist in peacetime."[1] In a special declaration the delegation of the United States contended that from twelve to twenty months are necessary for industrial resources to be converted and for mass production of armaments to take place. Only four cannon produced in the United States during the World War reached the front before the armistice, although a period of nineteen months had elapsed after the entry of the United States into the war.[2]

[1] *Report of Subcommission A*, p. 42.
[2] *Ibid.*, p. 20.

LIMITATION OF PERSONNEL AND MATERIAL

The opposing group was made up of Argentina, Belgium, Czechoslovakia, France, Italy, Japan, Poland, Rumania, and Yugoslavia. As can be seen, most of these countries have relatively large armies and relatively small potential. Their contention was that the conduct of modern war requires all the means at a country's disposal. It was, therefore, their view that comparisons should be made of ultimate war armaments as well as those available immediately upon mobilization. Ultimate war armaments, they said, "are in proportion to certain elements of a country's power in time of war which can be found in public documents, such as population, annual output of coal, steel, and petroleum."[1]

The radical differences of views on this subject made it impossible for the P.C. to draft any acceptable provision for considering potential in the matter of disarmament. The subject is not included in the draft convention. But it is certain to be present at the conference as an unseen influence, not directly mentioned, perhaps, but always a factor in the making of decisions, particularly as to the limitation or reduction of land and air material.

Attempts to Humanize War: Aërial Bombardment.—As a plan to limit the destructiveness of modern warfare the German government proposed to prohibit the use of the airplane for bombing purposes. According to this project, weapons of offense of any kind were not to be launched from aircraft.[2] M. Litvinoff, the Russian delegate, whose government and people feel uneasy over the prospect of a combined air attack by capitalist nations, gave the plan his full support. The French representative, M. Massigli, attacked the attempted regulation. A bombing airplane, he said, was like a long-range cannon. It was no more blind and undiscriminating in its slaughter and destruction than a heavy gun fired at a range of 120 to 150

[1] *Ibid.*, p. 42.
[2] *Minutes of the Sixth Session (First Part)*, p. 85.

kilometers. Furthermore, the abolition of the bombing plane would deprive the governments of a legitimate means of defense. Thus it would be impossible to use airplanes to blow up bridges in the path of an invading enemy. Other delegates objected on the ground that the P.C. did not exist for the purpose of codifying the laws of warfare but for limiting the personnel and material of the armed forces. Mr. Wilson, of the American delegation, opposed the plan because it brought up a complicated and endless problem at an inopportune time. The German proposal was accordingly voted down.

The Prohibition of Gas Warfare.—A more acceptable effort to set forth rules of international law regarding the conduct of war was incorporated in Article XXXIX of the draft treaty which deals with chemical and bacteriological warfare. The article reads:

> The High Contracting Parties undertake, subject to reciprocity, to abstain from the use in war of asphyxiating, poisonous or similar gases, and of all analogous liquids, substances or processes.
>
> They undertake unreservedly to abstain from the use of all bacteriological methods of warfare.

This is the third important international attempt to outlaw gas warfare since the World War. A treaty regarding submarine and gas warfare was signed as between the five naval powers at Washington in 1922 but failed because it was not ratified by France. A convention directed against gas and bacteriological warfare was drawn up at the Traffic in Arms Conference at Geneva in 1925 and was signed by forty-five states. It has now gone into effect for some twenty-six ratifying states.[1] The United States signed the 1925 convention but has not ratified it because of the inability to secure the two-thirds approval of the United States Senate. The Senate failed to give its approval after the American Legion and

[1] League of Nations, *"Tables, Diagrams and Graphs Showing the State of Signatures, Ratifications and Accessions Concluded under the Auspices of the League of Nations up to September 1st, 1930*, Geneva, 1930.

some of the chemical industries presented the view that gas warfare is not necessarily inhumane. If the conference of 1932 is successful in agreeing upon a treaty which follows the draft convention in the attempt to abolish chemical and bacteriological warfare, the problem will again be before the Senate.

The plan as adopted does not attempt to prohibit the preparation of material in time of peace for waging gas and bacteriological warfare, and for that reason was criticised by the Soviet delegation at the last meeting of the P.C.[1]

[1] *Minutes of the Sixth Session (Second Part)*, p. 402.

Chapter XVII

CONCLUSION

IN THE turmoil of these changing years there are powerful influences at work for and against the disarmament movement.

The historic spirit of nationalism is asking for the retention of war and its weapons. The adherents to this school subscribe to such conservative philosophy as appears in the quotation at the head of a chapter written by an eminent naval officer:

> The thing that has been, it is that which shall be; and that which is done is that which shall be done; and there is no new thing under the sun.[1]

An outstanding manifestation of nationalistic conflict is the bitter and persistent dispute between Germany and France over the treaty of peace. The Hitler movement which has gained considerable support in the last year demands among other things the abrogation of the Treaty of Versailles, the restoration of the colonies, and the union of all Germans in one Great Germany. The appeal which this program has made to the Teutonic youth creates the expectation that when Germans of a new generation, without personal memory of the war, assume control they will not tolerate peacefully the unequal burdens placed upon the Reich.

In response to this sentiment, the French reply that so long as there is no international police force for the maintenance of order France must not be led into a reduction of armaments below the necessities of her

[1] MAGRUDER: *The United States Navy*, p. 159.

Conclusion

security.[1] And thus we have two nations moving through time along such converging paths as will inevitably bring them into collision unless one or both of them change direction.

It is the doctrine of nationalism in France which most clearly threatens the disarmament movement. Any initiative in reduction must plainly come from the over-armed nations. If, because of the so-called necessities of her security, France refuses to make any substantial reduction, it is difficult to see at this time any hope for the world conference.

The doctrine of security may well be pushed to such an extreme that it will defeat its own purpose. A security which must be based on armaments many times as great as those of the rival country from which an attack is feared can be no real or permanent security at all. The present artificial military predominance of France was established with the aid of powerful allies and did not arise because of any superior strength of the French nation. It can continue for a decade or so by its own momentum; but it cannot be maintained indefinitely in the face of rising economic, social, and political forces in central and eastern Europe. The very fact that France seems to desire such a preponderance of armed power over her defeated enemy is a confession of doubt as to her own intrinsic vigor and ability to defend herself by military methods. National safety as a permanent matter for any country of Europe can be attained only by the creation of confidence and good feeling upon that divided and suspicious Continent. A refusal on the part of France to reduce her armaments would make the establishment of harmony and mutual respect impossible and would therefore undermine the security of France as well as of all other European nations.

[1] See the speech of President Doumergue, *New York Times*, April 9, 1931.

On the other hand, if under the guidance of far-sighted leaders, such as Briand, the French people should be willing to make substantial reductions in their armed forces, they would by this action manifest their faith in the future of the Continent of Europe. Through their leadership the success of the movement for lower armaments could be assured. Such a step would not necessarily be contrary to French policy. The French army, despite its hugeness as compared with neighboring land forces, has been substantially diminished since 1914.[1] The term of enlistment has been shortened from two years to one year, and the number in the standing army has been cut from 947,000 previous to the war to a strength of 523,000 provided for in the budget for 1930. A continuation of the policy of reduction might well appeal to the good sense of the French political leaders, because such an attitude would make possible the success of the world conference and would thereby aid in establishing general security upon the more permanent and healthful basis of mutual confidence.

Despite striking evidences of nationalistic rivalry, the spirit of internationalism has developed great strength in recent years, based on a rational understanding of the wisdom of coöperation. The calmer and more intelligent world leaders are striving sincerely to prevent a mass destruction of populations which, due to the increased facilities for aërial attack, has now become one of the probabilities of war. The movement for peace has gained practical and substantial support from the expanding economic forces of production and distribution which press outward across political boundaries. It is no mere wave of pacific or religious idealism, this crusade. It has the backing of large-scale business answering to the call of the profit motive. The ablest producers and distributors, who represent the more modern developments of

[1] WOODWARD: "Limitation of Land Armaments," p. 24.

Conclusion

industry and commerce, operate for and in an international market. They lead in the protest against the provincialism that sets up economic barriers along political frontiers or that threatens to throw the world into chaos over issues which are handed down from a period of local economy. The pressure of the international financier has in the last decade been applied more than once to compel the modification of the ardent policies of belligerent nationalism. In a large sense a great economic order is struggling to prevent its own destruction.[1]

At a time when the forces working for economic and political internationalism are becoming sufficiently strong to give rise to dreams of future world unity, there appears outside the circle of capitalist nations a rapidly developing economic system of a different character. Such success as has been achieved by the Russian five-year plan has made it possible that the next great rivalry will be not international but inter-systemic, not between states but between systems of production. Already the beginnings of a world-wide commercial conflict are seen in the protests which have arisen in a score of countries over Soviet sales at low prices. Russian leaders believe that their country must acquire productive machinery or perish. Accordingly, in order to obtain the means whereby they can finance the rapid purchase of production goods they have thrown quantities of foodstuffs and raw materials upon the markets of the world. And in the future there looms the possibility of a struggle for markets in manufactured articles as Russian factories come into full production.

All that has been said about the folly of a resort to arms for pseudo-economic reasons applies to this gathering

[1] For a good economic treatment of the difficulties presented by the conflicting forces of world interdependence and nationalism see Ernest Minor Patterson, *The World's Economic Dilemma*, Whittlesey House, McGraw-Hill Book Company, New York, 1930.

struggle. The test of the different systems of production should be applied in the laboratory of peace rather than on the confused and uncertain battlefield of war. The future era of production and distribution under which our grandchildren are to attain a standard of living and culture hardly reached by the most favored classes today must be born through the natural processes of economics rather than by the dangerous Cæsarian obstetrics of revolution. Here is probably the gravest problem that will confront the friends of peace during the next few decades. Disaster can be avoided only if the policies on each side are dictated by rational considerations and not by the bitter reprisals of such sentimentalists as emotional and unrealistic reactionaries, on the one side, or the equally emotional and unrealistic propagandists for the world revolution, on the other.

Despite the uncertainties which becloud the political world, the 1932 conference can open with fair prospects that it is to make a contribution to the movement for the international control of armaments. The Washington and London conferences and the Preparatory Commission in its six sessions have given some indication of the almost unlimited possibilities of the conference method. In the solution of problems of mutual interest among nations this method represents the substitution of intelligent direction for disorganization and chance.

In one decade, from 1921 to 1931, what may be called a legislative system of dealing with armaments has been brought into existence. The whole movement bears unmistakably the marks of progress. It is now definitely understood that the armaments of a nation are a subject which can be properly considered by an international gathering. The American who demands to know why Great Britain should have anything to say about the size of the United States navy and the proud Briton who asks the reverse question have gradually found themselves

Conclusion

to be in a defeated minority. These questions in their very nature are found to be international. The spirit of compromise by which "irreducible" demands are diminished for the purpose of arriving at harmonious agreements is an essential factor of success in the international conference; and in the field of arms limitation it has been proved to exist by a number of splendid mutual concessions and legislative measures some of which may be catalogued as follows:

1. The general compromise between the United States and Great Britain by which this country agreed to forego building programs, which could easily have been carried out, in return for Britain's agreement to relinquish first place and to accept parity in naval material.

2. The special compromise by which Great Britain reduced the number of cruisers in her program from seventy to fifty in return for a limitation of the number of 8-inch gun cruisers in the navy of the United States.

3. The compromise by which Japan agreed to accept a 60 per cent ratio in capital ships and aircraft carriers in return for a *status quo* agreement as to fortifications in the islands of the western Pacific.

4. The reduction of the Japanese demand at London for a full 70 per cent ratio in 8-inch gun cruisers in return for which reduction they received concessions including a ratio of more than 60 per cent in total auxiliary ships.

5. The escalator clause which made it possible for the British government, and consequently the United States and Japan, to sign the London Naval Treaty despite the seemingly insurmountable obstacle of the Franco-Italian dispute.

6. The numerous compromises that have been brought about in the Preparatory Commission of which an outstanding example is that between the advocates of the global and category methods of limiting naval tonnage.

The United States has thus far played a progressive and constructive part in matters of armament limitation and this policy has been strictly in line with our national interests from both the materialistic and idealistic points of view. The stake of the American people in the movement for world harmony is very real and very great. It is true that this country does not face the same dangers from large armaments as do the peoples of Europe whose frontiers may be crossed by rapidly moving armies and whose cities are in danger of destruction by bombs hurled from the air. The United States, however, has a great economic interest in the maintenance of peaceful conditions throughout the world; and the absence of an immediate danger of invasion leaves this country free to approach the problem in a comparatively rational frame of mind.

The commercial and financial stake of the United States in the matter has been pointed out. Mass production in this country has enrolled in its gigantic industries an army of machines with a productive power equivalent to that of several billions of human beings. For every man, woman, and child there are scores of steel slaves working tirelessly and uncomplainingly to produce the greatest output of goods that the world has known. From every corner of the globe come fleets of steamships bearing their cargoes of raw materials to be fed into the hoppers of American industrialism. The flow of manufactured goods passes outward in a steady stream from these factories to every continent.

The United States is at present the most conspicuously successful part of the world integrated system of specialized industry and trade. What this may eventually mean in raised standards of living and cultural advances for the general population is difficult to predict but gratifying to contemplate. Armaments, created to destroy life and wealth, belligerent nationalism which would disturb the peace and bring ruin to this system of production and commerce, are alike threats to the fulfillment of American hopes. As the world conference approaches can there be any doubt of the vital interests of the people of the United States in its successful outcome?

APPENDIX I

THE WASHINGTON NAVAL TREATY OF 1922

TREATY BETWEEN THE UNITED STATES OF AMERICA, THE BRITISH EMPIRE, FRANCE, ITALY AND JAPAN LIMITING NAVAL ARMAMENT

The United States of America, the British Empire, France, Italy and Japan;

Desiring to contribute to the maintenance of the general peace, and to reduce the burdens of competition in armament;

Have resolved, with a view to accomplishing these purposes, to conclude a treaty to limit their respective naval armament, and to that end have appoined as their Plenipotentiaries;

The President of the United States of America:

    Charles Evans Hughes,
    Henry Cabot Lodge,
    Oscar W. Underwood,
    Elihu Root,
        citizens of the United States;

His majesty the King of the United Kingdom of Great Britain and Ireland and of the British Dominions beyond the Seas, Emperor of India:

    The Right Honourable Arthur James Balfour, O. M., M. P., Lord President of His Privy Council;
    The Right Honourable Baron Lee of Fareham, G. B. E., K. C. B., First Lord of His Admiralty;
    The Right Honourable Sir Auckland Campbell Geddes, K. C. B., His Ambassador Extraordinary and Plenipotentiary to the United States of America;

and

  for the Dominion of Canada:
    The Right Honourable Sir Robert Laird Borden, G. C. M. G., K. C.;
  for the Commonwealth of Australia:

The United States and Disarmament

> Senator the Right Honourable George Foster Pearce, Minister for Home and Territories;
>
> for the Dominion of New Zealand:
>
> > The Honourable Sir John William Salmond, K. C., Judge of the Supreme Court of New Zealand;
>
> for the Union of South Africa:
>
> > The Right Honourable Arthur James Balfour, O. M., M. P.;
>
> for India:
>
> > The Right Honourable Valingman Sankaranarayana Srinivasa Sastri, Member of the Indian Council of State;
>
> The President of the French Republic:
>
> > Mr. Albert Sarraut, Deputy, Minister of the Colonies;
> > Mr. Jules J. Jusserand, Ambassador Extraordinary and Plenipotentiary to the United States of America, Grand Cross of the National Order of the Legion of Honour;
>
> His Majesty the King of Italy:
>
> > The Honourable Carlo Schanzer, Senator of the Kingdom;
> > The Honourable Vittorio Rolandi Ricci, Senator of the Kingdom, His Ambassador Extraordinary and Plenipotentiary at Washington;
> > The Honourable Luigi Albertini, Senator of the Kingdom;
>
> His Majesty the Emperor of Japan:
>
> > Baron Tomosaburo Kato, Minister for the Navy, Junii, a member of the First Class of the Imperial Order of the Grand Cordon of the Rising Sun with the Paulownia Flower;
> > Baron Kijuro Shidehara, His Ambassador Extraordinary and Plenipotentiary at Washington, Joshii, a member of the First Class of the Imperial Order of the Rising Sun;
> > Mr. Masanao Hanihara, Vice Minister for Foreign Affairs, Jushii, a member of the Second Class of the Imperial Order of the Rising Sun;
>
> Who, having communicated to each other their respective full powers, found to be in good and due form, have agreed as follows:

Chapter I

General Provisions Relating to the Limitation of Naval Armament

Article I. The Contracting Powers agree to limit their respective naval armament as provided in the present Treaty.

Article II. The Contracting Powers may retain respectively the capital ships which are specified in Chapter II, Part 1. On the coming into force of the present Treaty, but subject to the following provi-

Appendix I

sions of this Article, all other capital ships, built or building, of the United States, the British Empire and Japan shall be disposed of as prescribed in Chapter II, Part 2.

In addition to the capital ships specified in Chapter II, Part 1, the United States may complete and retain two ships of the *West Virginia* class now under construction. On the completion of these two ships the *North Dakota* and *Delaware* shall be disposed of as prescribed in Chapter II, Part 2.

The British Empire may, in accordance with the replacement table in Chapter II, Part 3, construct two new capital ships not exceeding 35,000 tons (35,560 metric tons) standard displacement each. On the completion of the said two ships the *Thunderer, King George V, Ajax* and *Centurion* shall be disposed of as prescribed in Chapter II, Part 2.

Article III. Subject to the provisions of Article II, the Contracting Powers shall abandon their respective capital ship building programs, and no new capital ships shall be constructed or acquired by any of the Contracting Powers except replacement tonnage which may be constructed or acquired as specified in Chapter II, Part 3.

Ships which are replaced in accordance with Chapter II, Part 3, shall be disposed of as prescribed in Part 2 of that Chapter.

Article IV. The total capital ship replacement tonnage of each of the Contracting Powers shall not exceed in standard displacement, for the United States 525,000 tons (533,400 metric tons); for the British Empire 525,000 tons (533,400 metric tons); for France 175,000 tons (177,800 metric tons); for Italy 175,000 tons (177,800 metric tons); for Japan 315,000 tons (320,040 metric tons).

Article V. No capital ship exceeding 35,000 tons (35,560 metric tons) standard displacement shall be acquired by, or constructed by, for, or within the jurisdiction of, any of the Contracting Powers.

Article VI. No capital ship of any of the Contracting Powers shall carry a gun with a calibre in excess of 16 inches (406 millimetres).

Article VII. The total tonnage for aircraft carriers of each of the Contracting Powers shall not exceed in standard displacement, for the United States 135,000 tons (137,160 metric tons); for the British Empire 135,000 tons (137,160 metric tons); for France 60,000 tons (60,960 metric tons); for Italy 60,000 tons (60,960 metric tons); for Japan 81,000 tons (82,296 metric tons).

Article VIII. The replacement of aircraft carriers shall be effected only as prescribed in Chapter II, Part 3, provided, however, that all aircraft carrier tonnage in existence or building on November 12, 1921, shall be considered experimental, and may be replaced, within the total tonnage limit prescribed in Article VII, without regard to its age.

Article IX. No aircraft carrier exceeding 27,000 tons (27,432 metric tons) standard displacement shall be acquired by, or constructed by, for or within the jurisdiction of, any of the Contracting Powers.

However, any of the Contracting Powers may, provided that its total tonnage allowance of aircraft carriers is not thereby exceeded, build not more than two aircraft carriers, each of a tonnage of not more than 33,000 tons (33,528 metric tons) standard displacement, and in order to effect economy any of the Contracting Powers may use for this purpose any two of their ships, whether constructed or in course of construction, which would otherwise be scrapped under the provisions of Article II. The armament of any aircraft carriers exceeding 27,000 tons (27,432 metric tons) standard displacement shall be in accordance with the requirements of Article X, except that the total number of guns to be carried in case any of such guns be of a calibre exceeding 6 inches (152 millimetres), except anti-aircraft guns and guns not exceeding 5 inches (127 millimetres), shall not exceed eight.

Article X. No aircraft carrier of any of the Contracting Powers shall carry a gun with a calibre in excess of 8 inches (203 millimetres). Without prejudice to the provisions of Article IX, if the armament carried includes guns exceeding 6 inches (152 millimetres) in calibre the total number of guns carried, except anti-aircraft guns and guns not exceeding 5 inches (127 millimetres), shall not exceed ten. If alternatively the armament contains no guns exceeding 6 inches (152 millimetres) in calibre, the number of guns is not limited. In either case the number of anti-aircraft guns and of guns not exceeding 5 inches (127 millimetres) is not limited.

Article XI. No vessel of war exceeding 10,000 tons (10,160 metric tons) standard displacement, other than a capital ship or aircraft carrier, shall be acquired by, or constructed by, for, or within the jurisdiction of, any of the Contracting Powers. Vessels not specifically built as fighting ships nor taken in time of peace under government control for fighting purposes, which are employed on fleet duties or as troop transports or in some other way for the purpose of assisting in the prosecution of hostilities otherwise than as fighting ships, shall not be within the limitations of this Article.

Article XII. No vessel of war of any of the Contracting Powers, hereafter laid down, other than a capital ship, shall carry a gun with a calibre in excess of 8 inches (203 millimetres).

Appendix I

Article XIII. Except as provided in Article IX, no ship designated in the present Treaty to be scrapped may be reconverted into a vessel of war.

Article XIV. No preparations shall be made in merchant ships in time of peace for the installation of warlike armaments for the purpose of converting such ships into vessels of war, other than the necessary stiffening of decks for the mounting of guns not exceeding 6 inch (152 millimetres) calibre.

Article XV. No vessel of war constructed within the jurisdiction of any of the Contracting Powers for a non-Contracting Power shall exceed the limitations as to displacement and armament prescribed by the present Treaty for vessels of a similar type which may be constructed by or for any of the Contracting Powers; provided, however, that the displacement for aircraft carriers constructed for a non-Contracting Power shall in no case exceed 27,000 tons (27,432 metric tons) standard displacement.

Article XVI. If the construction of any vessel of war for a non-Contracting Power is undertaken within the jurisdiction of any of the Contracting Powers, such Power shall promptly inform the other Contracting Powers of the date of the signing of the contract and the date on which the keel of the ship is laid; and shall also communicate to them the particulars relating to the ship prescribed in Chapter II, Part 3, Section I (b), (4) and (5).

Article XVII. In the event of a Contracting Power being engaged in war, such Power shall not use as a vessel of war any vessel of war which may be under construction within its jurisdiction for any other Power, or which may have been constructed within its jurisdiction for another Power and not delivered.

Article XVIII. Each of the Contracting Powers undertakes not to dispose by gift, sale or any mode of transfer of any vessel of war in such a manner that such vessel may become a vessel of war in the Navy of any foreign Power.

Article XIX. The United States, the British Empire and Japan agree that the status quo at the time of the signing of the present Treaty, with regard to fortifications and naval bases, shall be maintained in their respective territories and possessions specified hereunder:

(1) The insular possessions which the United States now holds or may hereafter acquire in the Pacific Ocean, except (a) those adjacent to the coast of the United States, Alaska and the Panama Canal Zone, not including the Aleutian Islands, and (b) the Hawaiian Islands;

(2) Hongkong and the insular possessions which the British Empire now holds or may hereafter acquire in the Pacific Ocean, east of the meridian of 110° east longitude, except (a) those adjacent to the coast of Canada, (b) the Commonwealth of Australia and its Territories, and (c) New Zealand;

(3) The following insular territories and possessions of Japan in the Pacific Ocean, to wit: the Kurile Islands, the Bonin Islands, Amami-Oshima, the Loochoo Islands, Formosa and the Pescadores, and any insular territories or possessions in the Pacific Ocean which Japan may hereafter acquire.

The maintenance of the status quo under the foregoing provisions implies that no new fortifications or naval bases shall be established in the territories and possessions specified; that no measures shall be taken to increase the existing naval facilities for the repair and maintenance of naval forces, and that no increase shall be made in the coast defences of the territories and possessions above specified. This restriction, however, does not preclude such repair and replacement of worn-out weapons and equipment as is customary in naval and military establishments in time of peace.

Article XX. The rules for determining tonnage displacement prescribed in Chapter II, Part 4, shall apply to the ships of each of the Contracting Powers.

Chapter II

Rules Relating to the Execution of the Treaty— Definition of Terms

Part 1. Capital Ships Which May be Retained by the Contracting Powers

In accordance with Article II ships may be retained by each of the Contracting Powers as specified in this Part.

Appendix I

Ships Which May Be Retained by the United States

Name	Tonnage
Maryland	32,600
California	32,300
Tennessee	32,300
Idaho	32,000
New Mexico	32,000
Mississippi	32,000
Arizona	31,400
Pennsylvania	31,400
Oklahoma	27,500
Nevada	27,500
New York	27,000
Texas	27,000
Arkansas	26,000
Wyoming	26,000
Florida	21,825
Utah	21,825
North Dakota	20,000
Delaware	20,000
Total tonnage	500,650

On the completion of the two ships of the *West Virginia* class and the scrapping of the *North Dakota* and *Delaware*, as provided in Article II, the total tonnage to be retained by the United States will be 525,850 tons.

Ships Which May Be Retained by the British Empire

Name	Tonnage
Royal Sovereign	25,750
Royal Oak	25,750
Revenge	25,750
Resolution	25,750
Ramillies	25,750
Malaya	27,500
Valiant	27,500
Barham	27,500
Queen Elizabeth	27,500
Warspite	27,500
Benbow	25,000
Emperor of India	25,000
Iron Duke	25,000
Marlborough	25,000
Hood	41,200
Renown	26,500
Repulse	26,500
Tiger	28,500
Thunderer	22,500
King George V	23,000
Ajax	23,000
Centurion	23,000
Total tonnage	580,450

THE UNITED STATES AND DISARMAMENT

On the completion of the two new ships to be constructed and the scrapping of the *Thunderer, King George V, Ajax* and *Centurion*, as provided in Article II, the total tonnage to be retained by the British Empire will be 558,950 tons.

SHIPS WHICH MAY BE RETAINED BY FRANCE

Name	Tonnage, metric tons
Bretagne	23,500
Lorraine	23,500
Provence	23,500
Paris	23,500
France	23,500
Jean Bart	23,500
Courbet	23,500
Condorcet	18,890
Diderot	18,890
Voltaire	18,890
Total tonnage	221,170

France may lay down new tonnage in the years 1927, 1929, and 1931, as provided in Part 3, Section II.

SHIPS WHICH MAY BE RETAINED BY ITALY

Name	Tonnage, metric tons
Andrea Doria	22,700
Caio Duilio	22,700
Conte di Cavour	22,500
Giulio Cesare	22,500
Leonardo da Vinci	22,500
Dante Alighieri	19,500
Roma	12,600
Napoli	12,600
Vittorio Emanuele	12,600
Regina Elena	12,600
Total tonnage	182,800

Italy may lay down new tonnage in the years 1927, 1929, and 1931, as provided in Part 3, Section II.

SHIPS WHICH MAY BE RETAINED BY JAPAN

Name	Tonnage
Mutsu	33,800
Nagato	33,800
Hiuga	31,260
Ise	31,260
Yamashiro	30,600
Fu-So	30,600
Kirishima	27,500
Haruna	27,500
Hiyei	27,500
Kongo	27,500
Total tonnage	301,320

Appendix I

Part 2. Rules for Scrapping Vessels of War

The following rules shall be observed for the scrapping of vessels of war which are to be disposed of in accordance with Articles II and III.

I. A vessel to be scrapped must be placed in such condition that it cannot be put to combatant use.

II. This result must be finally effected in any one of the following ways:

(a) Permanent sinking of the vessel;

(b) Breaking the vessel up. This shall always involve the destruction or removal of all machinery, boilers and armour, and all deck, side and bottom plating;

(c) Converting the vessel to target use exclusively. In such case all the provisions of paragraph III of this Part, except sub-paragraph (6), in so far as may be necessary to enable the ship to be used as a mobile target, and except sub-paragraph (7), must be previously complied with. Not more than one capital ship may be retained for this purpose at one time by any of the Contracting Powers.

(d) Of the capital ships which would otherwise be scrapped under the present Treaty in or after the year 1931, France and Italy may each retain two seagoing vessels for training purposes exclusively, that is, as gunnery or torpedo schools. The two vessels retained by France shall be of the *Jean Bart* class, and of those retained by Italy one shall be the *Dante Alighieri*, the other of the *Giulio Cesare* class. On retaining these ships for the purpose above stated, France and Italy respectively undertake to remove and destroy their conning-towers and not to use the said ships as vessels of war.

III. (a) Subject to the special exceptions contained in Article IX, when a vessel is due for scrapping, the first stage of scrapping, which consists in rendering a ship incapable of further warlike service, shall be immediately undertaken.

(b) A vessel shall be considered incapable of further warlike service when there shall have been removed and landed, or else destroyed in the ship:

(1) All guns and essential portions of guns, fire-control tops and revolving parts of all barbettes and turrets;

(2) All machinery for working hydraulic or electric mountings;

(3) All fire-control instruments and range-finders;

(4) All ammunition, explosives and mines;

(5) All torpedoes, war-heads and torpedo tubes;

(6) All wireless telegraphy installations;

(7) The conning tower and all side armour, or alternatively all

main propelling machinery; and

(8) All landing and flying-off platforms and all other aviation accessories.

IV. The periods in which scrapping of vessels is to be effected are as follows:

(*a*) In the case of vessels to be scrapped under the first paragraph of Article II, the work of rendering the vessels incapable of further warlike service, in accordance with paragraph III of this Part, shall be completed within six months from the coming into force of the present Treaty, and the scrapping shall be finally effected within eighteen months from such coming into force.

(*b*) In the case of vessels to be scrapped under the second and third paragraphs of Article II, or under Article III, the work of rendering the vessel incapable of further warlike service in accordance with paragraph III of this Part shall be commenced not later than the date of completion of its successor, and shall be finished within six months from the date of such completion. The vessel shall be finally scrapped, in accordance with paragraph II of this Part, within eighteen months from the date of completion of its successor. If, however, the completion of the new vessel be delayed, then the work of rendering the old vessel incapable of further warlike service in accordance with paragraph III of this Part shall be commenced within four years from the laying of the keel of the new vessel, and shall be finished within six months from the date on which such work was commenced, and the old vessel shall be finally scrapped in accordance with paragraph II of this Part within eighteen months from the date when the work of rendering it incapable of further warlike service was commenced.

Part 3. *Replacement*

The replacement of capital ships and aircraft carriers shall take place according to the rules in Section I and the tables in Section II of this Part.

Section I. *Rules for Replacement*

(*a*) Capital ships and aircraft carriers twenty years after the date of their completion may, except as otherwise provided in Article VIII and in the tables in Section II of this Part, be replaced by new construction, but within the limits prescribed in Article IV and Article VII. The keels of such new construction may, except as otherwise provided in Article VIII and in the tables in Section II of this Part, be laid down not earlier than seventeen years from the date of

APPENDIX I

completion of the tonnage to be replaced, provided, however, that no capital ship tonnage, with the exception of the ships referred to in the third paragraph of Article II, and the replacement tonnage specifically mentioned in Section II of this Part, shall be laid down until ten years from November 12, 1921.

(*b*) Each of the Contracting Powers shall communicate promptly to each of the other Contracting Powers the following information:

(1) The names of the capital ships and aircraft carriers to be replaced by new construction;

(2) The date of governmental authorization of replacement tonnage;

(3) The date of laying the keels of replacement tonnage;

(4) The standard displacement in tons and metric tons of each new ship to be laid down, and the principal dimensions, namely, length at waterline, extreme beam at or below waterline, mean draft at standard displacement;

(5) The date of completion of each new ship and its standard displacement in tons and metric tons, and the principal dimensions, namely, length at waterline, extreme beam at or below waterline, mean draft at standard displacement, at time of completion.

(*c*) In case of loss or accidental destruction of capital ships or aircraft carriers, they may immediately be replaced by new construction subject to the tonnage limits prescribed in Articles IV and VII and in conformity with the other provisions of the present Treaty, the regular replacement program being deemed to be advanced to that extent.

(*d*) No retained capital ships or aircraft carriers shall be reconstructed except for the purpose of providing means of defense against air and submarine attack, and subject to the following rules: The Contracting Powers may, for that purpose, equip existing tonnage with bulge or blister or anti-air attack deck protection, providing the increase of displacement thus effected does not exceed 3,000 tons (3,048 metric tons) displacement for each ship. No alterations in side armor, in calibre, number or general type of mounting of main armament shall be permitted except:

(1) in the case of France and Italy, which countries within the limits allowed for bulge may increase their armor protection and the calibre of the guns now carried on their existing capital ships so as not to exceed 16 inches (406 millimeters) and

(2) the British Empire shall be permitted to complete, in the case of the *Renown*, the alterations to armor that have already been commenced but temporarily suspended.

The United States and Disarmament

Section II. Replacement and Scrapping of Capital Ships
UNITED STATES

Year	Ships laid down	Ships completed	Ships scrapped (age in parentheses)	Ships retained, summary Pre-Jutland	Post-Jutland
			Maine (20), Missouri (20), Virginia (17), Nebraska (17), Georgia (17), New Jersey (17), Rhode Island (17), Connecticut (17), Louisiana (17), Vermont (16), Kansas (16), Minnesota (16), New Hampshire (15), South Carolina (13), Michigan (13), Washington (0), South Dakota (0), Indiana (0), Montana (0), North Carolina (0), Iowa (0), Massachusetts (0), Lexington (0), Constitution (0), Constellation (0), Saratoga (0), Ranger (0), United States (0).*	17	1
1922	....	A, B†	Delaware (12), North Dakota (12)......	15	3
1923	....	....	....	15	3
1924	....	....	....	15	3
1925	....	....	....	15	3
1926	....	....	....	15	3
1927	....	....	....	15	3
1928	....	....	....	15	3
1929	....	....	....	15	3
1930	....	....	....	15	3
1931	C, D	....	....	15	3
1932	E, F	....	....	15	3
1933	G	....	....	15	3
1934	H, I	C, D	Florida (23), Utah (23), Wyoming (22)..	12	5
1935	J	E, F	Arkansas (23), Texas (21), New York (21)	9	7
1936	K, L	G	Nevada (20), Oklahoma (20)..........	7	8
1937	M	H, I	Arizona (21), Pennsylvania (21)	5	10
1938	N, O	J	Mississippi (21).......................	4	11
1939	P, Q	K, L	New Mexico (21), Idaho (20)..........	2	13
1940	....	M	Tennessee (20).........................	1	14
1941	....	N, O	California (20), Maryland (20).........	0	15
1942	....	P, Q	2 ships West Virginia class............	0	15

* The United States may retain the *Oregon* and *Illinois*, for noncombatant purposes, after complying with the provisions of Part 2, III, (b).

† Two West Virginia class.

NOTE.—A, B, C, D, etc., represent individual capital ships of 35,000 tons standard displacement, laid down and completed in the years specified.

APPENDIX I

BRITISH EMPIRE

Year	Ships laid down	Ships completed	Ships scrapped (age in parentheses)	Ships retained, summary Pre-Jutland	Post-Jutland
			Commonwealth (16), Agamemnon (13), Dreadnought (15), Bellerophon (12), St. Vincent (11), Inflexible (13), Superb (12), Neptune (10), Hercules (10), Indomitable (13), Temeraire (12), New Zealand (9), Lion (9), Princess Royal (9), Conquerer (9), Monarch (9), Orion (9), Australia (8), Agincourt (7), Erin (7), 4 building or projected.*	21	1
1922	A, B†	....	....	21	1
1923	....	....	....	21	1
1924	....	....	....	21	1
1925	....	A, B	King George V (13), Ajax (12), Centurion (12), Thunderer (13)................	17	3
1926	....	....	....	17	3
1927	....	....	....	17	3
1928	....	....	....	17	3
1929	....	....	....	17	3
1930	....	....	....	17	3
1931	C, D	....	....	17	3
1932	E, F	....	....	17	3
1933	G	....	....	17	3
1934	H, I	C, D	Iron Duke (20), Marlborough (20), Emperor of India (20), Benbow (20).......	13	5
1935	J	E, F	Tiger (21), Queen Elizabeth (20), Warspite (20), Barham (20)..............	9	7
1936	K, L	G	Malaya (20), Royal Sovereign (20)......	7	8
1937	M	H, I	Revenge (21), Resolution (21)..........	5	10
1938	N, O	J	Royal Oak (22)......................	4	11
1939	P, Q	K, L	Valiant (23), Repulse (23).............	2	13
1940	....	M	Renown (24).........................	1	14
1941	....	N, O	Ramillies (24), Hood (21).............	0	15
1942	....	P, Q	A (17), B (17).......................	0	15

* The British Empire may retain the *Colossus* and *Collingwood* for noncombatant purposes, after complying with the provisions of Part 2, III, (b)

† Two 35,000-ton ships, standard displacement.

NOTE.—A, B, C, D, etc., represent individual capital ships of 35,000 tons standard displacement laid down and completed in the years specified.

The United States and Disarmament

France

Year	Ships laid down	Ships completed	Ships scrapped (age in parentheses)	Ships retained, summary Pre-Jutland	Post-Jutland
1922				7	0
1923				7	0
1924				7	0
1925				7	0
1926				7	0
1927	35,000 tons			7	0
1928				7	0
1929	35,000 tons			7	0
1930		35,000 tons	Jean Bart (17), Courbet (17)	5	(*)
1931	35,000 tons			5	(*)
1932	35,000 tons	35,000 tons	France (18)	4	(*)
1933	35,000 tons			4	(*)
1934		35,000 tons	Paris (20), Bretagne (20)	2	(*)
1935		35,000 tons	Provence (20)	1	(*)
1936		35,000 tons	Lorraine (20)	0	(*)
1937				0	(*)
1938				0	(*)
1939				0	(*)
1940				0	(*)
1941				0	(*)
1942				0	(*)

* Within tonnage limitations; number not fixed.

NOTE.—France expressly reserves the right of employing the capital ship tonnage allotment as she may consider advisable, subject solely to the limitations that the displacement of individual ships should not surpass 35,000 tons, and that the total capital ship tonnage should keep within the limits imposed by the present Treaty.

Italy

Year	Ships laid down	Ships completed	Ships scrapped (age in parentheses)	Ships retained, summary Pre-Jutland	Post-Jutland
1922				6	0
1923				6	0
1924				6	0
1925				6	0
1926				6	0
1927	35,000 tons			6	0
1928				6	0
1929	35,000 tons			6	0
1930				6	0
1931	35,000 tons	35,000 tons	Dante Alighieri (19)	5	(*)
1932	45,000 tons			5	(*)
1933	25,000 tons	35,000 tons	Leonardo da Vinci (19)	4	(*)
1934				4	(*)
1935		35,000 tons	Giulio Cesare (21)	3	(*)
1936		45,000 tons	Conte di Cavour (21), Duilio (21)	1	(*)
1937		25,000 tons	Andrea Doria (21)	0	(*)

* Within tonnage limitations; number not fixed.

NOTE.—Italy expressly reserves the right of employing the capital ship tonnage allotment as she may consider advisable, subject solely to the limitations that the displacement of individual ships should not surpass 35,000 tons, and the total capital ship tonnage should keep within the limits imposed by the present Treaty.

Appendix I

Japan

Year	Ships laid down	Ships completed	Ships scrapped (age in parentheses)	Ships retained, summary Pre-Jutland	Ships retained, summary Post-Jutland
			Hizen (20), Mikasa (20), Kashima (16), Katori (16), Satsuma (12), Aki (11), Settsu (10), Ikoma (14), Ibuki (12), Kurama (11), Amagi (0), Akagi (0), Kaga (0), Tosa (0), Takao (0), Atago (0). Projected program 8 ships not laid down.*	8	2
1922	..	..		8	2
1923	..	..		8	2
1924	..	..		8	2
1925	..	..		8	2
1926	..	..		8	2
1927	..	..		8	2
1928	..	..		8	2
1929	..	..		8	2
1930	..	..		8	2
1931	A	..		8	2
1932	B	..		8	2
1933	C	..		8	2
1934	D	A	Kongo (21)	7	3
1935	E	B	Hiyei (21), Haruna (20)	5	4
1936	F	C	Kirishima (21)	4	5
1937	G	D	Fuso (22)	3	6
1938	H	E	Yamashiro (21)	2	7
1939	I	F	Ise (22)	1	8
1940	..	G	Hiuga (22)	0	9
1941	..	H	Nagato (21)	0	9
1942	..	I	Mutsu (21)	0	9

*Japan may retain the *Shikishima* and *Asahi* for noncombatant purposes, after complying with the provisions of Part 2, III, (b).

Note.—A, B, C, D, etc., represent individual capital ships of 35,000 tons standard displacement, laid down and completed in the years specified.

Note Applicable to All the Tables in Section II.—The order above prescribed in which ships are to be scrapped is in accordance with their age. It is understood that when replacement begins according to the above tables the order of scrapping in the case of the ships of each of the Contracting Powers may be varied at its option; provided, however, that such Power shall scrap in each year the number of ships above stated.

The United States and Disarmament

Part 4. Definitions

For the purposes of the present Treaty, the following expressions are to be understood in the sense defined in this Part.

Capital Ship.—A capital ship, in the case of ships hereafter built, is defined as a vessel of war, not an aircraft carrier, whose displacement exceeds 10,000 tons (10,160 metric tons) standard displacement, or which carries a gun with a calibre exceeding 8 inches (203 millimetres).

Aircraft Carrier.—An aircraft carrier is defined as a vessel of war with a displacement in excess of 10,000 tons (10,160 metric tons) standard displacement designed for the specific and exclusive purpose of carrying aircraft. It must be so constructed that aircraft can be launched therefrom and landed thereon, and not designed and constructed for carrying a more powerful armament than that allowed to it under Article IX or Article X as the case may be.

Standard Displacement.—The standard displacement of a ship is the displacement of the ship complete, fully manned, engined, and equipped ready for sea, including all armament and ammunition, equipment, outfit, provisions and fresh water for crew, miscellaneous stores and implements of every description that are intended to be carried in war, but without fuel or reserve feed water on board.

The word "ton" in the present Treaty, except in the expression "metric tons," shall be understood to mean the ton of 2,240 pounds (1,016 kilos).

Vessels now completed shall retain their present ratings of displacement tonnage in accordance with their national system of measurement. However, a Power expressing displacement in metric tons shall be considered for the application of the present Treaty as owning only the equivalent displacement in tons of 2,240 pounds.

A vessel completed hereafter shall be rated at its displacement tonnage when in the standard condition defined herein.

Chapter III

Miscellaneous Provisions

Article XXI. If during the term of the present Treaty the requirements of the national security of any Contracting Power in respect of naval defence are, in the opinion of that Power, materially affected by any change of circumstances, the Contracting Powers will, at the request of such Power, meet in conference with a view to the reconsideration of the provisions of the Treaty and its amendment by mutual agreement.

Appendix I

In view of possible technical and scientific developments, the United States, after consultation with the other Contracting Powers, shall arrange for a conference of all the Contracting Powers which shall convene as soon as possible after the expiration of eight years from the coming into force of the present Treaty to consider what changes, if any, in the Treaty may be necessary to meet such developments.

Article XXII. Whenever any Contracting Power shall become engaged in a war which in its opinion affects the naval defence of its national security, such Power may after notice to the other Contracting Powers suspend for the period of hostilities its obligations under the present Treaty other than those under Articles XIII and XVII, provided that such Power shall notify the other Contracting Powers that the emergency is of such a character as to require such suspension.

The remaining Contracting Powers shall in such case consult together with a view to agreement as to what temporary modifications if any should be made in the Treaty as between themselves. Should such consultation not produce agreement, duly made in accordance with the constitutional methods of the respective Powers, any one of said Contracting Powers may, by giving notice to the other Contracting Powers, suspend for the period of hostilities its obligations under the present Treaty, other than those under Articles XIII and XVII.

On the cessation of hostilities the Contracting Powers will meet in conference to consider what modifications, if any, should be made in the provisions of the present Treaty.

Article XXIII. The present Treaty shall remain in force until December 31st, 1936, and in case none of the Contracting Powers shall have given notice two years before that date of its intention to terminate the Treaty, it shall continue in force until the expiration of two years from the date on which notice of termination shall be given by one of the Contracting Powers, whereupon the Treaty shall terminate as regards all the Contracting Powers. Such notice shall be communicated in writing to the Government of the United States, which shall immediately transmit a certified copy of the notification to the other Powers and inform them of the date on which it was received. The notice shall be deemed to have been given and shall take effect on that date. In the event of notice of termination being given by the Government of the United States, such notice shall be given to the diplomatic representatives at Washington of the other Contracting Powers, and the notice shall be deemed to have been given and shall take effect on the date of the communication made to the said diplomatic representatives.

Within one year of the date on which a notice of termination by any Power has taken effect, all the Contracting Powers shall meet in conference.

Article XXIV. The present Treaty shall be ratified by the Contracting Powers in accordance with their respective constitutional methods and shall take effect on the date of the deposit of all the ratifications, which shall take place at Washington as soon as possible. The Government of the United States will transmit to the other Contracting Powers a certified copy of the procès-verbal of the deposit of ratifications.

The present Treaty, of which the French and English texts are both authentic, shall remain deposited in the archives of the Government of the United States, and duly certified copies thereof shall be transmitted by that Government to the other Contracting Powers.

In faith whereof the above-named Plenipotentiaries have signed the present Treaty.

Done at the City of Washington the sixth day of February, One Thousand Nine Hundred and Twenty-Two.

[L. S.] CHARLES EVANS HUGHES
[L. S.] HENRY CABOT LODGE
[L. S.] OSCAR W. UNDERWOOD
[L. S.] ELIHU ROOT
[L. S.] ARTHUR JAMES BALFOUR
[L. S.] LEE OF FAREHAM
[L. S.] A. C. GEDDES
    R. L. BORDEN   [L. S.]
    G. F. PEARCE   [L. S.]
    JOHN W. SALMOND   [L. S.]
    ARTHUR JAMES BALFOUR [L. S.]
    V. S. SRINIVASA SASTRI   [L. S.]
    A. SARRAUT   [L. S.]
    JUSSERAND   [L. S.]
    CARLO SCHANZER   [L. S.]
[L. S.] V. ROLANDI RICCI
[L. S.] LUIGI ALBERTINI
[L. S.] T. KATO
[L. S.] K. SHIDEHARA
[L. S.] M. HANIHARA

APPENDIX II

THE LONDON NAVAL TREATY OF 1930

The President of the United States of America, the President of the French Republic, His Majesty the King of Great Britain, Ireland and the British Dominions beyond the Seas, Emperor of India, His Majesty the King of Italy, and His Majesty the Emperor of Japan,

Desiring to prevent the dangers and reduce the burdens inherent in competitive armaments, and

Desiring to carry forward the work begun by the Washington Naval Conference and to facilitate the progressive realization of general limitation and reduction of armaments,

Have resolved to conclude a Treaty for the limitation and reduction of naval armament, and have accordingly appointed as their Plenipotentiaries:

The President of the United States of America:
    Henry L. Stimson, Secretary of State;
    Charles G. Dawes, Ambassador to the Court of St. James;
    Charles Francis Adams, Secretary of the Navy;
    Joseph T. Robinson, Senator from the State of Arkansas;
    David A. Reed, Senator from the State of Pennsylvania;
    Hugh Gibson, Ambassador to Belgium;
    Dwight W. Morrow, Ambassador to Mexico;
The President of the French Republic:
    Mr. André Tardieu, Deputy, President of the Council of Ministers, Minister of the Interior;
    Mr. Aristide Briand, Deputy, Minister for Foreign Affairs;
    Mr. Jacques-Louis Dumesnil, Deputy, Minister of Marine;
    Mr. François Piétri, Deputy, Minister of the Colonies;
    Mr. Aimé-Joseph de Fleuriau, Ambassador of the French Republic at the Court of St. James;
His Majesty the King of Great Britain, Ireland and the British Dominions beyond the Seas, Emperor of India:
    for Great Britain and Northern Ireland and all parts of the British Empire which are not separate Members of the League of Nations:

The Right Honourable James Ramsay MacDonald, M.P., First Lord of His Treasury and Prime Minister;
The Right Honourable Arthur Henderson, M.P., His Principal Secretary of State for Foreign Affairs;
The Right Honourable Albert Victor Alexander, M.P., First Lord of His Admiralty;
The Right Honourable William Wedgwood Benn, D.S.O., D.F.C., M.P., His Principal Secretary of State for India;

for the Dominion of Canada:
Colonel The Honourable James Layton Ralston, C.M.G., D.S.O., K.C., a Member of His Privy Council for Canada, His Minister for National Defence;
The Honourable Philippe Roy, a Member of His Privy Council for Canada, His Envoy Extraordinary and Minister Plenipotentiary in France for the Dominion of Canada;

for the Commonwealth of Australia:
The Honourable James Edward Fenton, His Minister for Trade and Customs;

for the Dominion of New Zealand:
Thomas Mason Wilford, Esquire, K.C., High Commissioner for the Dominion of New Zealand in London;

for the Union of South Africa:
Charles Theodore te Water, Esquire, High Commissioner for the Union of South Africa in London;

for the Irish Free State:
Timothy Aloysius Smiddy, Esquire, High Commissioner for the Irish Free State in London;

for India:
Sir Atul Chandra Chatterjee, K.C.I.E., High Commissioner for India in London;

His Majesty the King of Italy:
The Honourable Dino Grandi, Deputy, His Minister Secretary of State for Foreign Affairs;
Admiral of Division The Honourable Giuseppe Sirianni, Senator of the Kingdom, His Minister Secretary of State for Marine;
Mr. Antonio Chiaramonte-Bordonaro, His Ambassador Extraordinary and Plenipotentiary at the Court of St. James;
Admiral The Honourable Baron Afredo Acton, Senator of the Kingdom;

His Majesty the Emperor of Japan:
Mr. Reijiro Wakatsuki, Member of the House of Peers;
Admiral Takeshi Takarabe, Minister for the Navy;

Appendix II

Mr. Tsuneo Matsudaira, His Ambassador Extraordinary and Plenipotentiary at the Court of St. James;

Mr. Matsuzo Nagaï, His Ambassador Extraordinary and Plenipotentiary to His Majesty the King of the Belgians;

Who, having communicated to one another their full powers, found in good and due form, have agreed as follows:

Part I

Article I. The High Contracting Parties agree not to exercise their rights to lay down the keels of capital ship replacement tonnage during the years 1931–1936 inclusive as provided in Chapter II, Part 3 of the Treaty for the Limitation of Naval Armament signed between them at Washington on the 6th February, 1922, and referred to in the present Treaty as the Washington Treaty.

This provision is without prejudice to the disposition relating to the replacement of ships accidentally lost or destroyed contained in Chapter II, Part 3, Section I, paragraph (c) of the said Treaty.

France and Italy may, however, build the replacement tonnage which they were entitled to lay down in 1927 and 1929 in accordance with the provisions of the said Treaty.

Article II. 1. The United States, the United Kingdom of Great Britain and Northern Ireland, and Japan shall dispose of the following capital ships as provided in this Article:

United States:
"Florida."
"Utah."
"Arkansas" or "Wyoming."

United Kingdom:
"Benbow."
"Iron Duke."
"Marlborough."
"Emperor of India."
"Tiger."

Japan:
"Hiyei."

(a) Subject to the provisions of sub-paragraph (b), the above ships, unless converted to target use exclusively in accordance with Chapter II, Part 2, paragraph II(c) of the Washington Treaty, shall be scrapped in the following manner:

One of the ships to be scrapped by the United States, and two of those to be scrapped by the United Kingdom shall be rendered unfit for warlike service, in accordance with Chapter II, Part 2, paragraph III(*b*) of the Washington Treaty, within twelve months from the coming into force of the present Treaty. These ships shall be finally scrapped, in accordance with paragraph II(*a*) or (*b*) of the said Part 2, within twenty-four months from the said coming into force. In the case of the second of the ships to be scrapped by the United States, and of the third and fourth of the ships to be scrapped by the United Kingdom, the said periods shall be eighteen and thirty months respectively from the coming into force of the present Treaty.

(*b*) Of the ships to be disposed of under this Article, the following may be retained for training purposes:

> by the United States: "Arkansas" or "Wyoming."
> by the United Kingdom: "Iron Duke."
> by Japan: "Hiyei."

These ships shall be reduced to the condition prescribed in Section V of Annex II to Part II of the present Treaty. The work of reducing these vessels to the required condition shall begin, in the case of the United States and the United Kingdom, within twelve months, and in the case of Japan within eighteen months from the coming into force of the present Treaty; the work shall be completed within six months of the expiration of the above-mentioned periods.

Any of these ships which are not retained for training purposes shall be rendered unfit for warlike service within eighteen months, and finally scrapped within thirty months, of the coming into force of the present Treaty.

2. Subject to any disposal of capital ships which might be necessitated, in accordance with the Washington Treaty, by the building by France or Italy of the replacement tonnage referred to in Article I of the present Treaty, all existing capital ships mentioned in Chapter II, Part 3, Section II of the Washington Treaty and not designated above to be disposed of may be retained during the term of the present Treaty.

3. The right of replacement is not lost by delay in laying down replacement tonnage, and the old vessel may be retained until replaced even though due for scrapping under Chapter II, Part 3, Section II of the Washington Treaty.

Article III. 1. For the purposes of the Washington Treaty, the definition of an aircraft carrier given in Chapter II, Part 4 of the said Treaty is hereby replaced by the following definition:

> The expression "aircraft carrier" includes any surface vessel of war, whatever its displacement, designed for the specific and exclusive purpose of

Appendix II

carrying aircraft and so constructed that aircraft can be launched therefrom and landed thereon.

2. The fitting of a landing-on or flying-off platform or deck on a capital ship, cruiser or destroyer, provided such vessel was not designed or adapted exclusively as an aircraft carrier, shall not cause any vessel so fitted to be charged against or classified in the category of aircraft carriers.

3. No capital ship in existence on the 1st April, 1930, shall be fitted with a landing-on platform or deck.

Article IV. 1. No aircraft carrier of 10,000 tons (10,160 metric tons) or less standard displacement mounting a gun above 6.1-inch (155 mm.) calibre shall be acquired by or constructed by or for any of the High Contracting Parties.

2. As from the coming into force of the present Treaty in respect of all the High Contracting Parties, no aircraft carrier of 10,000 tons (10,160 metric tons) or less standard displacement mounting a gun above 6.1-inch (155 mm.) calibre shall be constructed within the jurisdiction of any of the High Contracting Parties.

Article V. An aircraft carrier must not be designed and constructed for carrying a more powerful armament than that authorised by Article IX or Article X of the Washington Treaty, or by Article IV of the present Treaty, as the case may be.

Wherever in the said Articles IX and X the calibre of 6 inches (152 mm.) is mentioned, the calibre of 6.1 inches (155 mm.) is substituted therefor.

Part II

Article VI. 1. The rules for determining standard displacement prescribed in Chapter II, Part 4 of the Washington Treaty shall apply to all surface vessels of war of each of the High Contracting Parties.

2. The standard displacement of a submarine is the surface displacement of the vessel complete (exclusive of the water in non-watertight structure) fully manned, engined, and equipped ready for sea, including all armament and ammunition, equipment, outfit, provisions for crew, miscellaneous stores, and implements of every description that are intended to be carried in war, but without fuel, lubricating oil, fresh water or ballast water of any kind on board.

3. Each naval combatant vessel shall be rated at its displacement tonnage when in the standard condition. The word "ton," except in the expression "metric tons," shall be understood to be the ton of 2,240 pounds (1,016 kilos.).

The United States and Disarmament

Article VII. 1. No submarine the standard displacement of which exceeds 2,000 tons (2,032 metric tons) or with a gun above 5.1-inch (130 mm.) calibre shall be acquired by or constructed by or for any of the High Contracting Parties.

2. Each of the High Contracting Parties may, however, retain, build or acquire a maximum number of three submarines of a standard displacement not exceeding 2,800 tons (2,845 metric tons); these submarines may carry guns not above 6.1-inch (155 mm.) calibre. Within this number, France may retain one unit, already launched, of 2,880 tons (2,926 metric tons), with guns the calibre of which is 8 inches (203 mm.).

3. The High Contracting Parties may retain the submarines which they possessed on the 1st April, 1930, having a standard displacement not in excess of 2,000 tons (2,032 metric tons) and armed with guns above 5.1-inch (130 mm.) calibre.

4. As from the coming into force of the present Treaty in respect of all the High Contracting Parties, no submarine the standard displacement of which exceeds 2,000 tons (2,032 metric tons) or with a gun above 5.1-inch (130 mm.) calibre shall be constructed within the jurisdiction of any of the High Contracting Parties, except as provided in paragraph 2 of this Article.

Article VIII. Subject to any special agreements which may submit them to limitation, the following vessels are exempt from limitation:

(a) naval surface combatant vessels of 600 tons (610 metric tons) standard displacement and under;

(b) naval surface combatant vessels exceeding 600 tons (610 metric tons), but not exceeding 2,000 tons (2,032 metric tons) standard displacement, provided they have none of the following characteristics:

(1) mount a gun above 6.1-inch (155 mm.) calibre;
(2) mount more than four guns above 3-inch (76 mm.) calibre;
(3) are designed or fitted to launch torpedoes;
(4) are designed for a speed greater than twenty knots.

(c) naval surface vessels not specifically built as fighting ships which are employed on fleet duties or as troop transports or in some other way than as fighting ships, provided they have none of the following characteristics:

(1) mount a gun above 6.1-inch (155 mm.) calibre;
(2) mount more than four guns above 3-inch (76 mm.) calibre;
(3) are designed or fitted to launch torpedoes;
(4) are designed for a speed greater than twenty knots;
(5) are protected by armour plate;
(6) are designed or fitted to launch mines;

Appendix II

(7) are fitted to receive aircraft on board from the air;
(8) mount more than one aircraft-launching apparatus on the centre line; or two, one on each broadside;
(9) if fitted with any means of launching aircraft into the air, are designed or adapted to operate at sea more than three aircraft.

Article IX. The rules as to replacement contained in Annex I to this Part II are applicable to vessels of war not exceeding 10,000 tons (10,160 metric tons) standard displacement, with the exception of aircraft carriers, whose replacement is governed by the provisions of the Washington Treaty.

Article X. Within one month after the date of laying down and the date of completion respectively of each vessel of war, other than capital ships, aircraft carriers and the vessels exempt from limitation under Article VIII, laid down or completed by or for them after the coming into force of the present Treaty, the High Contracting Parties shall communicate to each of the other High Contracting Parties the information detailed below:

(a) the date of laying the keel and the following particulars:
classification of the vessel;
standard displacement in tons and metric tons;
principal dimensions, namely: length at water-line, extreme beam at or below water-line;
mean draft at standard displacement;
calibre of the largest gun.
(b) the date of completion together with the foregoing particulars relating to the vessel at that date.

The information to be given in the case of capital ships and aircraft carriers is governed by the Washington Treaty.

Article XI. Subject to the provisions of Article II of the present Treaty, the rules for disposal contained in Annex II to this Part II shall be applied to all vessels of war to be disposed of under the said Treaty, and to aircraft carriers as defined in Article III.

Article XII. 1. Subject to any supplementary agreements which may modify, as between the High Contracting Parties concerned, the lists in Annex III to this Part II, the special vessels shown therein may be retained and their tonnage shall not be included in the tonnage subject to limitation.

2. Any other vessel constructed, adapted or acquired to serve the purposes for which these special vessels are retained shall be charged against the tonnage of the appropriate combatant category, according to the characteristics of the vessel, unless such vessel conforms to the characteristics of vessels exempt from limitation under Article VIII.

3. Japan may, however, replace the minelayers "Aso" and "Tokiwa" by two new minelayers before the 31st December, 1936. The standard displacement of each of the new vessels shall not exceed 5,000 tons (5,080 metric tons); their speed shall not exceed twenty knots, and their other characteristics shall conform to the provisions of paragraph (b) of Article VIII. The new vessels shall be regarded as special vessels and their tonnage shall not be chargeable to the tonnage of any combatant category. The "Aso" and "Tokiwa" shall be disposed of in accordance with Section I or II of Annex II to this Part II, on completion of the replacement vessels.

4. The "Asama," "Yakumo," "Izumo," "Iwate" and "Kasuga" shall be disposed of in accordance with Section I or II of Annex II to this Part II when the first three vessels of the "Kuma" class have been replaced by new vessels. These three vessels of the "Kuma" class shall be reduced to the condition prescribed in Section V, sub-paragraph (b)2 of Annex II to this Part II, and are to be used for training ships, and their tonnage shall not thereafter be included in the tonnage subject to limitation.

Article XIII. Existing ships of various types, which, prior to the 1st April, 1930, have been used as stationary training establishments or hulks, may be retained in a nonseagoing condition.

Annex I. Rules for Replacement

Section I.—Except as provided in Section III of this Annex and Part III of the present Treaty, a vessel shall not be replaced before it becomes "over-age." A vessel shall be deemed to be "over-age" when the following number of years have elapsed since the date of its completion:

(a) For a surface vessel exceeding 3,000 tons (3,048 metric tons) but not exceeding 10,000 tons (10,160 metric tons) standard displacement:
 (i) if laid down before the 1st January, 1920: 16 years;
 (ii) if laid down after the 31st December, 1919: 20 years.

(b) For a surface vessel not exceeding 3,000 tons (3,048 metric tons) standard displacement:
 (i) if laid down before the 1st January, 1921: 12 years;
 (ii) if laid down after the 31st December, 1920: 16 years.

(c) For a submarine: 13 years.

The keels of replacement tonnage shall not be laid down more than three years before the year in which the vessel to be replaced becomes "over-age"; but this period is reduced to two years in the case of any replacement surface vessel not exceeding 3,000 tons (3,048 metric tons) standard displacement.

Appendix II

The right of replacement is not lost by delay in laying down replacement tonnage.

Section II.—Except as otherwise provided in the present Treaty, the vessel or vessels, whose retention would cause the maximum tonnage permitted in the category to be exceeded, shall, on the completion or acquisition of replacement tonnage, be disposed of in accordance with Annex II to this Part II.

Section III.—In the event of loss or accidental destruction a vessel may be immediately replaced.

Annex II. *Rules for Disposal of Vessels of War*

The present Treaty provides for the disposal of vessels of war in the following ways:

(i) by scrapping (sinking or breaking up);
(ii) by converting the vessel to a hulk;
(iii) by converting the vessel to target use exclusively;
(iv) by retaining the vessel exclusively for experimental purposes;
(v) by retaining the vessel exclusively for training purposes.

Any vessel of war to be disposed of, other than a capital ship, may either be scrapped or converted to a hulk at the option of the High Contracting Party concerned.

Vessels, other than capital ships, which have been retained for target, experimental or training purposes, shall finally be scrapped or converted to hulks.

Section I. *Vessels to Be Scrapped*

(a) A vessel to be disposed of by scrapping, by reason of its replacement, must be rendered incapable of warlike service within six months of the date of the completion of its successor, or of the first of its successors if there are more than one. If, however, the completion of the new vessel or vessels be delayed, the work of rendering the old vessel incapable of warlike service shall, nevertheless, be completed within four and a half years from the date of laying the keel of the new vessel, or of the first of the new vessels; but should the new vessel, or any of the new vessels, be a surface vessel not exceeding 3,000 tons (3,048 metric tons) standard displacement, this period is reduced to three and a half years.

(b) A vessel to be scrapped shall be considered incapable of warlike service when there shall have been removed and landed or else destroyed in the ship:

(1) all guns and essential parts of guns, fire control tops and revolving parts of all barbettes and turrets;

(2) all hydraulic or electric machinery for operating turrets;
(3) all fire control instruments and rangefinders;
(4) all ammunition, explosives, mines and mine rails;
(5) all torpedoes, war heads, torpedo tubes and training racks;
(6) all wireless telegraphy installations;
(7) all main propelling machinery, or alternatively the armoured conning tower and all side armour plate;
(8) all aircraft cranes, derricks, lifts and launching apparatus. All landing-on or flying-off platforms and decks, or alternatively all main propelling machinery;
(9) in addition, in the case of submarines, all main storage batteries, air compressor plants and ballast pumps.

(c) Scrapping shall be finally effected in either of the following ways within twelve months of the date on which the work of rendering the vessel incapable of warlike service is due for completion:

(1) permanent sinking of the vessel;
(2) breaking the vessel up; this shall always include the destruction or removal of all machinery, boilers and armour, and all deck, side and bottom plating.

Section II. Vessels to Be Converted to Hulks

A vessel to be disposed of by conversion to a hulk shall be considered finally disposed of when the conditions prescribed in Section I, paragraph (b), have been complied with, omitting sub-paragraphs (6), (7) and (8), and when the following have been effected:

(1) mutilation beyond repair of all propeller shafts, thrust blocks, turbine gearing or main propelling motors, and turbines or cylinders of main engines;
(2) removal of propeller brackets;
(3) removal and breaking up of all aircraft lifts, and the removal of all aircraft cranes, derricks and launching apparatus.

The vessel must be put in the above condition within the same limits of time as provided in Section I for rendering a vessel incapable of warlike service.

Section III. Vessels to Be Converted to Target Use

(a) A vessel to be disposed of by conversion to target use exclusively shall be considered incapable of warlike service when there have been removed and landed, or rendered unserviceable on board, the following:

(1) all guns;
(2) all fire control tops and instruments and main fire control communication wiring;
(3) all machinery for operating gun mountings or turrets;

Appendix II

(4) all ammunition, explosives, mines, torpedoes and torpedo tubes;
(5) all aviation facilities and accessories.

The vessel must be put into the above condition within the same limits of time as provided in Section I for rendering a vessel incapable of warlike service.

(b) In addition to the rights already possessed by each High Contracting Party under the Washington Treaty, each High Contracting Party is permitted to retain, for target use exclusively, at any one time:

> (1) not more than three vessels (cruisers or destroyers), but of these three vessels only one may exceed 3,000 tons (3,048 metric tons) standard displacement;
> (2) one submarine.

(c) On retaining a vessel for target use, the High Contracting Party concerned undertakes not to recondition it for warlike service.

Section IV. Vessels Retained for Experimental Purposes

(a) A vessel to be disposed of by conversion to experimental purposes exclusively shall be dealt with in accordance with the provisions of Section III(a) of this Annex.

(b) Without prejudice to the general rules, and provided that due notice be given to the other High Contracting Parties, reasonable variation from the conditions prescribed in Section III(a) of this Annex, in so far as may be necessary for the purposes of a special experiment, may be permitted as a temporary measure.

Any High Contracting Party taking advantage of this provision is required to furnish full details of any such variations and the period for which they will be required.

(c) Each High Contracting Party is permitted to retain for experimental purposes exclusively at any one time:

> (1) not more than two vessels (cruisers or destroyers), but of these two vessels only one may exceed 3,000 tons (3,048 metric tons) standard displacement;
> (2) one submarine.

(d) The United Kingdom is allowed to retain, in their present conditions, the monitor "Roberts," the main armament guns and mountings of which have been mutilated, and the seaplane carrier "Ark Royal," until no longer required for experimental purposes. The retention of these two vessels is without prejudice to the retention of vessels permitted under (c) above.

(e) On retaining a vessel for experimental purposes the High Contracting Party concerned undertakes not to recondition it for warlike service.

Section V. Vessels Retained for Training Purposes

(a) In addition to the rights already possessed by any High Contracting Party under the Washington Treaty, each High Contracting Party is permitted to retain for training purposes exclusively the following vessels:

> United States: 1 capital ship ("Arkansas" or "Wyoming");
> France: 2 surface vessels, one of which may exceed 3,000 tons (3,048 metric tons) standard displacement;
> United Kingdom: 1 capital ship ("Iron Duke");
> Italy: 2 surface vessels, one of which may exceed 3,000 tons (3,048 metric tons) standard displacement;
> Japan: 1 capital ship ("Hiyei"), 3 cruisers ("Kuma" class).

(b) Vessels retained for training purposes under the provisions of paragraph (a) shall, within six months of the date on which they are required to be disposed of, be dealt with as follows:

1. *Capital Ships.*—The following is to be carried out:

(1) removal of main armament guns, revolving parts of all barbettes and turrets; machinery for operating turrets; but three turrets with their armament may be retained in each ship;

(2) removal of all ammunition and explosives in excess of the quantity required for target practice training for the guns remaining on board;

(3) removal of conning tower and the side armour belt between the foremost and aftermost barbettes;

(4) removal or mutilation of all torpedo tubes;

(5) removal or mutilation on board of all boilers in excess of the number required for a maximum speed of eighteen knots.

2. *Other Surface Vessels Retained by France, Italy and Japan.*—The following is to be carried out:

(1) removal of one half of the guns, but four guns of main calibre may be retained on each vessel;

(2) removal of all torpedo tubes;

(3) removal of all aviation facilities and accessories;

(4) removal of one half of the boilers.

(c) The High Contracting Party concerned undertakes that vessels retained in accordance with the provisions of this Section shall not be used for any combatant purpose.

Appendix II

Annex III. Special Vessels

United States

Name and type of vessel	Displacement tons	Name and type of vessel	Displacement tons
Aroostook—Minelayer	4,950	Bridgeport—Destroyer tender	11,750
Oglala—Minelayer	4,950	Dobbin—Destroyer tender	12,450
Baltimore—Minelayer	4,413	Melville—Destroyer tender	7,150
San Francisco—Minelayer	4,083	Whitney—Destroyer tender	12,450
Cheyenne—Monitor	2,800	Holland—Submarine tender	11,570
Helena—Gunboat	1,392	Henderson—Naval transport	10,000
Isabel—Yacht	938		
Niagara—Yacht	2,600		91,493

France

Name and type of vessel	Displacement tons	Name and type of vessel	Displacement tons
Castor—Minelayer	3,150	Nancy—Despatch vessel	644
Pollux—Minelayer	2,461	Calais—Despatch vessel	644
Commandant-Teste—Seaplane carrier	10,000	Lassigny—Despatch vessel	644
Aisne—Despatch vessel	600	Les Eparges—Despatch vessel	644
Marne—Despatch vessel	600	Remiremont—Despatch vessel	644
Ancre—Despatch vessel	604	Tahure—Despatch vessel	644
Scarpe—Despatch vessel	604	Toul—Despatch vessel	644
Suippe—Despatch vessel	604	Épinal—Despatch vessel	644
Dunkerque—Despatch vessel	644	Liévin—Despatch vessel	644
Laffaux—Despatch vessel	644	(—)—Netlayer	2,293
Bapaume—Despatch vessel	644		28,644

British Commonwealth of Nations

Name and type of vessel	Displacement tons	Name and type of vessel	Displacement tons
Adventure—Minelayer (United Kingdom)	6,740	Marshal Soult—Monitor (United Kingdom)	6,400
Albatross—Seaplane carrier (Australia)	5,000	Clive—Sloop (India)	2,021
Erebus—Monitor (United Kingdom)	7,200	Medway—Submarine depot ship (United Kingdom)	15,000
Terror—Monitor (United Kingdom)	7,200		49,561

The United States and Disarmament

Italy

Name and type of vessel	Displacement tons	Name and type of vessel	Displacement tons
Miraglia—Seaplane carrier	4,880	Monte Novegno—Ex-monitor	500
Faà di Bruno—Monitor	2,800	Campania—Sloop	2,070
Monte Grappa—Monitor	605		
Montello—Monitor	605		11,960
Monte Cengio—Ex-monitor	500		

Japan

Name and type of vessel	Displacement tons	Name and type of vessel	Displacement tons
Aso—Minelayer	7,180	Iwate—Old cruiser	9,180
Tokiwa—Minelayer	9,240	Kasuga—Old cruiser	7,080
Asama—Old cruiser	9,240	Yodo—Gunboat	1,320
Yakumo—Old cruiser	9,010		
Izumo—Old cruiser	9,180		61,430

Part III

The President of the United States of America, His Majesty the King of Great Britain, Ireland and the British Dominions beyond the Seas, Emperor of India, and His Majesty the Emperor of Japan, have agreed as between themselves to the provisions of this Part III:

Article XIV. The naval combatant vessels of the United States, the British Commonwealth of Nations and Japan, other than capital ships, aircraft carriers and all vessels exempt from limitation under Article VIII, shall be limited during the term of the present Treaty as provided in this Part III, and, in the case of special vessels, as provided in Article XII.

Article XV. For the purpose of this Part III the definition of the cruiser and destroyer categories shall be as follows:

Cruisers. Surface vessels of war, other than capital ships or aircraft carriers, the standard displacement of which exceeds 1,850 tons (1,880 metric tons), or with a gun above 5.1-inch (130 mm.) calibre.

The cruiser category is divided into two sub-categories, as follows:

(*a*) cruisers carrying a gun above 6.1-inch (155 mm.) calibre;

(*b*) cruisers carrying a gun not above 6.1-inch (155 mm.) calibre.

Destroyers. Surface vessels of war the standard displacement of which does not exceed 1,850 tons (1,880 metric tons), and with a gun not above 5.1-inch (130 mm.) calibre.

Article XVI. 1. The completed tonnage in the cruiser, destroyer and submarine categories which is not to be exceeded on the 31st December, 1936, is given in the following table:

APPENDIX II

Categories	United States	British Commonwealth of Nations	Japan
Cruisers: (a) with guns of more than 6.1-inch (155 mm.) calibre..........	180,000 tons (182,880 metric tons)	146,800 tons (149,149 metric tons)	108,400 tons (110,134 metric tons)
(b) with guns of 6.1-inch (155 mm.) calibre or less.............	143,500 tons (145,796 metric tons)	192,200 tons (195,275 metric tons)	100,450 tons (102,057 metric tons)
Destroyers........	150,000 tons (152,400 metric tons)	150,000 tons (152,400 metric tons)	105,500 tons (107,188 metric tons)
Submarines........	52,700 tons (53,543 metric tons)	52,700 tons (53,543 metric tons)	52,700 tons (53,543 metric tons)

2. Vessels which cause the total tonnage in any category to exceed the figures given in the foregoing table shall be disposed of gradually during the period ending on the 31st December, 1936.

3. The maximum number of cruisers of sub-category (a) shall be as follows: for the United States, eighteen; for the British Commonwealth of Nations, fifteen; for Japan, twelve.

4. In the destroyer category not more than sixteen per cent of the allowed total tonnage shall be employed in vessels of over 1,500 tons (1,524 metric tons) standard displacement. Destroyers completed or under construction on the 1st April, 1930, in excess of this percentage may be retained, but no other destroyers exceeding 1,500 tons (1,524 metric tons) standard displacement shall be constructed or acquired until a reduction to such sixteen per cent has been effected.

5. Not more than twenty-five per cent of the allowed total tonnage in the cruiser category may be fitted with a landing-on platform or deck for aircraft.

6. It is understood that the submarines referred to in paragraphs 2 and 3 of Article VII will be counted as part of the total submarine tonnage of the High Contracting Party concerned.

7. The tonnage of any vessels retained under Article XIII or disposed of in accordance with Annex II to Part II of the present Treaty shall not be included in the tonnage subject to limitation.

Article XVII. A transfer not exceeding ten per cent of the allowed total tonnage of the category or sub-category into which the transfer is to be made shall be permitted between cruisers of sub-category (b) and destroyers.

Article XVIII. The United States contemplates the completion by 1935 of fifteen cruisers of sub-category (a) of an aggregate tonnage of

150,000 tons (152,400 metric tons). For each of the three remaining cruisers of sub-category (*a*) which it is entitled to construct the United States may elect to substitute 15,166 tons (15,409 metric tons) of cruisers of sub-category (*b*). In case the United States shall construct one or more of such three remaining cruisers of sub-category (*a*), the sixteenth unit will not be laid down before 1933 and will not be completed before 1936; the seventeenth will not be laid down before 1934 and will not be completed before 1937; the eighteenth will not be laid down before 1935 and will not be completed before 1938.

Article XIX. Except as provided in Article 20, the tonnage laid down in any category subject to limitation in accordance with Article XVI shall not exceed the amount necessary to reach the maximum allowed tonnage of the category, or to replace vessels that become "over-age" before the 31st December, 1936. Nevertheless, replacement tonnage may be laid down for cruisers and submarines that become "over-age" in 1937, 1938 and 1939, and for destroyers that become "over-age" in 1937 and 1938.

Article XX. Notwithstanding the rules for replacement contained in Annex I to Part II:

(*a*) The "Frobisher" and "Effingham" (United Kingdom) may be disposed of during the year 1936. Apart from the cruisers under construction on the 1st April, 1930, the total replacement tonnage of cruisers to be completed, in the case of the British Commonwealth of Nations, prior to the 31st December, 1936, shall not exceed 91,000 tons (92,456 metric tons).

(*b*) Japan may replace the "Tama" by new construction to be completed during the year 1936.

(*c*) In addition to replacing destroyers becoming "over-age" before the 31st December, 1936, Japan may lay down, in each of the years 1935 and 1936, not more than 5,200 tons (5,283 metric tons) to replace part of the vessels that become "over-age" in 1938 and 1939.

(*d*) Japan may anticipate replacement during the term of the present Treaty by laying down not more than 19,200 tons (19,507 metric tons) of submarine tonnage, of which not more than 12,000 tons (12,192 metric tons) shall be completed by the 31st December, 1936.

Article XXI. If, during the term of the present Treaty, the requirements of the national security of any High Contracting Party in respect of vessels of war limited by Part III of the present Treaty are in the opinion of that Party materially affected by new construction of any Power other than those who have joined in Part III of this Treaty, that High Contracting Party will notify the other Parties

APPENDIX II

to Part III as to the increase required to be made in its own tonnages within one or more of the categories of such vessels of war, specifying particularly the proposed increases and the reasons therefor, and shall be entitled to make such increase. Thereupon the other Parties to Part III of this Treaty shall be entitled to make a proportionate increase in the category or categories specified; and the said other Parties shall promptly advise with each other through diplomatic channels as to the situation thus presented.

Part IV

Article XXII. The following are accepted as established rules of International Law.

(1) In their action with regard to merchant ships, submarines must conform to the rules of International Law to which surface vessels are subject.

(2) In particular, except in the case of persistent refusal to stop on being duly summoned, or of active resistance to visit or search, a warship, whether surface vessel or submarine, may not sink or render incapable of navigation a merchant vessel without having first placed passengers, crew and ship's papers in a place of safety. For this purpose the ship's boats are not regarded as a place of safety unless the safety of the passengers and crew is assured, in the existing sea and weather conditions, by the proximity of land, or the presence of another vessel which is in a position to take them on board.

The High Contracting Parties invite all other Powers to express their assent to the above rules.

Part V

Article XXIII. The present Treaty shall remain in force until the 31st December, 1936, subject to the following exceptions:

(1) Part IV shall remain in force without limit of time;
(2) the provisions of Articles 3, 4 and 5, and of Article XI and Annex II to Part II so far as they relate to aircraft carriers, shall remain in force for the same period as the Washington Treaty.

Unless the High Contracting Parties should agree otherwise by reason of a more general agreement limiting naval armaments, to which they all become parties, they shall meet in conference in 1935 to frame a new treaty to replace and to carry out the purposes of the present Treaty, it being understood that none of the provisions of the present Treaty shall prejudice the attitude of any of the High Contracting Parties at the conference agreed to.

Article XXIV. 1. The present Treaty shall be ratified by the High Contracting Parties in accordance with their respective constitutional methods and the ratifications shall be deposited at London as soon as possible. Certified copies of all the *procès-verbaux* of the deposit of ratifications will be transmitted to the Governments of all the High Contracting Parties.

2. As soon as the ratifications of the United States of America, of His Majesty the King of Great Britain, Ireland and the British Dominions beyond the Seas, Emperor of India, in respect of each and all of the Members of the British Commonwealth of Nations as enumerated in the preamble of the present Treaty, and of His Majesty the Emperor of Japan have been deposited, the Treaty shall come into force in respect of the said High Contracting Parties.

3. On the date of the coming into force referred to in the preceding paragraph, Parts I, II, IV and V of the present Treaty will come into force in respect of the French Republic and the Kingdom of Italy if their ratifications have been deposited at that date; otherwise these Parts will come into force in respect of each of those Powers on the deposit of its ratification.

4. The rights and obligations resulting from Part III of the present Treaty are limited to the High Contracting Parties mentioned in paragraph 2 of this Article. The High Contracting Parties will agree as to the date on which, and the conditions under which, the obligations assumed under the said Part III by the High Contracting Parties mentioned in paragraph 2 of this Article will bind them in relation to France and Italy; such agreement will determine at the same time the corresponding obligations of France and Italy in relation to the other High Contracting Parties.

Article XXV. After the deposit of the ratifications of all the High Contracting Parties, His Majesty's Government in the United Kingdom of Great Britain and Northern Ireland will communicate the provisions inserted in Part IV of the present Treaty to all Powers which are not signatories of the said Treaty, inviting them to accede thereto definitely and without limit of time.

Such accession shall be effected by a declaration addressed to His Majesty's Government in the United Kingdom of Great Britain and Northern Ireland.

Article XXVI. The present Treaty, of which the French and English Texts are both authentic, shall remain deposited in the archives of His Majesty's Government in the United Kingdom of Great Britain and Northern Ireland. Duly certified copies thereof shall be transmitted to the Governments of all the High Contracting Parties.

In faith whereof the above-named Plenipotentiaries have signed the present Treaty and have affixed thereto their seals.

Appendix II

Done at London, the twenty-second day of April, nineteen hundred and thirty.

[SEAL] HENRY L. STIMSON.
[SEAL] CHARLES G. DAWES.
[SEAL] CHARLES F. ADAMS.
[SEAL] JOSEPH T. ROBINSON.
[SEAL] DAVID A. REED.
[SEAL] HUGH GIBSON.
[SEAL] DWIGHT W. MORROW.
[SEAL] ARISTIDE BRIAND.
[SEAL] J. L. DUMESNIL.
[SEAL] A. DE FLEURIAU.
[SEAL] J. RAMSAY MACDONALD
[SEAL] ARTHUR HENDERSON.
[SEAL] A. V. ALEXANDER.
[SEAL] W. WEDGWOOD BENN.
[SEAL] PHILIPPE ROY.
[SEAL] JAMES E. FENTON.
[SEAL] T. M. WILFORD.
[SEAL] C. T. TE WATER.
[SEAL] T. A. SMIDDY.
[SEAL] ATUL C. CHATTERJEE.
[SEAL] G. SIRIANNI.
[SEAL] A. C. BORDONARO.
[SEAL] ALFREDO ACTON.
[SEAL] R. WAKATSUKI.
[SEAL] TAKESHI TAKARABE.
[SEAL] T. MATSUDAIRA.
[SEAL] M. NAGAI.

APPENDIX III

SUMMARY OF THE DRAFT CONVENTION DRAWN UP BY THE PREPARATORY COMMISSION

The High Contracting Parties agree to limit and, so far as possible, to reduce their respective armaments as provided in the present Convention.

Part I. Personnel

Chapter A. Effectives.—The average daily effectives of each of the High Contracting Parties shall not exceed the figures laid down in the skeleton tables annexed to this chapter. The limits shall apply (1) to the land, sea, and air armed forces, and (2) to formations organized on a military basis, which include police forces of all kinds, gendarmerie, forest guards, etc., which are capable of being employed for military purposes without measures of mobilization. Skeleton tables are provided in which the maximum figures are to be filled in for each of the High Contracting Parties. (Trained reserves are not included in the forces to be limited.)

Chapter B. Period of Service of Conscripts.—A skeleton table is set forth in which the maximum total period of service for conscripts is to be filled in for each of the High Contracting Parties. A place is also provided for the insertion of the maximum period of service which cannot be exceeded by any party.

Part II. Material

Chapter A. Land Armaments.—The annual expenditure of each High Contracting Party on the upkeep, purchase, and manufacture of war material for land armaments shall be limited to the figures laid down for such party.

Chapter B. Naval Armaments.—The global tonnage of the vessels of war (other than exempt vessels) of each of the High Contracting Parties shall not exceed the figure laid down for such party in the annexed skeleton table.

Appendix III

In a second table each of the High Contracting Parties is to show the manner in which it intends to distribute its tonnage by categories. But transfers are to be allowed after due notice. In a third table the maximum tonnage to be fixed for each party in each category is to be shown. Thus the difference between Table II and Table III will show the amount of transfers that can be made by each power into each category. The amount of transfers for each power will depend upon the size of its navy. Powers whose total tonnage does not exceed 100,000 tons (figures inserted by way of illustration) will have full freedom of transfer as regards surface ships. As regards other powers, the amount of transfer should vary in inverse ratio to the amount of the total tonnage.

Certain maximum specifications for war vessels are to be provided. The figures inserted in the draft convention are by way of illustration and are taken from the Washington and London treaties. Thus capital ships are not to be of more than 35,000 tons or to have guns of more than 16 inches in caliber. Aircraft carriers are to be limited to 27,000 tons and guns of 8 inches in caliber, submarines to 2,000 tons and guns of 5.1 inches. No preparations shall be made in merchant vessels in time of peace for the installation of warlike armaments for the purpose of converting such ships into vessels of war, other than the necessary stiffening of decks for the mounting of guns not exceeding 6.1 inches in caliber. The convention follows the London Treaty in its definition of exempt vessels and also in rules for replacement and disposal of vessels of war.

The annual expenditure of each High Contracting Party on the upkeep, purchase, and manufacture of war material for naval armaments shall be limited to the figures laid down for such party.

Chapter C. Air Armaments.—The number and total horsepower of the airplanes, capable of use in war, in commission, and in immediate reserve in the land, sea, and air armed forces and formations organized on a military basis of each High Contracting Party shall not exceed the figures laid down in the annexed skeleton tables. Similar figures for dirigibles (except that the words "in immediate reserve" are omitted) shall be inserted and the total volume of dirigibles is to be limited.

The High Contracting Parties shall not attempt to regulate civil aviation for military purposes by prescribing the embodiment of military features in commercial aircraft. Preparations for installing armaments in civil aircraft shall not be made in time of peace. Civil aviation enterprises shall not be required to employ personnel specially trained for military purposes. Air lines principally established for military rather than economic, administrative, or social purposes shall not be subsidized. The conclusion of economic agreements between civil aviation undertakings in different countries shall be encouraged as far as possible by the High Contracting Parties.

Part III. Budgetary Expenditures

The total annual expenditures of each of the High Contracting Parties on his land, sea, and air forces and formations organized on a military basis shall be limited to the figures laid down for such party.

Part IV. Exchange of Information

Skeleton tables are included for the obtaining of information regarding the average daily number of each category of effectives in the land, sea, and air armed forces and formations organized on a military basis. These facts are to be reported to the Secretary General of the League of Nations. Other items to be reported are:

The number of youths who have compulsorily received preparatory military training.

The legal provisions regarding the length of enrollment of conscripts in the different periods of service.

The total expenditures on the upkeep, purchase, and manufacture of war materials for the land and sea armed forces and formations organized on a military basis.

With regard to war vessels under construction: (a) the date of laying down the keel together with the tonnage, dimensions, etc.; (b) the date of completion together with similar particulars for that date.

The names and tonnage of merchant vessels whose decks have been stiffened for the mounting of guns.

The number and total horsepower of aircraft in the land, sea, and air armed forces and formations organized on a military basis and also the total volume in the case of dirigibles.

The number and total horsepower of civil aircraft registered within the jurisdiction of each of the High Contracting Parties and the amounts expended on civil aviation by the governments and the local authorities.

The total amounts expended on land, sea, and air armaments.

Part V. Chemical Arms

The High Contracting Parties undertake, subject to reciprocity, to abstain from the use in war of asphyxiating, poisonous, or similar gases, and of all analogous liquids, substances, or processes. They undertake unreservedly to abstain from the use of all bacteriological methods of warfare.

APPENDIX III

Part VI. Miscellaneous

Chapter A. Permanent Disarmament Commission.—The numbers of members of the commission and the governments which are to appoint them will be determined by the conference. The members shall not represent their governments.

The commission is to be set up at the seat of the League of Nations and shall meet for the first time on the summons of the Secretary General of the League within three months after the entry into force of the convention. It shall draw up its own rules and elect its officers. Thereafter its regular sessions shall be on the date fixed by its rules. Extraordinary sessions shall be called on application of a High Contracting Party and upon summons by the president of the commission.

Any High Contracting Party not having a member of its nationality on the commission shall appoint a member to sit at meetings which deal with questions specially affecting the interests of such party.

Reports of the commission shall be sent to all High Contracting Parties and to the Council of the League of Nations and shall be published. The commission shall receive all of the information required to be sent to the Secretary General by the High Contracting Parties and shall make at least one report each year.

Chapter B. Derogations.—If a change in circumstances constitutes in the opinion of any High Contracting Party a menace to its national security, such High Contracting Party may suspend, so far as it concerns itself, any part of the present convention not expressly designed to apply in the event of war, provided that it shall notify the other parties and the Permanent Disarmament Commission through the Secretary General of the League and that it shall give a full explanation of the circumstances. The other High Contracting Parties shall promptly advise as to the situation thus presented.

Chapter C. Procedure Regarding Complaints.—If any High Contracting Party is of the opinion that another party is violating the convention it may lay the matter, through the Secretary General of the League, before the Permanent Disarmament Commission. The commission shall hear the interested parties and report to all the High Contracting Parties and to the Council of the League of Nations. If the High Contracting Parties directly concerned are members of the League of Nations, the Council of the League shall take the appropriate action under the Covenant of the League.

Chapter D. Final Provisions.—The present convention shall not affect the provisions of previous treaties under which certain of the High Contracting Parties have agreed to limit their land, sea, or air armaments and have thus fixed in relation to one another their respective rights and obligations in this connection. The following High Contracting Parties (place left open here for optional signature of those who are parties to previous treaties) declare that the limits fixed for their armaments under the present convention are accepted by them in relation to the obligations referred to, the maintenance of such provisions being for them an essential condition for the observance of the present convention.

If a dispute arises between two or more of the High Contracting Parties concerning the convention and cannot be adjusted directly or by other friendly settlement the parties will, at the request of any one of them, submit such dispute to the decision of the Permanent Court of International Justice or to an arbitral tribunal chosen by them.

The number of years during which the convention is to be in force is to be determined by the conference. Provisions are made that within a certain time before the expiration of this term a conference of the High Contracting Parties shall be called by the Council of the League after taking cognizance of the opinion of the Permanent Disarmament Commission and of the intentions of those High Contracting Parties who are non-members of the League. This conference shall re-examine and, if necessary, revise the convention. If technical transformations or special circumstances render an earlier conference desirable, such a meeting may be called at the request of a High Contracting Party with the concurrence of the Permanent Disarmament Commission. Such earlier meeting cannot be called, however, until after a certain number of years (to be fixed) from the entry into force of the convention.

INDEX

A

Adams, Charles F., delegate to London Conference, 190
Aggressor nation, trade with, by United States, 97, 113
Air material, limitation of, 296
Aircraft, bombardment by, prohibition of, 301
   civilian, 297-300
   in coast defense, 41
   commerce destruction by, 44, 88
   danger of, to United States, 67
   threat of, to Panama Canal, 71
Aircraft carriers, definition of, 210
   treaty limitation of, 147
Allies, financial plight of, in 1917, 107
American Revolution, naval character of, 16-19
Angell, Norman, quoted, 48
Anglo-Japanese Alliance, 154-156
Athens, ancient, economic dependence of, 79
Auxiliary combat craft, failure to limit at Washington Conference, 148-150

B

Baker, P. J. Noel, quoted, 298
Balfour, Arthur J., quoted, 149
Beard, Charles A., quoted, 7, 47, 121
Bernstorff, Count von, quoted, 265, 287
Blockade, effect of, in Germany, 80
Bolles, Albert S., quoted, 101
Borah, William E., proposes naval conference, 139
   quoted, 96, 136

Bridgeman, William C., quoted, 169, 171
Britten, Fred A., quoted, 97
Brouckère, Senator de, quoted, 252, 299
Budgetary limitation, for air material, advocated, 274
   applied to land material, 267
   applied to naval material, 268
   arguments against, 270
   arguments for, 267
Buell, R. L., quoted, 157
Business, conflict of, with nationalism, 6, 306
Bywater, Hector, opinion of, 76
   quoted, 134

C

Capital ship, abolition of, opposed by United States, 189, 209
   comparison of British and American tonnage in, 208
   reduction in size of, proposed, 295
   replacements of, postponed, 206
   replacements under Washington Treaty, table, 204
   tonnage of, destroyed under Washington Treaty, 147
   under London Treaty, 207
   to be reached under Washington Treaty, 146
   retained under Washington Treaty, 145
   scrapped under London Treaty, 207
Capitalism and war, 6, 119, 306
Capper Resolution, 113
Category-global dispute, 292-295

Category method of naval limitation,
  arguments for, 293
  defined, 292
Cecil, Viscount, delegate to Geneva
  Conference, 166
  favors budgetary limitation of air
    material, 274
  opinion of, on attitude of British
    cabinet, 172
  quoted, 293
Chamberlain, Sir Austen, quoted, 182
China, boycott by, 53
  coming importance of, 39, 75
  exploitation of, by force, 53
Churchill, Winston, quoted, 137, 171
Civil aviation, 297–300
Coast defense, increased means of, 40
Coffee, 81
Commerce, international, growth of,
    46
  neutral, 100, 104
  protection of, in Far East, 232
  in modern war impossible, 44
Commerce raiders, 42, 86
Commercial revolution, effect of,
    on sea power, 25
Communist-capitalist war, possi-
    bility of, 307
Conference method in international
    affairs, 58, 140
Consultation agreement, 114, 202
Convertible merchant ships, 175
Coolidge, Calvin, calls Geneva Con-
    ference of 1927, 164
  quoted, 112
Coronel, Battle of, 87
Covenant of the League of Nations,
    provisions of, regarding dis-
    armament, 239*ff*.
Cruisers, controversy regarding 8-
    inch gun, 168*ff*.
  distribution of, in war, 88
  landing-on type proposed, 211
  London Treaty provisions regard-
    ing, compared with General
    Board's program, table, 213

Cruisers, number of, desired by Great
    Britain, 168, 185
  race in construction of, 161
  6-inch gun and 8-inch gun com-
    pared, 214
  tonnage under London Treaty,
    table, 212
Cushendun, Lord, quoted, 260
Customs duties, increase of, during
    neutrality, 101

D

Dalton, Hugh, 253
Dawes, Charles G., 185, 186, 189
Destroyer leaders, 216
Destroyers, tonnage of, under Lon-
    don Treaty, table, 216
Domestic safety as standard for
    armaments, 238
Draft Convention of the Preparatory
    Commission, completed, 253
  summary of, 348*ff*.
Draft Treaty of Mutual Assistance,
    246
Dreadnought, effect of, on naval
    competition, 128
Dulles, Allen W., proposal of, for
    fleet comparison, 181

E

Economic factors in United States
    declaration of war in 1917, 111
Economic internationalism, 6, 46,
    78, 306
Emery, E. S., quoted, 171
Escalator clause, 203, 221
European armies, 281
  table showing, 283
European political alignments, 255

F

Fiske, Rear Admiral Bradley A.,
    opinion of, 180
Foodstuffs, 78*ff*.
Four Power Pacific Treaty, 157

INDEX

France, aims of, at London Conference, 196-198
  artificial military superiority of, 305
  desire of, for security, 245, 304
  favors budgetary limitation, 266
  favors consideration of civil aviation, 298
  of war potential, 301
  favors global method, 292
  interest of, in Mediterranean, 196
  naval dispute of, with Italy, 197, 201, 222
  naval needs of, 199, 200
  opposes limitation of land material, 288
  of submarines, 149
  of trained reserves, 284
  opposes prohibition of aërial bombardment, 301
  opposes publicity of land material, 275
  opposes Russian plan for disarmament, 259
  opposes separate consideration of naval material, 292
  reductions in army of, 306
  tentative arms agreement of, with Great Britain, 179
Freedom of seas, 102, 105
Fry, Sir Edward, quoted, 125

G

Gas warfare, proposal to prohibit, 302
Geneva Conference of 1927, 161-178
  British position at, 168
  delegations to, 165
  Japanese position at, 177
  question of parity at, 171
  United States proposals at, 168
  value of, 178
Geneva Protocol for arbitration, security, and disarmament, 246
German merchant "used" for naval expansion, 127

German Navy Act of 1900, 126
  of 1912, 132
German sailors sink ships at Scapa Flow, 241
Germany, disarmament of, in Treaty of Peace, 241
  favors limitation of land material, 288
  of trained reserves, 284
  naval competition of with Great Britain before 1914, 126-132
  opposed disarmament in 1899, 122
  in 1907, 124
  opposes consideration of civil aviation, 298
  of war potential, 300
  protest of, against failure of disarmament, 242, 264, 265
Gibson, Hugh, delegate to London Conference, 190
  proposes yardstick formula, 182
  quoted, 226, 262, 270, 276, 278, 285, 298
Global method of naval limitation, 292
  arguments for, 293
Great Britain, aims of, at London Conference, 191-193
  alliances of, before 1914, 128-129
  cruisers necessary for security of, 168, 185
  dominions of, attitude toward Japan, 156, 186
  favors abolition of submarine, 148, 217
  favors category method, 293
  favors limitation of air budgets, 274
  of naval budgets, 269
  favors reduction in size of capital ship, 205
  interest of, in Mediterranean, 192
  Labor government of, cuts cruiser program, 185
  views of, 192
  losses of, in World War, 49, 80, 87, 92

355

Great Britain, naval competition of, with Germany before 1914, 126
 naval successes of, 13
 naval traditions of, 191
 opposes consideration of war potential, 300
 opposes Russian plan for disarmament, 260
 position of, at Geneva, 256
  regarding limitation of naval effectives, 290
  regarding separate treatment of naval material, 291
  regarding trained reserves, 285, 286
 sea power of, 32–36
 strained relations of, with United States following 1927, 179
 tentative arms agreement of, with France, 179
Grotius, advocates freedom of seas, 30

H

Hague Conference, of 1899, calling of, 121
  disarmament discussion at, 122
  failure of disarmament in, 123
 of 1907, calling of, 124
  disarmament discussion in, 125
  failure of disarmament in, 125
Haldane, Viscount, quoted, 40
 visit of, to Berlin in 1912, 131
Hale, Frederick, quoted, 210
Hall, W. G. Carlton, quoted, 180
Harding, Warren G., invited powers to naval conference, 139
Hartford Convention, 103
Henderson, Arthur, quoted, 253, 296
History, sea power, theory of, 9–61
 theories of, 10
Hitlerism, 252, 304
 success of, hastens work of League, 252
Holland, sea power of, 29–32

Hoover, Herbert C., conference of, with Prime Minister MacDonald, 187
 interest of, in disarmament, 286
 quoted, 5, 182, 183, 184
Howland, C. P., sea law proposals of, 181
Hughes, Charles E., conference diplomat, 141
 program of, at Washington, 143
 quoted, 142

I

Imperialism, not profitable to United States, 73–76
Indirect method of disarmament, 244–250
Industrialists, attitude of, 6
Industrialized war methods, 83, 287
Inter-allied loans, aid of, to export trade, 110
Intercontinental equality, 52
International organization, growth of, 58
International supervision of disarmament, 277
Investments, influence of, 6, 46–48
Italy, aims of, at London Conference, 196–198
 favors consideration of civil aviation, 298
 of war potential, 301
 favors direct limitation of land material, 288
 favors global method, 292
 interest of, in Mediterranean, 197
 naval dispute of, with France, 197, 201, 222
 opposes limitation of trained reserves, 284
 opposes publicity of land material, 275
 stresses naval needs, 199
 uncertain position of, 255, 288

INDEX

J

Japan, aims of, at London Conference, 193-195
American expedition to, in 1853, 53
cruiser construction of, 161, 230
demand of, for *status quo* in Pacific fortifications, 151
desire of, for 70 per cent ratio, 195, 203, 231
favors consideration of war potential, 301
improbability of capture of Hawaii by, 76
interest of, in naval reduction, 194
militarism in, 194
naval ratio of, under London Treaty, 231
opposes abolition of submarine, 195, 218
opposes direct limitation of land material, 288
opposes publicity for land material, 275
and Philippines, 74
position of, at Geneva Conference of 1927, 177
regarding naval effectives, 290
regarding separate treatment of naval material, 291
Jefferson, Thomas, quoted, 99

K

Kenworthy, J. M., quoted, 163
Kenworthy, J. M., and George Young, quoted, 143, 167
Keynes, John M., economic prediction of, 52
Krüger, Fritz-Konrad, quoted, 127

L

Lamont, Thomas W., quoted, 107
Land effectives, limitation of, 281
Land material, importance of, 287
limitation of, 287-290
position of United States upon, 289
Land power, growth of, 37-42
Landing-on platforms, permitted under London Treaty, 211
Landing-on type of cruiser proposed, 211
Latin America, commercial importance of, to United States, 93
Law, growth of, on sea, 56
Lawlessness on sea in former times, 56
League of Nations, approach of, to disarmament, 237*ff*.
coöperation of United States with, suggested, 115
Council of, calls world disarmament conference, 254
Covenant of, disarmament provisions in, 239
disarmament machinery of, 242*ff*.
disarmament sentiment during inception of, 238
importance of, 58
indirect method of, 244-250
Litvinoff, Maxime, quoted, 258, 264
Locarno Treaty of Mutual Guarantee, 249
London Conference, American-Japanese negotiations at, 203
calling of, 187
crisis at, 201
opening of, 199
results of, 221, 223
London Naval Treaty of 1930, 199-225
text of, 329*ff*.

M

MacDonald, James Ramsay, addresses United States Senate, 186
conference of, with President Hoover, 187
McNutt, Paul V., protest of, on cruiser postponement, 183
Madariaga, Salvador de, opinion of, regarding Washington Conference, 159
quoted, 243

357

Magruder, Rear Admiral Thomas P., book of, referred to, 304
  quoted, 15
Mahan, Alfred T., brief biography of, 11
  doctrine of, 4, 9*ff.*
  quoted, 15, 130
  writings of, 12
Markets, loss of in war, 91
Marque, letters of, 56
Minerals, difficulties of war trade in, 86
  necessity of importing, 84
  value of, in war, 83
Morrow, Dwight, delegate to London Conference, 190
Multilateral Treaty for the Renunciation of War, 60, 113
Munitions industry, profits of, in 1916, 106
Mutsu, the, 144

N

Napoleonic Wars, profits of neutral trade in, 100
National safety as standard for armaments, 239
Naval attack on coast, difficulty of, 40
Naval bases, advantage of nearness to, 69
  of United States, 74, 76, 174
Naval defense, general, 68
  local, 68
Naval effectives, limitation of, 290
Naval expansion, possible injury of, to American trade, 94
Naval material, separate consideration of, 291
Naval officer, diplomatic rôle of, 55
Naval problem, relative character of, 226
Naval tonnage of United States, Great Britain, and Japan in 1929, table, 188
Naval tonnage of United States, Great Britain, and Japan (*see also* Capital ships; Aircraft carriers; Cruisers; Destroyers; Submarines).
Naval vessels, rising cost of, 269
  unlimited classes of, 222
Navies, and abolition of piracy, 57
  and invasion, 69
Navigation, progress in before 1500 aids commerce, 22
Neutral merchants, profits of, 98
Neutral rights, doctrine of, 95*ff.*
Neutrality, a questionable economic policy, 97, 102, 107, 112
Nicholas II, reasons of, for calling Hague Conference of 1899, 121

O

Ocean barrier increased by Washington Treaty, 152
Oceanic types of nations, threatened by private war system, 78

P

Pacific, Four-power Treaty regarding, 157
  non-fortification agreement regarding, 151
Page, Walter Hines, quoted, 108
Panama affair, 54
Panama Canal, protection of, 70–72
Paris Peace Conference and disarmament, 239
Parity, between United States and Great Britain, 145, 171, 188, 227
  conceded by Prime Minister MacDonald, 187
  meaning of, 228
  opposed by Winston Churchill, 171
Peace, surest protector of trade, 93
Peace movement, 6, 120, 306
Peace treaties, question of, 264
Pearl Harbor, 76
Permanent Advisory Commission, 242

# Index

Permanent Disarmament Commission, project for, 279
Philippine Islands, defenses in, becoming obsolete, 74
 liability of, in national defense, 72-76, 154
Piracy, 24
Poortugael, General den Beer, quoted, 122
Portugal, sea power of, 26-28
Preparatory Commission for Disarmament Conference, 250ff.
Prestige as motive in war, 51
Privateering, abolition of, in 1856, 57
Publicity of armaments, 274-277

R

Ratios in naval tonnage, 144, 226-233
Raw materials in war time, 83-86
Reed, David A., delegate to London Conference, 190
 supports London Treaty in United States Senate, 191
Robinson, Joseph T., delegate to London Conference, 190
 supports London Treaty in United States Senate, 191
Rodgers, Rear Admiral W. L., quoted, 96
Russia, commercial policy of, 307
 favors drastic disarmament, 258, 282
 favors limitation of trained reserves, 285
 favors prohibition of aerial bombardment, 301
 favors reduction in size of capital ships, 295
 plan of, for drastic disarmament, 259
 to limit land material, 288-289
 position of, on gas warfare, 303
 second plan of, for disarmament, 263
 supports German bloc, 255

S

Sailing ships and commercial revolution, 22
Schwarzhoff, Colonel Gross von, quoted, 123
Sea police, 57
Sea power, age of, 21-36
 theory of, 9-61
 twilight of national, 37-61
Security, French desire for, 245, 304
 in League program, 244
 of United States from naval attack, 70
Seibold, Louis, quoted, 144
Self help, national, 60
Senators as treaty negotiators, 190
Shearer, William B., 175, 176, 183
Shipbuilding, progress in, before 1500, 22
Shipping, growth of, during neutrality, 100
Shipping interests, opposition of, to War of 1812, 103
Smuts, Jan C., quoted, 60
Spain, sea power of, 28
Spengler, Oswald, quoted, 9
Spofford, Wolcott, quoted, 16
Standard ton, 145
Steel, necessary war material, 85
Stimson, Henry L., delegate to London Conference, 189
Stock market, depressed by war rumors in 1916, 106
Subcommittee A of the Preparatory Commission, 251
Submarines, attacks of, on British commerce, 80
 attempt to limit tonnage of, at Washington, 149
 British opposition to, 148, 217
 destructions of commerce by, 43, 87
 French defense of, 218
 Japanese defense of, 218

359

Submarines, regulation of, attempted at Washington, 150
  under London Treaty, 219
  restriction of size of, 220
  tonnage agreed to under London Treaty, 220
Sugar, sources of American supply of, 82
Sullivan, Mark, quoted, 144
Swanson, Claude, A., quoted, 135

T

Tarbell, Ida, quoted, 144
Temporary Mixed Commission, 243
Theatricals of diplomacy, 167
Trade routes, defense of, 89
Trained reserves, limitation of, 283–287
  French group opposes, 284
  Germany favors, 284
  no provision for, in draft treaty, 286
Transfers of tonnage from categories, 217, 294

U

United States, advance of, in Pacific halted, 153
  aims of, at London Conference, 187–191
  considers consultation pact, 202
  Cruiser Act of 1929, 179
  defense of territory of, 65–77
  distances between naval bases of, 174
  fails to ratify gas warfare treaty, 302
  favors category method, 292
  favors 8-inch gun cruisers, 173–175
  favors publicity of armaments, 276
  foodstuffs, commerce in, 80–82
  and Great Britain, naval ratios of, 144, 171, 188, 227, 229
  and Japan, naval ratios of, 144, 203, 231, 233

United States, Naval Act of 1916, 5, 133–139
  effect of, upon Great Britain, 136
  upon Japan, 138
  naval budget of, as affected by London Treaty, 224
  naval power of, in Far East, 232
  naval tonnage of, under London Treaty, 207, 213, 216, 220, 224
  Navy, General Board of, 185, 209
  not concerned in controversy over peace treaties, 265
  not product of sea power, 65
  opposes abolition of capital ship, 189, 209
  opposes budgetary limitation, 270
  opposes consideration of civil aviation, 297
  of war potential, 300
  opposes prohibition of aërial bombardment, 302
  position of, on international supervision, 278
  on limitation of land material, 289
  of trained reserves, 285
  in relation to European factions, 256
  proposals of, at Geneva Conference of 1927, 168
  refusal of, to consider security pact, 202
  stake of, in world disarmament, 310
  strained relations of, with Great Britain after 1927, 179

W

War of 1812, effect of, on United States trade, 100–103
War of 1914, effect of, on United States trade, 103–112
War potential, 300
Wars for economic reasons, 45, 48–51
Washington, George, letters of, regarding sea power, 17

INDEX

Washington Conference, 140–160
  calling of, 139
  naval ratios agreed upon at, 144
  speech of Charles E. Hughes at, 142
  submarine discussion at, 148
Washington Naval Treaty, effect of, on American policy in Pacific, 154
  opinions on, 158
  text of, 311*ff*.
Wilson, Hugh R., opposes proposal to prohibit aërial bombardment, 302

Wilson, Woodrow, calls for large navy, 4
  proposal of, for armament reduction, 238
  for freedom of seas, 95
World Court, 60, 249
World War, cost of, to United States, 112

Y

Yardstick formula, 182
Yarnell, Rear Admiral H. E., quoted, 172

361

JX
1974
.W57
1973